C000181952

IRAQ AND THE CRIMES OF AGGRESSIVE WAR

From the torture of detainees at Abu Ghraib to unnecessary military attacks on civilians, this book is an account of the violations of international criminal law committed during the U.S. invasion and occupation of Iraq. Taking stock of the entire war, it uniquely documents the overestimation of the successes and underestimation of the failings of the Surge and Awakening policies. The authors show how an initial cynical framing of the American war led to the creation of a new Shia-dominated Iraq state, which in turn provoked powerful feelings of legal cynicism among Iraqis, especially the Sunni. The predictable result was a resilient Sunni insurgency that reemerged in the violent aftermath of the 2011 withdrawal.

Examining more than a decade of evidence, this book makes a powerful case that the American war in Iraq constituted a criminal war of aggression.

John Hagan is the John D. MacArthur Professor of Sociology and Law at Northwestern University and codirector of the Center on Law and Globalization at the American Bar Foundation. His previous Cambridge University Press books are *Mean Streets: Youth Crime and Homelessness* (with Bill McCarthy) and *Darfur and the Crime of Genocide* (with Wenona Rymond-Richmond). Hagan is an elected member of the American Academy of Arts and Sciences and the Royal Society of Canada.

Joshua Kaiser is a Law and Social Science Fellow at the American Bar Foundation and a JD-PhD candidate in law and sociology at Northwestern University. His research focuses on the sociology and criminology of state control and state violence, both in the United States and internationally.

Anna Hanson is currently a doctoral candidate in the sociology department at Northwestern University. Her research focuses on issues of terrorism and human rights.

CAMBRIDGE STUDIES IN LAW AND SOCIETY

Cambridge Studies in Law and Society aims to publish the best scholarly work on legal discourse and practice in its social and institutional contexts, combining theoretical insights and empirical research.

The fields that it covers are: studies of law in action; the sociology of law; the anthropology of law; cultural studies of law, including the role of legal discourses in social formations; law and economics; law and politics; and studies of governance. The books consider all forms of legal discourse across societies, rather than being limited to lawyers' discourses alone.

The series editors come from a range of disciplines: academic law, sociolegal studies, sociology, and anthropology. All have been actively involved in teaching and writing about law in context.

Series Editors
Chris Arup, *Monash University, Victoria*
Sally Engle Merry, *New York University*
Susan Silbey, *Massachusetts Institute of Technology*

A list of books in the series can be found at the back of this book.

Iraq and the Crimes of Aggressive War

THE LEGAL CYNICISM OF CRIMINAL MILITARISM

JOHN HAGAN

Northwestern University

American Bar Foundation

JOSHUA KAISER

Northwestern University

American Bar Foundation

ANNA HANSON

Northwestern University

CAMBRIDGE
UNIVERSITY PRESS

CAMBRIDGE
UNIVERSITY PRESS

32 Avenue of the Americas, New York, NY 10013-2473, USA

Cambridge University Press is part of the University of Cambridge.

It furthers the University's mission by disseminating knowledge in the pursuit of education, learning, and research at the highest international levels of excellence.

www.cambridge.org
Information on this title: www.cambridge.org/9781107507012

© John Hagan, Joshua Kaiser, and Anna Hanson 2015

This publication is in copyright. Subject to statutory exception and to the provisions of relevant collective licensing agreements, no reproduction of any part may take place without the written permission of Cambridge University Press.

First published 2015

Printed in Great Britain by Clays Ltd, St Ives plc

A catalog record for this publication is available from the British Library.

Library of Congress Cataloging in Publication Data
Hagan, John, 1946–
Iraq and the crimes of aggressive war : the legal cynicism of criminal militarism / John Hagan, Joshua Kaiser, Anna Hanson.
pages cm. – (Cambridge studies in law and society)
Includes bibliographical references and index.
ISBN 978-1-107-10453-2 (hardback) – ISBN 978-1-107-50701-2 (paperback)
1. Iraq War, 2003–2011 – Atrocities. 2. Iraq War, 2003–2011 – Moral and ethical aspects.
3. War crimes – Iraq. I. Kaiser, Joshua, 1985– II. Hanson, Anna, 1985– III. Title.
DS79.767.A87H34   2015
341.6'9–dc23   2015002803

ISBN 978-1-107-10453-2 Hardback
ISBN 978-1-107-50701-2 Paperback

Cambridge University Press has no responsibility for the persistence or accuracy of URLs for external or third-party Internet Web sites referred to in this publication and does not guarantee that any content on such Web sites is, or will remain, accurate or appropriate.

To initiate a war of aggression, therefore, is not only an international crime; it is the supreme international crime differing only from other war crimes in that it contains within itself the accumulated evil of the whole.

–Judgment of the International Military
Tribunal at Nuremberg, 1946

We are not prepared to lay down a rule of criminal conduct against others which we would be unwilling to have invoked against us.

–Justice Robert Jackson, Chief Prosecutor for the
International Military Tribunal at Nuremberg, 1945

I see mostly normal men, trying to do good, beaten down by horror, by their inability to quell their own rages, by their masculine posturing and their so-called hardness, their desire to be tougher, and therefore crueler, than their circumstance.

–Phil Klay, Iraq War Veteran and Author of *Redeployment*, 2014

Contents

Prologue

The first assault in the U.S.-led Iraq War was spearheaded by two F-117 Nighthawks dropping four 2,000-pound Bunker Buster bombs and four ships firing forty Tomahawk cruise missiles. They targeted a compound outside Baghdad where U.S. intelligence mistakenly believed Saddam Hussein was visiting his sons. Saddam apparently had not been there in almost twenty years. This assault killed the war's first civilian bystander.

The first strike was followed two days later by the Shock and Awe launch of 1,700 air sorties with hundreds more cruise missiles. Arab-American journalist Anthony Shadid reported from the ground that "Baghdad's residents . . . were terrified. In the three hour blitz, at times bringing a new blast every ten seconds, Saddam's garrisons and the symbols of his three-decade rule were shattered" (Shadid 2005:61). The British *Guardian* newspaper called Shock and Awe terrorism by another name (Whitaker 2003). Iraq Body Count estimated that more than 6,000 civilians were killed in the ensuing first phase of the U.S.-led invasion.

A 1974 UN General Assembly resolution defines a war of aggression as the "serious and dangerous" use of force by one nation against another.[1] However, this definition is too inclusive. We argue in the first chapter of this book that the genocide in Sudan's Darfur region was one among numerous instances where another state justifiably could and should have used force to stop the killing of civilians. There are also circumstances in which one state is justified in defending another state against attack, for example, when Germany invaded an undefended Poland to begin World War II. The 1974 UN definition is too broad for purposes of criminal prosecutions or social scientific research, and there is no cumulative case law to clarify the definition of aggressive war.

The unformed nature of today's law of aggressive war is similar in some ways to the laws about unethical business practices encountered in the

1950s by Edwin Sutherland, the famous American criminologist who coined the term "white collar crime" that today still frames much discourse about financial illegality. Sutherland (1949) included within his study of white collar crime the actions of U.S. corporations who illegally traded with Germany during World War II. Yet Sutherland and following social scientists contributed little beyond this to the socio-legal study of aggressive war. Our book seeks to advance this underdeveloped social science of wars of aggression.

Our approach is a social scientific analog to the political philosophy of Michael Walzer (1977) and his just and unjust war theory of crimes of international aggression. Walzer (2007) cites legal definitions of aggressive war – from Nuremberg, through the UN General Assembly, to the Rome Treaty. However, he emphasizes that these definitions do not sufficiently specify the events and circumstances that are necessary to circumscribe prosecutorial and trial applications of the concept of aggressive war.

Following the still new International Criminal Court, we begin by defining aggressive war as the use of armed force against another state without the justification of self-defense or authorization by the UN Security Council.[2] Examples of aggressive war include unprovoked and unauthorized attacks by armed forces, bombardments, and blockades. But Walzer (2012:35) argues that more attention is needed to the factors and circumstances that initiate war – *ad bellum* – to conclude whether a war is just or unjust. He further insists that what comes *after* a war is also a crucial part of whether it should or should not be fought in the first place. Foreseeable consequences of war – *post bellum* – must also be considered.

Our own contribution is a social scientific theory and empirical causal analysis built on this approach, with particular attention to consequences of war, based on extensive social science surveys and interview evidence gathered in Iraq – the most extensively reported but still infrequently empirically studied international conflict recently involving the United States. We bring social science data to bear in documenting both the background and consequences – *ad bellum* and *post bellum* – of the U.S.-led invasion of Iraq.

Of course, it would be naïve in the extreme to believe that this exercise in social science alone could lead to prosecutions and convictions for aggressive war in an international criminal court of law. In any case, Walzer (2007:642; see also Hagan 2010: chapter 2) argues against hasty judgments and further suggests that there is a "moral continuum" along which just and unjust instances of international aggression can be located. He concludes that "the American war in Iraq falls somewhere in between – closer in my view to the unjust pole" (2007:642). We go further: we argue that the *ad bellum* and *post bellum* evidence we consider supports a conclusion that the American war in Iraq was an unjust form of criminal militarism that constituted a war of aggression.

Thus we believe that our study of the American war in Iraq can inform and is relevant to judgments and decisions about criminal prosecution and convictions. There are obviously normative elements as well as social scientific aspects of the work presented in this book. To call acts of war instances of legal cynicism and criminal militarism – as we do – involves normative conclusions about what should count as crimes as well as efforts to objectively assemble and access evidence about these putative crimes.

Some will probably say we are simply "witnesses for the prosecution" – which we could conceivably be – but if this is so then our goal is to be open and objective social scientific witnesses. There are ample witnesses for the defense. Former and present CIA directors George Tenet and John Brennan began meeting in April 2014 with aides to plan how they would respond to the declassification of a 6,300-page, 6 million-dollar, and long-withheld Senate Intelligence Committee report on U.S. torture practices during the Iraq War.[3] Despite earlier misleading denials by Director Brennan, the CIA Inspector General subsequently confirmed that its employees broke into a private Senate computer server to secretly monitor its work. Few expected the Tenet-Brennan defense to be an open and objective response to charges that the CIA misled Congress and the public about the legality and effectiveness of U.S. torture policies.

We see our approach as consistent with Howard Becker's (1967) position that in choosing sides of an argument about aggressive war we can usefully acknowledge and advance *both* our value positions and our commitment to standards of social science. We see our study as expanding on the challenge Walzer articulates when he suggests that "surely this is [the kind of] work that must be done before the ICC [International Criminal Court] can think about prosecuting political leaders for the crime of aggression – or for any lesser crimes" (2007:642).

In his 2002 West Point speech elaborating his new War on Terror, President Bush used his presidential authority to issue a normative call to action in defense of American lives and liberty. He announced that "our security will require all Americans to be forward-looking and resolute, to be ready for pre-emptive action when necessary to defend our liberty and to defend our lives." This formulation implicitly acknowledged the important requirement that there be an actual threat to justify a preemptive war, and the Bush administration set out to provide this justification. Yet the ad hoc character of the administration's claims and justifications revealed the legal cynicism of the preemptive policy that led to the Iraq War – which is the focus of this book.

Legal cynicism is a normless condition of skepticism in which rules of law are not regarded as binding (Sampson and Bartusch 1998:782). This lawlessness can generate fear in an effected population – as it did in Iraq – for the safety of individuals and their families. Legal cynicism can also be more broadly understood as a cultural frame or orientation in which law is viewed by a population as illegitimate, unresponsive, and ineffectual in providing security – that is, as "ill equipped to ensure public safety" (Kirk and Papachristos 2011:1191). We further borrow from these perspectives in viewing criminal militarism as a cultural frame or orientation in which laws of war are neglected or ignored.

Legal cynicism and criminal militarism originate with bureaucratic, political, and military elites and their agents, whose actions can be a source of perceptions of illegitimacy and injustice among nonelite populations. These subgroups often find and feel themselves to be poorly protected, ill-served, and mistreated by legal authorities (Ivkovic and Hagan 2006; Hagan, Shedd, and Payne 2005; Hagan and Albonetti 1982). Legal cynicism unfolds in ways that sometimes constrain but also more notably create possibilities for response strategies – including collective violence – among the affected subgroups (Lamont and Small 2008:81). Legal cynicism is a key cause of strategic responses that we argue is crucial to understanding sources of sectarian violence in Iraq.

Closer to home, in the United States, Chicago's neighborhoods with high rates of homicide are also places of acute legal cynicism. David Kirk and Andrew Papachristos find that residents in socially and economically disadvantaged neighborhoods of this city collectively "come to understand that the dominant societal institutions (of which the police and justice system are emblematic) will offer them little in the way of security" (2011:1198). This legal cynicism about law enforcement leads residents in affected neighborhoods to see it as acceptable and appropriate to resort to self-protection as "self-help" (Black 1983). Because this self-help can take the form of homicide, this is a provocative thesis. We examine related arguments in the culminating chapters of this book about the effects of unnecessary violent attacks by U.S./coalition forces on Arab Sunni civilians in Iraq. These chapters reveal that such attacks were sources of legal cynicism that led to widespread social support for Sunni militancy and insurgent violence.

Legal cynicism can have state-based political origins that are deeply embedded and difficult to discern. The roots of legal cynicism in Iraq included foreign and domestic political elites – from U.S. President Bush to Iraqi Prime Minister Maliki – who facilitated and enabled highly organized criminal militarism in Iraq. Indeed, there are persuasive arguments that the militarism that led to the American invasion of Iraq had elite intellectual roots that extended beyond state actors, for example, as reflected in the post-9/11 call in the *Wall Street Journal* and elsewhere for a "World War IV" against Syria, Iraq, and Iran, which were famously included in the "axis of evil" identified by President George Bush in his 2002 State of the Union Address.

> The World War IV idea was initially put forward in the *Wall Street Journal* in November 2001 by Eliot A. Cohen, who later took a leave from the School of Advanced International Studies at Johns Hopkins to accept a position in the Bush State Department. The idea was expanded on in a *Commentary* article in February 2002 by Norman Podhoretz, the magazine's editor from 1960 to 1995. (Mills 2009:105)

These public intellectuals argued that the United States needed to wage a World War IV that would be similar in length and difficulty to the Cold War, which they thought of as World War III. They called on America to use its military might to forestall future threats to its security. Insofar as many such alleged threats formed false foundations for the war in Iraq, they exemplify an extreme form of criminal militarism.

We argue that this kind of militaristic thinking had legally cynical causes and consequences. Legally cynical, state-based politics often involve less noticed and therefore less predictable processes than do those in simplified, individual-level cause-and-effect models. Yet these deeply embedded paths of influence can also be durable and consequential – often in ways both antici-pated and unanticipated. Several parts of this book examine the anticipated and unanticipated consequences of the covert as well as overt legally cynical policies of the Bush administration during the near decade-long American combat presence in Iraq.

For example, we explore the responses of Iraqi judges to the legal rea-soning – which many critics and scholars regarded as legally cynical – that justified U.S. torture practices used in Abu Ghraib prison, but which were routinely cloaked in classified and tendentious opinions and memos. We also investigate Arab Sunnis' fear in Baghdad of the lack of effective protection by legal authorities against Shia militia attacks aimed at taking over their com-munities. Indeed, many Arab Sunnis in Baghdad became convinced of the legally cynical view that Shia militia had taken over the Iraqi security ministry and were a government-based source of attacks on their communities. These chapters document and explain the successive and ongoing ways legal cyni-cism initially emerged, was enabled, and then also evolved into retaliatory, revengeful forms of criminal militarism in Iraq.

A militaristic form of legal cynicism initially helped to set the conditions and to form the possibilities for going to war in Iraq. Congress's 2002 "Joint

Resolution to Authorize the Use of United States Armed Forces against Iraq" claimed that Iraq was "a continuing threat to the national security of the United States" because it had "a significant chemical and biological weapons capacity" and was "seeking a nuclear weapons capability."[4] In Great Britain, a "Downing Street Memo" warned about the speciousness of these claims and that "the intelligence and facts were being fixed around the policy."[5] UN Secretary-General Kofi Annan declared in September 2004 that the ensuing war was "illegal" from the point of view of the UN Charter.

On at least two occasions, only days after the 9/11 attacks, President Bush expressed (with no apparent supporting evidence) his belief that Saddam Hussein and Iraq were involved in these attacks on America (see Baker 2013:135; Packer 2006:41). In advance of the war, the vice president of the United States leaked false claims about Iraqi weapons of mass destruction that were presented as newsworthy in *New York Times* articles written by Judith Miller (e.g., 2001). In the final months before the invasion, Bill Keller (2003), the executive editor of the *New York Times*, supported the invasion of Iraq with an op-ed proclaiming his membership in "The I-Can't-Believe-I'm-a-Hawk Club."

The weak evidentiary foundation for the war in Iraq was itself evidence of a criminal militarism grounded in legal cynicism. The justification for the war consisted of three essential claims. The first claim alleged the complicity of Saddam Hussein's regime in the 9/11 attacks based on a reported meeting of the Iraqi consul in Prague with 9/11 hijacker Mohamed Atta. The FBI was never able to find any evidence for this claim, and despite persistent assertions by Vice President Cheney, President Bush acknowledged the absence of confirming evidence before and after the invasion.[6] The second and most important claim was that Iraq was in possession of extensive stocks of biological and chemical weapons of mass destruction (WMDs). UN preinvasion and U.S. post-invasion inspections could not find WMD stockpiles.[7] The third claim was that Iraq was obtaining capacity to make nuclear weapons, as evidenced by the acquisition of "yellow cake" uranium. The UN Atomic Energy Agency reported shortly before the U.S. invasion that this claim was based on a forged letter.[8] Even Bush administration advisors, such as Richard Haass (2009), would later say that although the first Gulf War of George H. W. Bush was a necessity, the second Iraq War of George W. Bush was a choice. This was a chosen and unnecessary war: a war of aggression.

A war of aggression is among the most serious forms of criminal militarism, and Justice Robert Jackson observed at the post–World War II Nuremberg Trials that "we are not prepared to lay down a rule of criminal conduct against others which we would be unwilling to have invoked against us." The Nuremberg Tribunal insisted that to initiate a war of aggression is not only an international crime – "it is the supreme international crime differing only from other war crimes in that it contains within itself the accumulated evil of the whole." This "accumulated evil" – in the *post bellum* form of unfolding, widespread, and systematic criminal consequences of the aggression – is the main subject of this book. The accumulated evil concept anticipates a path dependency[9] and a negative trajectory of unnecessary violence that the unfolding policy decision to go to war in Iraq amply fulfilled.

The chapters of this book track a trajectory of legal cynicism and criminal militarism that especially affected Iraq's Arab Sunnis. Uniquely advantaged during Saddam Hussein's authoritarian regime, the Arab Sunnis were in turn marginalized in the U.S.-led formation of the new Iraqi state. Iraq's Arab Sunnis disproportionately experienced the aftermath of the invasion and occupation, including torture, killing, displacement, and community insecurity that resulted from the war of aggression. The Arab Sunnis responded to their collective reversal of fortune with a resilient insurgent militancy. Seen through the "constraint and possibility" lens of legal cynicism, the former constraints – the invasion, occupation, torture, killing, displacement, and insecurity – made the militancy of the Sunnis insurgency not only a possible outcome, but actually the likely outcome of regime change in Iraq.

Wars of aggression are first and foremost recognized for their carnage and killing. This is why priority is given to establishing interim and final counts of the dead. Thus the results of criminal militarism in Iraq are best known through estimates of mortality. This is how and why the Web site of Iraq Body Count became such a widely cited news source in the reporting of the Iraq War. However, it is also essential to understand the further ways wars of aggression can be devastatingly destructive of the long-term fates of states and societies.

Thus wars of aggression are also characterized by their longer-term goals, which have to do with repressing and controlling surviving population groups. The goals of the U.S. occupation and presence in Iraq involved quickly achieving compliance and collaboration in establishing an American-designed democracy. This conspicuously failed and the U.S. forces remained in Iraq far longer and at far greater expense than predicted by the Bush administration. After a briefly stunned and slightly optimistic period following the 2003 invasion, the occupation entered its chaotic period of lawless looting. This was followed from 2004 through 2007 by the rising levels of violence that ultimately verged on civil war and the subsequent surge of U.S. forces. After this peak and a subsequent decline in violence, an interim period of relative peace and security lasted from 2008 through 2011, coinciding with the phased and final departure of American combat forces. Then the renewal of insurgent violence began in 2012.

Instead of producing a smooth transition to an American-designed demo-cratic society, the American war of aggression resulted in a massive and fearful period of population displacement that impacted in largest numbers the Arab Sunni population of Baghdad and beyond, as well as the development of an even more threatening and stubbornly resilient and militant Arab Sunni resistance and insurgency. Although it is typically suggested that these outcomes were produced by the lack of American planning and preparation for the occupation, we argue that these outcomes actually reflected a more predetermined set of policies that were destined to fail based on their belligerent origins and false assumptions. These included the assumed wisdom of removing all or most of the prior regime's Arab Sunni Ba'ath Party members from elected and non-elected positions in government and the demobilization of the Iraqi military.

The war of aggression began by privileging in its planning an ex-patriot Shia elite opposition who were mostly in exile until the invasion, while at the same time putatively insisting not only on defeating but also on largely disenfranchising a growing nonelite Shia Sadrist movement and the Arab Sunnis who were largely dismissed as the enemy constituency of Saddam Hussein. The criminally militaristic aggressiveness of the American-instigated war presupposed a Shia leadership that, given its savage mistreatment under Saddam, would willingly collaborate in forcefully defeating and dismissing the previously ascendant Arab Sunnis. This war of aggression did not include a robust effort to rehabilitate or reintegrate the Arab Sunnis into Iraq's economy and governance. The Bush administration's prejudgment of an emergent Arab Sunni resistance was expressed in Donald Rumsfeld's metaphor characterizing these "dead enders" as the "remnants of a dying cause."

The representative of the Coalition Provisional Authority (CPA) in Sunni Anbar province, Keith Mines (2012), commented that the head of the CPA, Paul Bremer, was "taken in by the Shia and Kurds, feeling like the Sunnis had lost for legitimate reasons ... and so could be ignored or even treated badly." Bremer also clumsily and dismissively stumbled into a policy of aggressively and ineffectively opposing a Shia Sadrist movement that was cynical about the U.S. invasion and occupation from the outset. Bremer was an assertive and uncompromising agent of the war of aggression.

Despite substantial amounts of frequently excellent journalism, there is relatively little empirical documentation or theoretical explanation of war crimes in Iraq – even, and perhaps most notably by criminologists, who might have been expected to take a special responsibility and interest. This book provides the social scientific underpinnings of a theoretical and empirical criminology of the Iraq War. Our focus is on the varied crimes that the legal cynicism and criminal militarism of this war produced.

The Iraq War and the Vietnam War to which it is often compared involved the perpetration of major crimes that have formed violently aggressive bookends of American foreign policy since World War II. Yet the American public and scholars who study crime have shown little inclination to remember or analyze these wars as crime scenes. Americans prefer to remember their wars victoriously, rather than dwell on their failures, and we argue that doing so is a virulent form of legal cynicism and denial that metastasizes in unexpected ways, including the perpetuation of a militaristic framing of American foreign policy that encourages repeated involvement in foreign wars.

Even Barak Obama, who ran for president to a large extent based on his early opposition to the Iraq War, has perhaps surprisingly displayed an inclination toward victorious denial in his observations about the Vietnam War – the conflict that produced many of the generals who would later lead the Iraq War. "Let it be remembered," President Obama reminded the Minneapolis American Legion Veterans of the Vietnam War in August 2011, "that you won every major battle of that war. Every single one."[10] This was not an idle or passing thought. Less than a year later, in May 2012, President Obama repeated nearly the exact same words in a commemoration of the fiftieth anniversary of the Vietnam War at the Vietnam Veterans' Memorial on Washington Mall. With the 2012 election campaign approaching, and several million Vietnam veterans among the electorate, there is reason to ask whether these victorious claims involved elements of a politically motivated and targeted militarism.

The claim that the U.S. military won all the major battles in Vietnam is relevant – and indeed predictive – of subsequent claims of the victorious results of the 2007 surge of troops in Iraq. In his first book about the Iraq War, journalist Thomas Ricks (2006:129) quotes a North Vietnamese officer as responding to the claim that the United States won all the major battles by saying, "that may be so, but it is also irrelevant." His point was that North Vietnam won the war by gaining the support of the people and communities the war was literally and figuratively fought over. In this respect, there is an important similarity in the Vietnamese and Iraq experiences. Several months into the Iraq War, Ricks noted that the Americans, as before in Vietnam, "had no idea who the enemy really was. Nor did they know much about what Iraqis thought of them" (2006:129).

The Americans, especially their commanding officers and diplomatic core, were isolated in the cocoon of Baghdad's Green Zone, or what Rajiv Chandraskaran (2006) aptly called *The Imperial Life in the Emerald City*. George W. Bush (2003a) rushed to claim "mission accomplished" after the U.S. invasion, perhaps to further confirm his father's militaristic assertion after the first Gulf War that "By God, we've kicked the Vietnam Syndrome once and for all." But the occupation of Iraq that followed the invasion proved a distinctly different challenge than the earlier Gulf War.

David Petraeus and his plan for the 2007 surge of more troops and a new counterinsurgency strategy drew directly on his Vietnam experience. We argue in this book that the surge was part of this long-term problem and did not provide its solution. The surge of forces in Iraq became the new hope for reversing the chaos and killing that burst explosively out of control in 2005 and 2006. The surge initially elevated the Iraqi and American death tolls, but when the killing entered a period of decline, it immediately sparked new claims of victory.

Two veterans of American politics as well as Vietnam, former infantryman Chuck Hagel and Navy bomber pilot John McCain, took up their long-lasting disagreements about the lessons of war in a revealing 2013 congressional confirmation hearing for Hagel's appointment as defense secretary. This confrontation recalled earlier disputes about the winning of battles, but now in the context of the surge of troops in Iraq.

Battle Scars

The congressional hearing began with Senator McCain acknowledging that he and Senator Hagel were old friends but that nonetheless he questioned Hagel's professional judgment and worldview on national security. McCain started his questioning of Hagel by citing an earlier exchange between Hagel and Secretary Condoleezza Rice about the proposed surge.

> SENATOR MCCAIN: In January of 2007, in a rather bizarre exchange with Secretary Rice ... You said, quote, "matter of fact, I have to say, Madam Secretary, I think the speech given last night by this President [Bush] represents the most dangerous foreign policy blunder in this country since Vietnam. If it's carried out, I will resist it."
>
> And then of course you continued on and on for months afterwards talking about what a disaster the surge would be, even to the point where the surge was succeeding....
>
> Do you – do you stand by that – those comments, Senator Hagel?
>
> MR. HAGEL: Well, I would defer to the judgment [of history] to sort that out, but I'll–
>
> SENATOR MCCAIN: I want to know if you were right or wrong. That's a direct question. I expect a direct answer.

MR. HAGEL: ... As to the comment I made about the most dangerous foreign policy decision since Vietnam – was about not just the surge but the overall war of choice going into Iraq. That particular decision that was made on the surge, but more to the point, our war in Iraq, I think was the fundamentally bad, dangerous decision since Vietnam.

SENATOR MCCAIN: It's fundamental difference of opinion, Senator Hagel.... I think history has already made a judgment about the surge, sir, and you're on the wrong side of it.

MR. HAGEL: Well, I don't know if that would have been required and cost us over a thousand American lives and thousands of [wounded].

SENATOR MCCAIN: So you don't know if that would have been required? OK.

Senator William Nelson followed McCain in the questioning by asking Hagel how his combat experience in Vietnam now shaped his response as a senator to the Iraq War. Hagel referred directly to his role on the ground as an enlisted infantryman, indirectly comparing this experience to McCain's view from above as an officer and a bomber pilot.

MR. HAGEL: In 1968, when Tom and I served there, was the worst year we had. Those who may not recall that year – we sent over 16,000 dead Americans home. Now that's unfathomable in the world we live in today, 16,000 dead Americans. I saw that from the bottom.... And it directly goes to Senator McCain's question about the surge....

So I did question a surge.... I always ask the question, is this going to be worth the sacrifice, because there will be a sacrifice. In the surge case in Iraq, we lost almost 1,200 dead Americans during the surge, and thousands of wounded. Now, was it required? Was it necessary? Senator McCain has his own opinion on that, shared by others. I'm not sure.

I don't see the lens of every world event and whether we should use American power through the lens of Vietnam. But it's part of me. It is part of that lens. I think that's for the better. I think we need to be cautious with our power.

This encounter between McCain and Hegel is a telling reflection of how U.S. domestic politics about the projection of military power frame and propel American foreign policy. It is important to take this backdrop of the Iraq War into account. However, it is notable that the congressional confirmation hearing mainly considered American deaths and losses in Iraq. One of the goals of this book is to move beyond exclusively American preoccupations and to draw from Iraqi civilians and their accounts of their experiences to better understand how the "accumulation of evil" of this war unfolded.

In broad outline, the developmental arc of legal cynicism and criminal militarism that is a central focus of this book builds from the massively violent Shock and Awe American attack and invasion of Iraq, then descends into the anarchy and looting associated with the U.S.-decreed de-Bat'athification of government ministries and demobilization of Iraq's military, lurches forward through policies ranging from clandestine torture to violent attacks by U.S. forces disproportionately targeting the Arab Sunni population of Iraq, and ultimately devolves into an ongoing American-guided elite bargaining process that produced a Shia-dominated and increasingly authoritarian yet constitutionally embedded and democratically elected regime headed by Prime Minister Nouri al-Maliki. The legal cynicism and criminal militarism of this conflict is a still-unfolding process whose evolution we document and analyze across the chapters and with the help of the sociohistorical and statistical data sources introduced next.

THE SOCIOHISTORICAL AND STATISTICAL APPROACH OF THIS BOOK

We begin in Chapter 1 with the regime of terror imposed by Saddam Hussein and the evolution of the Ba'ath Party's legal authoritarianism in the three decades before the U.S. invasion. We then consider in Chapter 2 how the American war of aggression, despite the Iraqi public's relief in being rid of Saddam, provoked growing expressions of legal cynicism from civilians. These early signs of a legal cynicism about the U.S.-led war and occupation were not randomly distributed – they were concentrated among the Arab Sunnis, who from the outset distrusted the occupation's Coalition Provisional Authority. We give particular attention in Chapter 3 to the legal cynicism that the American torture policy brought to Iraq and its impact on a little considered but crucial group, the Iraqi judiciary.

In terms of criminal violence, the peak of the Iraq War was the unleashing of Muqtada al-Sadr's Shia leadership of the Mahdi Army described in Chapter 4. It is essential to our understanding of this war of aggression to better explain how the concentration of this violence in Baghdad led to the permanent displacement of many Arab Sunnis from the neighborhoods of Iraq's dominant city. The explosive post-invasion growth of al-Sadr's criminal militia was a response to the brutal repression of the Shia under Saddam, the U.S. refusal to support a Shia rebellion against Saddam after the first Gulf War, and the post-invasion U.S.-led elite exclusion of al-Sadr from U.S./coalition planning, which intensified his opposition to the invasion and occupation.

Throughout the war, Shia and especially Arab Sunni civilians reported violent and unnecessary attacks by U.S./coalition forces in their neighborhoods. We focus in Chapter 5 on the impact of these attacks in undermining perceived security and safety and fostering legal cynicism, again especially in Arab Sunni communities, even during the period when war violence was decreasing in Iraq in 2008 and 2009. In Chapter 6, we examine how this experience of violence and insecurity in spite of – and often as a result of – the U.S. troop presence led to the acceptance among the Arab Sunnis of insurgent attacks on American forces and then on Iraqi security and military forces as well as politicians and civilians in Iraq.

The findings we report in this book draw from a unique combination of surveys and interviews conducted in Iraq. We begin in Chapter 1 with a massive U.S. State Department-funded interview study, the Iraq History Project (IHP), which consists of almost 7,000 interviews based on a saturation sample of Iraqi human rights victims during the period when Saddam Hussein's Ba'ath Party ruled Iraq from 1968 to 2003. These interviews were conducted from 2007 to 2008.[11]

We examine the criminal violence imposed by Saddam's regime on Iraq's northern Kurdish and southern Shia groups during the 1980s and 1990s. We then document the more bureaucratized and specifically targeted violence applied in the decade that followed the first Gulf War. This first chapter addresses the possibility that Saddam became a more sophisticated and calculating human rights abuser over the course of his regime, as he shifted to the use of a more brutally bureaucratized form of legal authoritarianism that relied on the security agencies, courts, and prisons of Iraq.

Chapter 2 draws on a Gallup Poll (GP) Survey conducted in Baghdad six months after the invasion with a randomized probability survey of 1,200 households.[12] The significance of local communities and their sectarian identities was already apparent at this stage, with respondents living in Shia neighborhoods expressing confidence and hope about the U.S.-led Coalition Provisional Authority (CPA). Nonetheless, the post-invasion chaos and breakdown of social order was increasingly apparent, and a sense of illegitimacy reflecting a growing legal cynicism was building with significantly more respondents overall – but led by Baghdad's Arab Sunnis – saying that the American invasion was wrong and had made things worse. We explore how hope and fear collided in creating the foundation of a legally cynical fear and despair during this initial post-invasion period.

When the U.S.-led invasion could not be justified as a preemptive war of self-defense against weapons of mass destruction, President Bush risked provoking an even more widely shared and skeptical sense of legal cynicism by promising to bring American-style democracy and the rule of law to Iraq.

During this period, media reports of U.S.-led torture at Abu Ghraib prison provided gruesome and highly publicized evidence of the consequences of the legal cynicism and criminal militarism that the American invasion and occupation imposed on Iraq. We report in Chapter 3 on a unique opportunity to observe how American torture practices impacted the thinking of Iraqi judges – who it was hoped would be effective sources of independence from political influence. The hope was that the judiciary would spread Bush's promised rule of law in Iraq. Our opportunity was an invitation from a European legal institute to evaluate a State Department program for Iraqi judges. Our study included more than eighty randomly chosen judges flown to the institute from Iraq in 2004 and 2005.

We developed a sentencing experiment based on hypothetical torture cases to address the question of whether the coalition could successfully encourage rule of law standards of judicial independence among Iraq's judges. The Bush administration's evolving interpretations of torture law presented a legal challenge for Iraqi judges: put briefly, they could either collaborate compliantly with the U.S.-led coalition and its tendentiously reasoned torture policy, or they could resist its normative imperatives. We examined how legal cynicism undermined rule of law expectations of judicial independence.

In the sentencing experiment we designed, the majority of the Iraqi judges complied and collaborated with the U.S. position by choosing lenient sentences for U.S. perpetrators of torture. However, a number of the sampled Iraqi judges also resisted the American position on torture by urging punitive sentences. Like the Sunni respondents in the previous chapter who shortly after the invasion expressed their doubts about the U.S.-led Coalition Provisional Authority, these resistant judges signaled an inclination toward legal cynicism by recommending severe punishment for U.S. soldiers involved in torture in Iraq.

Chapter 4 explores the way the U.S. war of aggression unleashed sectarian violence. It is one thing to say the war unleashed sectarian conflict, but it is another to explain how this happened. Shia leader Muqtada al-Sadr led a large militia, the Mahdi Army, with criminal militarist tactics as well as organized criminal capacities. These criminal tactics and capacities were applied in taking over Sunni Arab neighborhoods, using threats and harassment to selectively displace residents from their homes in Sunni and mixed areas of Baghdad.

To demonstrate how this occurred, we joined the Gallup Baghdad survey (GP) introduced in Chapter 3 with 805 Baghdad interviews from a second Soros Foundation-supported part of the Iraq History Project called the Current Violations Initiative (CVI). During the very period when President Bush was celebrating "mission accomplished," residents were fleeing Arab Sunni Baghdad neighborhoods. They feared Iraqi security police and U.S. forces would not protect them from al-Sadr's Shia militia. Their legally cynical fears were confirmed as formerly Sunni Baghdad became a Shia-controlled city – a situation the U.S. surge consolidated when it doubled down its offensive operations in 2007.

The consolidation of Shia control over formerly Sunni neighborhoods was perceived by Arab Sunnis as a legally cynical and long-feared dismissal of their legitimate rights to live among their own in Baghdad. When al-Sadr announced a unilateral ceasefire in August 2007, the result locked into place the Shia domination of Baghdad and created a new set of political and electoral opportunities for al-Sadr's mass movement. Al-Sadr's rapid shift from the leadership of a violent militia to the role of parliamentary politician was an audaciously successful act of legal cynicism.

In Chapter 5, we analyze how in the final years before the American withdrawal the Shia and Arab Sunni communities came to further occupy separate and unequal places in Iraqi society. These ethnic communities had effectively changed positions of power since the era of Saddam Hussein. The Arab Sunnis blamed the Americans' criminal militarism for their reversal of fortune. We examine how the new circumstances in Iraq influenced the experience of war violence and feelings of security within and between Arab Sunni and Shia communities.

Many of the findings are as expected, but some are surprising. We use a unique data set developed by a consortium of news organizations that sampled more than 8,000 Iraqis from neighborhood communities representing the different sectarian groups of Iraq. This data set included a period lasting from the beginning of the surge in early 2007 to seven months after its completion in 2009.[13]

Although we show that large segments of both Shia and the Arab Sunni civilian groups perceived that they were subjects of unnecessary violent attacks by U.S.-led forces during the surge and after, the Arab Sunnis felt that their neighborhoods were especially vulnerable to this American-initiated violence. There were clear overlaps between the widespread and systematic patterns of reported attacks on civilians observed in our data analysis and incidents reported in the controversial WikiLeaks War Logs and other sources.

The focus of our analysis in Chapter 5 is on the period from 2008 through 2009 when violence declined and the Sunni and Shia sectarian communities in Iraq nonetheless continued to move apart. This period established what we call "a separate peace" that left the Shia feeling much more secure than the Arab Sunnis. The Sunnis feared for their security and the safety of their families. So that even in the best of times after the invasion and occupation, fear and insecurity persisted, signaling the lingering tensions of a smoldering legal cynicism in the Arab Sunni neighborhoods.

In Chapter 6, we step back in order to look more closely in earlier survey data from the autumn of 2007 at how feelings of legal cynicism played a crucial role in building widespread support among the Arab Sunni population for resistance against the U.S./coalition presence in Iraq. We find persuasive evidence that reported unnecessary attacks by U.S./coalition forces on civilians were perceived by the Arab Sunnis as an unjust form of collective punishment. That is, we find that the reported attacks led to widespread feelings of collective legal cynicism in predominately Arab Sunni communities. This legal cynicism then mediated and intensified the broad support in these communities for insurgent attacks on the U.S./coalition forces.

We also find evidence of transference of legal cynicism about U.S./coalition forces to a similar kind of cynicism about Iraqi government/forces, with the reporting of unnecessary attacks of the Iraqi Police on Arab Sunnis playing a central role. An implication is that the renewal of an insurgency in 2012 had its deeper foundation in the legal cynicism that we observed was pervasive in Arab Sunni communities in 2007. Our conclusion is that the effects of tactics and strategies that were part of the U.S.-led war of aggression in Iraq are likely to prove long-lasting.

In each chapter of this book, we make use of qualitative interview material. Some of this interview material is quoted at length. Our goal in doing this is to fully reveal the emotional intensity of many of these interviews in a way that quantitative analysis alone cannot entirely convey.

Before the Iraq War began, there was obviously no way to know exactly how it would turn out. Now we know a great deal more about how it turned out. We have arrived at a point when it is important to take stock of the Iraq War. Yet there is an inclination in American society to stoically and stubbornly move forward following our armed conflicts, in Iraq as elsewhere, regardless of the outcomes.

While the impulse to move on is understandable, it is also important to learn from our experiences, and we argue it is especially important to learn from the strategies and tactics of criminal militarism involved in waging an aggressive war such as the conflict in Iraq – a war launched and waged with an attitude of legal cynicism linked to violating important and consequential principles of international law. As Justice Jackson suggested at Nuremberg, criminally aggressive wars are so serious not only because they are unjustified, but also because they unleash such powerfully destructive forces. These forces have unanticipated and extensive criminal consequences. Among the most serious and neglected of these consequences in American society is the cyclical perpetuation of legally cynical orientations that reproduce and sustain the criminal militarism of unjustified and unnecessary wars of aggression.

1

The Reign of Terror

A CONTENTIOUS CENTURY

Modern Iraq was created by foreign powers following World War I, when Britain unified three administrative regions of the former Ottoman Empire – Mosul province (northern Iraq), Baghdad province (central Iraq), and Basra province (southern Iraq) – under the control of a king. The British mandate ended in 1932, but the country continued to be ruled by the same royal family until they were overthrown in 1958 with the establishment of the Republic of Iraq. Fast forward a half century and the Islamic State in 2014 staged a symbolic renunciation of the British-drawn border between Syria and Iraq. This border was marked with an earthen berm that the soldiers of the previously named ISIS (or ISIL) bulldozed. They then tweeted a photograph of their victorious fighters dancing and waving flags in celebration of their ambitions to create a new caliphate. Saddam Hussein would have been enraged.

The Iraqi people lived under the authoritarian rule of the Ba'ath Party and Saddam Hussein for more than three decades. The Ba'ath Party first seized control of Iraq with its pan-Arabist ideology in 1963. It then briefly lost and later retook control in 1968. Saddam assumed complete control of Iraq and the Ba'ath Party in 1979, resulting in nearly a quarter century of his violent nationalist autocratic rule. His criminal militarism consumed massive amounts of national resources fighting domestic insurgencies, real and imagined, mostly arising from perceived threats connected to ethnic-religious identities and Iraq's complicated history.

The population of Iraq is strikingly diverse, with many groups tracing their history back hundreds if not thousands of years, long before Britain and France drew its post–World War I borders (Batatu 1978). Iraq's underlying group identities and social structures were historically grounded in differences of religious practice, such as the split between Sunni and Shia adherents of Islam. Added to this were a multitude of other groups, including the Yazidis, Sabean Mandeans, Jews, Shabak Shia, and a variety of Christian groups, including Assyrians, Chaldeans, Syriacs, Armenians, Catholics, and Protestants (Davis 2005).

Saddam Hussein served as deputy secretary of the Ba'ath Party and vice president of Iraq from 1968 until 1979, when he took over as president. The political system in Iraq under Saddam was a highly repressive single-party state with power concentrated in the autocratic rule of the presidency. From 1979 until the U.S.-led invasion, and intermittently with covert American assistance, Saddam ruled not only as president, but also as prime minister, chairman of the Revolutionary Command Council (RCC), and secretary-general of the Regional Command of the Ba'ath Party. He and his inner circle of party members exercised complete control over all key political and military power centers in Iraq.

CREATING A REPUBLIC OF FEAR

Saddam Hussein exercised his control through Iraq's military forces and increasingly its security agencies – a vast bureaucratic network that organized interconnected surveillance, control, infiltration, and intelligence gathering throughout the nation. The military systematically relied on force as its essential instrument, using weapons of mass destruction, at times with American support, to systematically exterminate and eliminate political opposition. Over time, Saddam's security agencies more selectively and systematically arrested, interrogated, tortured, sexually victimized, assassinated, and executed political opponents – and members of their families – to punish and deter dissent. Thus the Iraqi government under Saddam at first relied primarily on crude repression by its military forces, while it later developed a more complex legal authoritarian apparatus to bureaucratically organize state cruelty and terror. One of Saddam's early and most persistent critics, Kanan Makiya (1998), called the regime the "Republic of Fear."

While this Ba'athist regime was not entirely ethnic in its sectarian structure and membership, its key leaders were disproportionately Sunni Arabs linked to Saddam Hussein's inner circle of loyalists. This provided many social, political, and economic advantages for the Arab Sunni minority in Iraq, which made up only about 20 percent of Iraq's population. The resulting state policies marginalized and brutally subordinated several groups, including the majority Shia who constituted about 60 percent of Iraq's population and the non-Arab Sunni Kurds who formed nearly 20 percent.

Beginning in the late 1960s, thousands of allegedly "Iranian" Shia were deported from Iraq, and it is believed that in the 1970s as many as 150,000 Shia, identified by the authorities as Iranian, were forcibly expelled (Tripp 2010). The repression of Iraq's Shia and Kurdish groups increased substantially during the Iran–Iraq War. The war began in September 1980 and continued for eight years, ending in August 1988. An estimated 1 million people died in the hostilities (Coughlin 2002).

The conflict marked a return to brutal military tactics not witnessed on such a large scale since World War I, including the use of chemical weapons. It is now increasingly evident that President Ronald Reagan and former CIA director, vice president, and then president George H. W. Bush facilitated the use of these weapons of mass destruction within Iraq (Harris and Aid 2013a, 2013b; Gibson 2010; Hiltermann 2004).

As early as 1983, the Reagan administration authorized Iraq's purchase of poisonous chemicals and biological viruses, including anthrax and the bubonic plague. The Reagan administration further provided essential intelligence reports to guide Iraq's battlefield strategies, described later in this chapter. Saddam Hussein launched devastating chemical attacks during the Reagan and George H. W. Bush presidencies. During this period, the United States feared Iran more than Iraq. This led Presidents Reagan and Bush to facilitate genocidal chemical attacks by Hussein's military forces, as we further explain later.

Saddam's regime focused its brutality internally against its own Kurdish and Shia populations, as well as externally killing, injuring, detaining, and torturing millions of victims (e.g., Human Rights Watch 1990; Amnesty International 1985). Saddam's Ba'ath Party first targeted the Kurdish population through a low-intensity civil war that ended with a negotiated settlement in 1975. Despite the agreement, the regime continued large-scale deportations that moved possibly hundreds of thousands of Kurds from the oil-rich north of Iraq to the Arab south. In March 1987, Hussein named his cousin, Ali Hassan al-Majid, also known as "Chemical Ali," secretary of the Bureau for the Organization of the North, with orders to use any means necessary to "solve the Kurdish problem and slaughter the saboteurs" (Coughlin 2002:224).

The Iraqi Army razed more than 700 Kurdish villages and relocated the residents. This process culminated in the Anfal operations in which at least 50,000 and perhaps as many as 130,000 people, including many women and children, were systematically killed in an eight-month period (Tripp 2010:236). Al-Majid was an unapologetic genocidal killer. He ordered the armed forces to "kill any human being or animal present" in the Kurdish areas, "to fire at will, without restrictions," and to "carry out random bombardments ... in order to kill the largest number of persons" (Human Rights Watch 1990).

"so that no living soul will survive"

In the last years of the long 1980–8 Iraq–Iran War, Saddam Hussein met frequently with his military advisors to receive encouragement and advice. Although Iraq was winning back territory by the late 1980s, and Saddam relished these victories, he was also obsessed about isolated defeats. The Iranian siege of an Iraqi military base near Halabja in the northern Kurdish region of Iraq was among these temporary losses.

Looking back a month after he ordered the massive attacks that destroyed Halabja, resulting in a historic loss of life, Saddam confided to his officers that even this genocidal killing could not fully calm his obsessions: "I regard Halabja as an Iraqi city and regard it very dearly, and every single atom of dust is dear, but I get upset. I am upset because of the manner in which we lost Halabja." Saddam was convinced of the need to further overwhelm his enemies with unmistakable brutality: "We need this stage. We need to deliver a message, an overt one that could not be camouflaged" (Woods, Palkki, and Stout 2011:158–9).

Saddam's advisors urged a preemptive strike that would end the Iranians' will to fight – a year before the chemical strike came against Halabja. A close advisor ironically asked the same question President Bush later posed: "Why aren't we preemptive?" He responded that "it is not necessary to wait for a disruption in our forces or a strategic breach.... [W]e can abort the enemy's attacks now" (Woods et al. 2011:151). Another advisor went further, arguing that "we should choose an important city and we should mount a heavy chemical strike, equivalent to an atomic weapon, and totally annihilate that city, so that no living soul will survive" (Woods et al. 2011:148). Saddam had used chemical weapons on villages before, but it was another year before he ordered the fateful attack on Halabja.

Leaving no question about command responsibility, Saddam repeatedly warned that "the chemical weapon cannot be used unless I give the order to use it!" (Woods et al. 2011:128). He explained to his aides the potential effects of the chemicals: "Yes, it exterminates by the thousands [pause]. It exterminates by the thousands and restrains them from drinking or eating the food available, and [inaudible] from leaving the city for a period of time until it is fully decontaminated – nothing; he cannot sleep on a mattress, eat, drink, or anything. They will leave [inaudible] naked" (Woods et al. 2011:235).

This was the period in which the Reagan and Bush administrations facilitated Iraq's use of weapons of mass destruction in its war with Iran. Yet for nearly a decade following, the United States continued to cite CIA intelligence that exclusively assigned responsibility for the chemical attacks to Iraq. The cruel irony of this dissemblance was that use of these chemical weapons was later cynically cited as part of the American case for the 2003 invasion of Iraq.

In March 1988, Saddam gave the order for the chemical attack. Iraqi soldiers were deployed in Halabja. However, the Iranians had laid siege to a nearby Iraqi military base and on March 13 attacked and bombarded the city. The Iraqi soldiers began to flee and Iranian forces temporarily occupied the city. The Kurds who lived in Halabja were caught in the middle and had special reason to fear a subsequent assault by Saddam's forces. These forces had already destroyed many villages surrounding Halabja. Iraq's military now launched its air attack on the city itself.

In the box entitled "Chemical Killing," we report an eyewitness account of the Iraqi attacks on Halabja provided in an Iraq History Project (IHP) interview with an eleven-year-old girl, Hawbash. (We use pseudonyms for interview respondents throughout this book.) At first, Hawbash stayed with her family in the basement of a neighbor's house. Her father met with their relatives and they then decided to take refuge in a large government building where 300–400 people were already hiding.

Soon the Iraqi forces began air attacks to retake the city. Bombs began to explode near the building in which Hawbash and her family had taken refuge. "We all held each other. I will never forget the shouting and screaming of the people in the basement. It was so loud that no one could hear another."

Chemical Killing

Eventually the bombing stopped and they ventured outside. As they emerged from the building, they saw that a main wall had collapsed. They gradually realized from the dead and dying they saw around them that the bombs contained deadly chemicals. They knew they must flee:

We had three vehicles. Before we went outside, my mother soaked our heads in water and put a wet cloth against our mouths. I had a school handkerchief covering my face. Then, we ran out of the house to the vehicles. I saw white smoke rising.

I saw people fall onto the ground and die. I watched people hang onto our pickup, try to climb inside and then fall off and die.

Then, the drivers of our vehicles became confused. The chemicals affected us. My cousin, who was driving the pickup, fell unconscious and crashed into a wall. He died and became a martyr. Everyone inside the cab was injured and unconscious, including my parents, brothers, and sisters. Another cousin and I were conscious and alive.

My cousin said, "Let's run to my uncles' home."

I said, "I can't leave my family."

This was a day in which no one cared about anyone else.

I stayed there with my parents, brothers, and sisters. I sat there alone. I touched my parents' faces and shook them to see if they were alive. I didn't want to believe that they had died. I kept shaking them and hoping they would start breathing. It was useless.

I wanted to die. I wanted to be like them, laid out in the back of the truck. I kept thinking that my father and my older brothers were stronger than me, so how could they die and leave me here alive? I thought to myself, "They should save me. It shouldn't be me here trying to save them."

I was unable to sleep, even for a second. I just sat there looking at the dead bodies. I also watched the jets bombing the Sazanyan area where the people had fled. I counted the bombs. I felt as if I was dreaming. . . .

After the sun rose, my aunt went to my brother's home and the rest of us stayed near the pickup, hoping some of the others would wake up. There is a well-known photo of myself, my brother, my cousin, and my aunt sitting behind the pickup truck. That picture was published in a magazine. . . .

I was eleven years old. I had never hurt anyone. My family was innocent. We had done nothing. In the space of a few days, my life grew dark and became a nightmare.

Members of Hawbash's family were among an estimated 5,000 killed. A month later, Saddam again ordered the massive use of chemical weapons to expel the Iranians from al-Fao, the site of important oil terminals southeast of Basra that were a focal point for much of the Iraq–Iran War. U.S. intelligence had learned that Iranian troops were massing in the area and were preparing a spring 1988 offensive to overtake Basra. When President Reagan was informed, he warned his defense secretary that "an Iranian victory is unacceptable" (Harris and Aid 2013a, 2013b).

The U.S. intelligence was passed on to Iraq, providing the essential details for "targeting packages" to organize Iraqi strikes. Saddam drew from his American-enhanced chemical stocks for the attacks. Retired U.S. Air Force officer Rick Francona, who was in Baghdad during the 1988 strikes, reported that "The Iraqis never told us they intended to use nerve gas. They didn't have to. We already knew" (Harris and Aid 2013a, 2013b).

Aside from chemical weapons and artillery bombardments, Saddam committed more than 100,000 soldiers to retaking al-Fao. Again, Saddam saw the massive use of chemical weapons as a key instrument for not only exterminating and eliminating his enemies, but also for demonstrating to his own people his overwhelming capacity to prevail. He explained his thinking about what he called the "al-Fao effect" by drawing on a conversation with his wife:

> There is no message more important than Al-Fao.... I have told you about my wife. After the Al-Fao events, her mood changed, as a human being.... I mean, imagine the extent of the influence Al-Fao will have. I listen to her. I mean, she is exuberant in following Al-Fao. I mean, this is proof of the Al-Fao effect. She is a citizen, she is not in the leadership, she is not a politician, except within a small margin. So this is really a story to be told. (Woods et al. 2011:160)

However, Halabja and al-Fao were only a part of Saddam's reign of terror – albeit the part for which this regime is most widely reviled. Saddam's regime would over time become more bureaucratically efficient in its development and use of weapons of repression.

MASS ATROCITIES FOLLOWING THE FIRST GULF WAR

The Iraq–Iran War left Iraq with an economy in shambles, a huge conscripted military, and massive debt, which provoked a crisis in 1990 when Iraq refused repayment of its accumulated wartime borrowings to Kuwait. Attempts at negotiations between the two countries in July 1990 failed, and in August 1990 Saddam Hussein ordered Iraq's invasion of Kuwait, crushing its small army with tanks and a commitment of 100,000 Iraqi troops (Coughlin 2002:253). Significantly, Saddam held back some of his troops, especially his most loyal and effective Republican Guard, which was concentrated to the north in and around Baghdad.

President George H. W. Bush had by this point decided that Saddam Hussein was beyond his control and a threat to American interests in the region. He used his diplomatic experience to bring together the American-led international coalition that waged the first Gulf War and easily forced Iraq's army out of Kuwait.

Confronted with this humiliating defeat and weakened by Iraq's massive loss of lives from previous wars, Saddam's Ba'athist regime now faced the prospect of serious domestic insurrection. The threats came from both the Shia-dominated provinces in the south and the predominately Kurdish provinces in the north.

Saddam's strikes against both regions were savage. His forces heavily bombed Kurdish civilian areas in the north, and they engaged in widespread arrests, torture, arbitrary executions, and targeted killings of civilians fleeing the region (Coughlin 2002:281). By the end of April 1991, some 2 million Kurds had fled to the neighboring mountains and taken refuge across the Iraq border in Turkey.

The Kurds finally benefited from the belated protection provided by U.S. and British forces, and from their own increasing success in repelling and expelling the regime's army from the three provinces collectively known as Kurdistan. The Kurdish north emerged by the early 1990s as a semiautonomous region, at last freed from Saddam's direct rule and repression. This autonomy would spare the Kurdish north from most of the violence that would later follow the 2003 U.S. invasion of Iraq. The Shia of southern Iraq were neither protected nor spared in this way.

Saddam Hussein was determined to hold on to southern Iraq, and the Shia in this region were his unceasing targets for repression after the first Gulf War. As the battered remnants of Saddam Hussein's defeated army returned from Kuwait through Shia-populated southern Iraq, President George H. W. Bush publicly called for Iraqis to rise up and overthrow Saddam. He urged, "There is another way for the bloodshed to stop: And this is for the Iraqi military and the Iraqi people to take matters into their own hands and force Saddam Hussein, the dictator, to step aside."

Many Iraqis believed that the victorious American forces in southern Iraq would assist their uprising. They assumed that at least the American helicopter gunships located on bases in southern Iraq would provide air cover for their rebellion. Instead, the U.S. forces pulled back into their bases with orders not to intervene. George H. W. Bush was persuaded that Iran would gain control of Iraq if the Shia actually succeeded in toppling Saddam's Sunni-dominated regime, and this outcome became his overriding concern.

In a 2001 interview with the Public Broadcasting System (PBS), Bush's foreign policy advisor, Brent Scowcroft, explained that the administration still saw it as in the U.S. interest to maintain Iraq – even with Saddam in control and engaging in mass atrocities and killing his own citizens – as a counter to Iran. From a human rights perspective, this was a legally cynical rationalization for inaction; but for Bush's political realist policy advisor, Scowcroft, inaction was the only logical course to follow.

PBS: Didn't we see their military killing people?

SCOWCROFT: Yes.

PBS: And we didn't intervene.

SCOWCROFT: Of course not.

PBS: Not from the air.

SCOWCROFT: Of course not.

PBS: We didn't cut off their gasoline supplies?

SCOWCROFT: First of all, one of our objectives was not to have Iraq split up into constituent ... parts. It's a fundamental interest of the United States to keep a balance in that area, in Iraq.

This strategic concern in 1991 about the destabilizing consequences and advantages to Iran of Saddam's downfall deterred the first President Bush in ways that would not subsequently dissuade the second President Bush from the legally cynical decision to invade and occupy Iraq in 2003.

Great Britain's former prime minister, Gordon Brown, agreed with this characterization of Bush and Scowcroft's thinking. However, Brown also brought the specter of the past defeat in Vietnam into the picture. He observed that the U.S. military leadership "were united in seeing the whole [first Gulf War] campaign as a chance to redress the Viet Nam Syndrome, as they called it ... They had no heart for going to Baghdad, getting involved in a civil war, or anything else that would detract from a battlefield achievement designed to rehabilitate the military's image and self-esteem." Brown (2013) concluded that "I have no doubt that the entire military pushed in Washington for non-involvement."

SADDAM'S MILITARY REPRESSION AND LEGAL AUTHORITARIANISM

Unaware that they would be attempting to overthrow Saddam and his remaining loyal and heavily armed forces with neither American military intervention nor assistance, the Shia resistance seized control of important southern Iraqi cities following the first Gulf War. The first revolt occurred in Basra in early March 1991, and the revolt then spread throughout the Shia south, including the holy cities of Najaf and Karbala.

Undeterred by the American military who discretely pulled back into their southern Iraqi bases, Saddam's most trusted Republican Guard troops viciously launched their attack from the north with helicopter gunships and tanks. Within days, they seized the momentum in ruthlessly suppressing the rebellion, targeting rebels and civilians alike (Tripp 2010:246). The success of the Shia resistance in briefly gaining control of several important southern cities was quickly reversed. The losses instilled a lastingly cynical sense of victimhood among the defeated Shia.

Following the 1991 uprisings, the Iraqi government continued its military and political repression of the southern Shia. The government reversed reforms that it had previously implemented and intensified its repression. For example, Saddam Hussein rescinded secular programs that had opened some jobs to women. This reaffirmed Islamic traditions and enhanced Saddam's standing among local tribal and religious groups.

By 1994, the government had fully institutionalized its repression through state decrees, surveillance, torture, and brutal punishments that included rapes, sexual assaults, and executions for alleged crimes and infractions against the regime. The security agencies now bore the brunt of responsibility, taking over from a thoroughly depleted and exhausted military. War making gave way to a bureaucratic form of state making based on a legal authoritarian use of the justice system that legitimated its brutality with arrests, confessions, and trials. What remained the same was the cruel repression of the Shia.

The trials took place in courts in which the UN Special Rapporteur reported that "the judiciary is wholly subservient to and dependent upon an unaccountable executive in the institutions of the RCC [Revolutionary Command Council] and the President" (Abdullah 2013:82). This was the same judiciary that would later be the focus of U.S. efforts at "reeducation" in the rule of law, an effort we analyze in Chapter 3 of this book. The UN Special Rapporteur reported in 2001 that an estimated 4,000 women and girls had died in a brutal reinforcement of traditional gender roles that included a government-authorized resurgence of "honor killings." These killings were unimpeded and therefore indirectly enabled by Iraq's courts. A presidential decree exempted men from prosecution and punishment for these killings (Tripp 2010:256). A reinforced legal authoritarianism took hold.

Saddam Hussein's authoritarian state now relied on a vast, multifaceted, ever-present, and constantly domineering security apparatus that involved numerous agencies whose bureaucratic roles and responsibilities both competed and overlapped in a multilayered, fail-safe system of repression. The security apparatus worked outside the military chain of command and the regular army. This apparatus consisted of five agencies designated as Special Security (al-Amin al Khas), General Security (al-Amin), General Intelligence (al-Mukhabarat), Military Intelligence (al-Istikhbarat), and Military Security (al-Askari) (Marashi 2002).

The General Security Directorate had the most power. It managed an enormous system of personal files and a huge network of spies and informants, insinuating itself into the everyday lives of Iraqi citizens. It coordinated operations with the civilian police force, maintained a unit in every police station, and had branches in every Iraqi governorate. The General Security Directorate was the fully empowered coercive arm of the state. It maintained its own set of detention facilities, including Abu Ghraib, where the political prisoners most feared by the regime were held.

THE TOLL OF VICTIMIZATION

The General Security Directorate was a highly specialized agency. It legitimated its use of torture to extract confessions with the legal authoritarian cover of summary court proceedings, often justifying its activities as protecting the presidency and the Iraqi state. Although it is impossible to know the full extent of all the human rights violations that were committed in the name of Saddam's regime, a sense of the scale of this terror is provided through interviews conducted by the Iraq History Project. The massive IHP consists of almost 7,000 interviews conducted in 2007 and 2008 with human rights victims of the regime of Saddam Hussein.

IHP is the most comprehensive study of human rights victims in Iraq. It used a chain-referral methodology employing a heterogeneous group of more than forty-three interviewers to identify respondents dispersed throughout the country. Interviewers developed referral chains through displacement and refugee camps, political prisoners' associations, human rights groups, courts, word-of-mouth contacts, and social networks – that is, it mobilized a broad array of interviewers and referrals designed to diversify representation in a saturation sampling of concentrations of human rights victims.

IHP began by gathering interviews in the Kurdish region in northern Iraq. Following an initial five-month pilot phase, the project trained additional interviewers who worked in Baghdad as well as the governorates of Anbar, Babylon, Basrah, Diyala, Dohuk, Irbil, Karbala, Kirkuk, Missan, Muthanna, Najaf, Ninewa, Qadissiya, Salah al-Din, Sulaimaniya, Thi-Qar, and Wassit. Interviewers varied in gender and religious/ethnic background. They ranged in age and occupation and included physicians, professors, lawyers, and journalists. Interviewers were encouraged to disperse and diversify their recruits and referrals.

Figure 1.1 displays the vast incidence and prevalence of human rights violations documented in the 6,982 IHP interviews for the period from 1968 to 2003. These are reports by survivors, so killings are not fully indicated. Individual respondents reported multiple victimizations involving themselves and others. The most common violations reported in the preinvasion regime of Saddam Hussein included assaults and beatings, detentions, displacement, and torture.

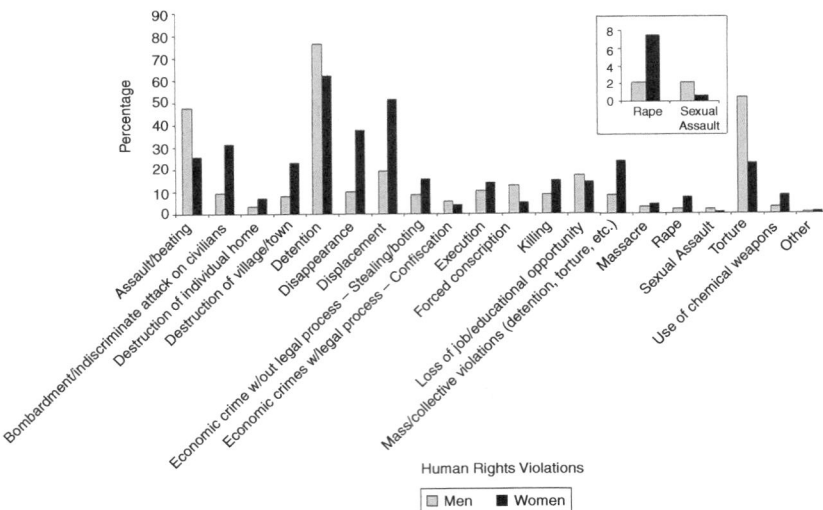

FIGURE 1.1. Variation in Reported Human Rights Violations, circa 1968–2003

Nearly 50 percent or more of the men interviewed reported assaults and beatings (47.7%), detentions (76.2%), and torture (61.9%). More than half of the women (51.5%) reported displacement, and more than a fifth of the women reported assaults and beatings (25.8%), the destruction of villages and towns (22.9%), or torture (22.6%).

More than 7 percent (7.5%) of the women and more than 2 percent (2.6%) of the men reported rapes of themselves and others. About 2 percent (2.3%) of the men and less than 1 percent (0.6%) of the women reported sexual assaults on themselves and others. The gender-specific pattern of women reporting being vaginally raped and men being anally sexually assaulted (usually with objects) replicates systematic gender differences also found in prior studies of sexual violence, thus providing a form of "divergent validation" (John and Benet-Martinez 2000) of the IHP interviews (Zawati 2007). Both forms of sexual violence are recognized as rape in international criminal law, although rape is infrequently named as a crime in Iraq, and when acknowledged is almost always called torture.

The female victims of the rapes had no doubts about the origins and purposes of these acts and linked them to the Sunni-dominated Ba'athist regime. One woman lamented that "when I saw this man and thought about what was going to happen, I wished I was dead. I also wished that I'd just joined the Ba'ath Party." A male victim asked, "How could this happen? What type of criminal regime were we living under?"

VICTIMS AND PERPETRATORS

The IHP numbers indicate the enormity and barbarity of the regime's human rights violations, while testimonials by individuals further convey the torment and terror inflicted. In addition to victims, IHP also included sixty-two perpetrators among its interviews. In the instance recounted in "Learning to Torture," Jasim describes how he became involved in the work of the Security Directorate and what this work entailed. Jasim's experience is an inside account of how this legal authoritarian regime imposed its terror by sexually abusing and torturing Shia members of the Dawa political party to which Nouri al-Maliki, Iraq's longest-serving prime minister, belonged. Many of Maliki's closest Dawa colleagues were tortured and killed, presaging the subsequent mistreatment of Arab Sunnis by Maliki's government. The vicious repression of the Dawa Party can be understood as one source of a long-lasting Shia legal cynicism about both Saddam and the American government that had tolerated and supported him.

Learning to Torture

A relative of Jasim's mother had asked if he wanted to work in the Security Directorate. He agreed and was taken to a large building with many rooms and hallways. He was assigned to the Operations Room and told he would be a torturer. He was told he would be punishing criminals who threatened the security and stability of the state. There were bloodstains on the walls. He was left to observe Abu Husam, an experienced torturer:

> I felt ill as I watched Abu Husam torturing people. It was hard for me to control myself.
>
> A short while later, they brought in a woman who refused to inform on her husband, who was a member of the Dawa Party. Abu Husam undressed her. He made her sit on a chair and tied her down. He connected electric wires to her hands, feet, and breasts. He began to shock her. She was shaking and screaming. She began to drool and then she fainted. Abu Husam took her out of the chair, dressed her, and called the guards to take her away.
>
> At that moment, I hated myself. I knew that soon I would become like this man.
>
> At the end of my training that day, Nazem came in and ordered me to go home. When he saw my condition, he took me home and we

spoke. "What happened to you, Jasim? This is only the first day. You were only watching. What would you be like if it were you that had been working?"

"What did those people do?" I asked. "They did a terrible, unforgivable thing. They want to overthrow the government. They want to destabilize the country. If that happened, there would be chaos, terror, killing, and looting. Don't believe that any of them are innocent! We are the innocent ones!"

He dropped me home. My mother saw I was sad and asked, "Is there something wrong, son?"

I looked in her eyes, shining with happiness, seeing me return from my first day at work and filled with the hope that we would soon have a better, more settled life. I couldn't tell her what happened that day. "Nothing, Mother, I am just not used to this new job." "Everybody finds things difficult at the beginning," she said, "but they get used to it."

I spent that night thinking about how I was supposed to hold the cable and beat people. I was filled with pain. Then, I remembered Nazem's words, saying those people were criminals and traitors. I began to tell myself that they deserved what was happening because they had betrayed our nation. I convinced myself that they must be punished. Soon, the three days of training were over and the day I was to start working had arrived. I didn't sleep that night. I knew that from then on I would be a torturer. . . .

The first person I was to torture was a man in his forties who was accused of joining the Dawa Party. I held the cable, but my hand was trembling. How could I beat this man who was older than me and whose eyes were begging for mercy?

Abu Husam shouted at me, "Don't let your hands shake! Don't be a coward!"

I raised the cable to beat the man, but I couldn't find the strength to hit him. Then, Abu Husam slapped me hard in the face. An officer who was in the room said, "You're a soldier here. Those who volunteer to work in the Security Directorate are the servants of the government. They follow orders. This time, I will have mercy on you. Your punishment will be minimal."

He turned to Abu Husam and said, "Carry out the orders!" Abu Husam tied my hand down and hit it with a metal pipe until it broke. After my hand healed, I returned to work. This time, the officer decided to supervise me personally. I was forced to torture a woman with electricity. I undressed her and connected her private parts to wires in the way Abu Husam had done. I shocked her until she fainted. I don't know how my heart could be filled with such cruelty.

"Well done!" said the officer. "That's the way to do it! Those people are a plague! They're trying to destroy our country. You must show them no mercy!" His words filled me with complicated feelings. After that day, I committed many violations as a torturer. I rented a house for my family. When they said, "good job!" it meant a lot to me.

The officer ordered me to torture a man who was a member of the insurgents. I connected his penis to high voltage. I was merciless. I disconnected the wires and he urinated. His urine was mixed with blood. Then, I broke one of his legs.

We had an arrangement with a lieutenant colonel that whenever a beautiful girl was sent, I was to beat her. Then, I would take her to his room to spend the night. I would stand next to the door and listen to the woman screaming or begging him to leave her alone. I could hear how he would beat them. He raped so many women.

At this time, I drank heavily. I tried not to think about all the things I was doing. It was my job.

Jasim eventually left the Security Directorate for medical reasons and sought solace in his religion. Although Jasim is the voice of only one perpetrator, his account suggests the bureaucratized organization and viciousness of the role that the security agencies played in the institutionalized repression of civilians during Saddam's regime. A further understanding of the role of the security agencies can be obtained from the Iraq History Project's aggregated reports of victim and perpetrator identities.

Rape was among the most viciously practiced crimes in the regime of Saddam Hussein after the first Gulf War. Figure 1.2 indicates that rapes in particular were highly concentrated, with Shia identified as the victims in more than 80 percent of all cases reported. Kurdish and Sunni victims combined account for about 16 percent of the rapes in this figure. These data reveal the degree to which Saddam's regime used rape to torture, terrorize, and repress the majority Shia group in Iraq, adding to the trauma of their growing sense of victimhood.

Figure 1.3 identifies the perpetrators of rape. Although a wide array of state actors engaged in rapes, more than 80 percent of those reported as perpetrators by victims were employees of the General Security Directorate. Ba'ath Party members were also involved, but this category overlaps with

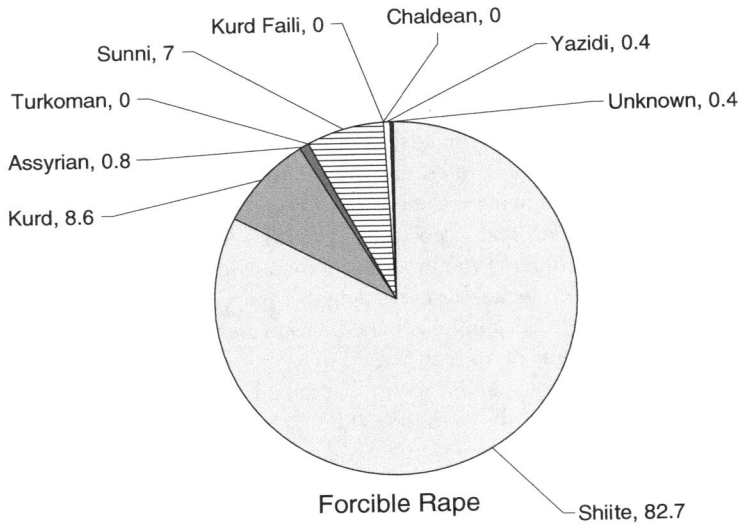

FIGURE 1.2. Ethnic Backgrounds of Victims of Forcible Rape, circa 1968–2003

the General Security Directorate. Thus the General Security Directorate personnel were primarily responsible. This figure reveals that regular army forces played only a small role as perpetrators of rape. Yet military forces and the Ba'ath Party members in general were summarily dismissed in the early stage of the American-led coalition occupation of Iraq described in the following chapter.

The dominant figure in addition to Saddam responsible for the record of human rights violations of the regime, from 1968 to 2003, was Saddam's previously introduced cousin and fellow Sunni clan member, Ali Hassan al-Majid. As noted earlier, al-Majid was more infamously known as "Chemical Ali" for his leading role in the Anfal genocide. However, al-Majid held numerous posts in the regime, including minister of defense, minister of the interior, director of general security, and chief of the Iraqi Intelligence Service. When the regular army was responsible for conducting deportations and mass killings during the wars, al-Majid moved into the leading military role. When General Security assumed the major responsibility for the detentions, torture, and rapes during the closing years of the regime, al-Majid again played a leading role.

After the U.S. invasion of Iraq, President Bush often referred to Saddam's "rape rooms" in offering a humanitarian justification for the Iraq War. However, in the lead-up to the war, the focus was instead on the urgent threat Iraq posed to America's security.

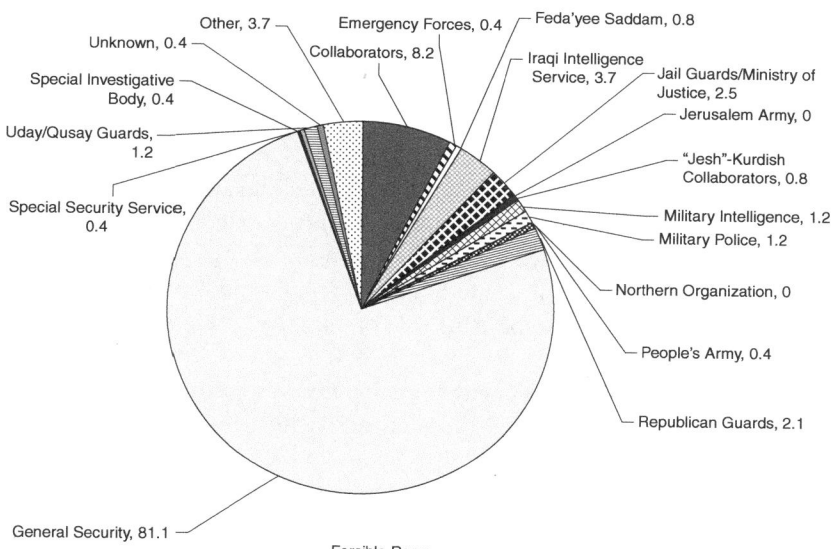

FIGURE 1.3. Institutional Affiliations of Perpetrators of Forcible Rape, circa 1968–2003

PREEMPTIVE WAR AND HUMANITARIAN INTERVENTION

The two dominant rationales for American military involvement in international conflicts since the Vietnam War are humanitarian intervention and preemptive war. Bill Clinton's commitment of U.S. air power in the Balkan conflict in the 1990s was justified as humanitarian intervention, while George W. Bush's argument for the invasion of Iraq was preemptive war, which also became known as the Bush Doctrine. The most salient difference between these commitments of military force is on whose behalf the commitment is ostensibly being made. Humanitarian intervention is a centuries-old idea in law and responds in a universalistic way to threats of harm to citizens in other countries, such as the Bosnians in the Balkans. Because the UN has never formally ratified humanitarian intervention, it has sometimes been depicted as illegal but morally necessary and legitimate (see Hurd 2013). Preemptive war responds to perceived threats to our own citizens rather than citizens of other nations, such as following 9/11.

If the United States had invaded Iraq in 1988, when Saddam ordered the chemical attack on Kurdish populations, or in 1991, when Saddam ordered the military attacks on Shia and Kurdish civilians who rose up against his rule following the first Gulf War in Kuwait, the American commitment of forces could have been justified as humanitarian intervention. However, in 2003, Saddam was not engaged in mass atrocities.

For the previous decade, Saddam had ruled Iraq through the more selectively targeted and bureaucratized terror of his legal authoritarian General Security agency. This bureaucratization of violent repression represented what Walzer has called "ordinary brutality," which he argues is not a justified basis for another state's military attack (2007:640). He reasons that if such bureaucratized brutality were justifiable grounds for attack, "there would be far more occasions than it is safe to have – and far too much 'waste in brief mortality.' States cannot impose the risks of war on other states, except in cases of humanitarian urgency."

To be sure, Saddam's security bureaucracy was a criminal organization guilty of grievous crimes. But these crimes against Iraq's citizens were not the announced rationale for the invasion, and a large-scale military invasion would likely not have been regarded as a proportionate response to this threat. Earlier economic sanctions and no-fly zones were imposed with this rationale. The new presumed threat to Americans introduced by the Bush administration to justify its war in Iraq was Saddam's weapons of mass destruction. The preoccupation with Iraq's possible possession of weapons of mass destruction intensified after the 9/11 attack on the World Trade Center in New York City. It took the form of the preemptive claim of self-defense.

The rationale was spelled out by George W. Bush in his 2002 speech at West Point justifying a new policy of preemptive war. Paul Wolfowitz could not have been clearer in explaining, "The truth is that for reasons that have a lot to do with the U.S. government bureaucracy, we settled on the one issue that everyone could agree on, which was weapons of mass destruction." In advance of the invasion, the British head of foreign intelligence confirmed the weak evidence for this threat by saying, "The intelligence and facts were being fixed around the policy." Yet Condoleezza Rice joined the call for war by dubiously warning of the nuclear danger: "the smoking gun in the shape of a mushroom cloud" (Packer 2006: chapter 2).

The Bush administration's assertions about weapons of mass destruction, including the prospect of nuclear weapons, were the primary self-defense rationale for its preemptive war in Iraq. The United States used an implicit self-defense claim to counter the prohibition of international law against wars of aggression and to justify the invasion of Iraq without the permission of the UN Security Council. Unanimous Security Council support was the safeguard against aggressive war that the international community had put into place after World War II.

The administration's self-defense claim anticipated finding weapons of mass destruction that the United States asserted Saddam Hussein had stockpiled in Iraq. Yet before CIA Director George Tenet offered his hyperbolic "slam dunk" assessment that the weapons were there to be found, even the CIA had expressed reservations about the credibility of reports by Iraqi defectors and had questioned alternative evidence cited by the Pentagon. The Bush administration's preemptive war doctrine would prove a legally cynical rationalization for an aggressive policy of criminal militarism.

Swedish diplomat Hans Blix, who served as the United Nations' chief weapons inspector before the invasion, reported that there were about 700 inspections, and that none of these inspections revealed weapons of mass destruction. Blix himself acknowledged the difficulties of proving a negative – that there were no weapons of mass destruction anywhere – conceding that they might eventually be found somewhere. However, there was a logical problem as well. Saddam Hussein's regime actually *did have* such weapons during the first Gulf War, yet these weapons were not used by the regime on the battlefield in Kuwait. This undermined the argument that even if Saddam still had these weapons, that he would use them against the United States. In Walzer's terms, there was no "extremity in real time" to the putative threat posed to Americans by Saddam's regime (2007:640). There was no immediacy or extremity that justified the risks of deadly consequences that the U.S.-led war in Iraq posed. The Bush administration negligently ignored the risks of this war's consequences that we demonstrate in this book.

Brazilian diplomat Jose Bustani was another source of skepticism about the perceived threat that Saddam Hussein's presumed weapons of mass destruction posed to the United States or others. Bustani was appointed by the United Nations to establish the Organization for the Prohibition of Chemical Weapons in The Hague. In late 2001, Iraq indicated that it wanted to join the Chemical Weapons Convention, and inspectors made plans to visit Iraq in January 2002. However, by spring 2002 the U.S. undersecretary of state, John Bolton, demanded Bustani's resignation, saying the United States was unhappy with his undertaking "ill-considered initiatives" without consulting the United States, which with Japan contributed about half the agency's budget (Simons 2013).

Former foreign minister of Brazil Celso Lafer received a private message from Colin Powell that "I have people in the administration who don't want Bustani to stay." "My view," Lafer explained, "is that the neocons wanted the freedom to act without multilateral constraints and, with Bustani wanting to act with more independence, this would limit their freedom of action" (Simons 2013:A12).

Bustani refused to resign and was ousted in a close and unusual vote in which nearly half of the member states abstained. He maintained that the United States thought he would be an obstacle to the administration's invasion plans. His experts had told him that Iraq's chemical weapons were destroyed in the 1990s, after the Gulf War. He insisted "everybody knew there weren't any," and that "An inspection would make it obvious there were no weapons to destroy. This would completely nullify the decision to invade" (Simons 2013:A12). To Bustani, the legal cynicism of the WMD claim was obvious.

After the invasion, David Kay, the U.S. government's chief weapons inspector, was also unable to find evidence that Saddam Hussein's government had stockpiled the purported weapons. However, the Bush administration had preempted the scheduled completion of UN inspections and invaded Iraq without Security Council authorization. By the terms of international law, the U.S. invasion of Iraq marked the intentional initiation of a war of aggression.

There are no certain answers to vexing moral questions provoked by this invasion. For example, was the greater crime the *ad bellum* preemptive rush to what international law calls aggressive war? Or was it the prospect of the *post bellum* collateral crimes that would follow the onset of this war – which at Nuremberg was called "the accumulated evil of the whole"? We are concerned with both *ad bellum* and *post bellum* aspects of the war in Iraq, and also with what Walzer (2012; 2004) has called the longer-term *jus post bellum* – the justice of what follows war – which has proven a long and deadly aftermath.

Colin Powell warned that the responsibilities associated with the Iraq War could be long term with his reference to the "Pottery Barn" rule that "you break it, you own it." Donald Rumsfeld offered his glib defense of the criminal aftermath of the Iraq War by concluding that "stuff happens and it's untidy, and freedom's untidy, and free people are free to make mistakes and commit crimes and do bad things" (see Hare 2004).

FREEDOM FROM PLANNING AND THE GREATER THREAT

In this case, freedom was also a rationalization for the absence of a plan: there was a plan for the invasion, but little preparation for the occupation that followed. The planning for the invasion began at least as early as January 1998, when a group called Project for the New American Century, including Donald

Rumsfeld and Paul Wolfowitz, wrote an open letter to President Clinton calling for regime change in Iraq. By the end of the year, in December 1998, President Clinton authorized the bombing of installations where chemical weapons had been produced in Iraq. The Iraq Survey Group Final Report later indicated that this bombing had destroyed Saddam's diminishing capacity to produce chemical weapons.

Nonetheless, the Twin Tower attacks of 9/11 renewed anxiousness within the Bush administration to topple Saddam Hussein, with the argument that there was a never proven connection between his assumed possession of weapons of mass destruction and the 9/11 attacks. Saddam's presumed weaponry was now more urgently seen as the threat that America must remove in a preemptive fashion.

There was little consideration of a nascent sectarian conflict between the Arab Sunni and Shia groups that Saddam's regime was both provoking and struggling to repressively contain. Haddad (2011) describes in *Sectarianism in Iraq* how following the first Gulf War the Shia developed a collective sense of victimhood. The massive killings, arrests, and rapes during and after the Shia uprising in southern Iraq had produced a rising collective sense of grievance and anger.

During this same period, Arab Sunnis also felt a rising sense of victimization from the increasing weight of international economic sanctions on Iraq. Following the first Gulf War in Kuwait, the United Nations supported by the United States imposed economic sanctions that were keenly felt by all groups. However, the Arab Sunnis had fared best in the earlier years of Saddam's regime, and they therefore had the most to lose from the sanctions.

Expressions of Shia and Sunni identities increasingly emerged as ways of articulating these alternative experiences of victimization and rising resentments. *There was no apparent American awareness that emerging sectarian identification and separation could present a greater future danger than the weapons that the administration insisted Saddam possessed and threatened to use against America.*

To the extent the administration had a plan, it was to overturn the regime and create a temporary government to which the rebuilding of the Iraqi state could be left within several months of arrival. However, as the Iraqi Army withdrew and dispersed ahead of the advancing U.S.-led forces, the once powerful Iraqi state quickly withered and withdrew along with it. What Rumsfeld saw as freedom looked more ominously like a void with nothing substantial planned to fill it. Significantly, President Bush placed the Department of Defense and Donald Rumsfeld rather than the State Department and Colin Powell in charge of post-invasion Iraq.

Rumsfeld initially picked a retired lieutenant, Jay Garner, to lead the transition. Garner had no well-developed plan and was soon replaced by Paul Bremer, a civilian and former diplomat. He was responsible for establishing the Coalition Provisional Authority (CPA) and an interim government council with very limited responsibilities. Bremer (2006) was appointed as presidential envoy to Iraq and compared his powers, which included ruling by decree, to those exercised by General Douglas MacArthur in postwar Japan. He presided over the dismissal of the Iraqi military and Ba'ath Party members from the top layers of the government. These last remaining institutions with a semblance of limited inter-sectarian leadership were cast aside without consideration of what could replace them. Iraq moved from liberation to an occupation that was intended to be short-lived but that led to a U.S. military presence that lasted longer than any previous American war.

The preemptive war had gone even more quickly than imagined, but without a discovery of the stockpile of weapons of mass destruction that had been its motivating cause. With Iraq's military disassembled, its government in shambles, and no real plan by which the coalition forces could fill the resulting void, looters took advantage of the vacuum and soon walked away with the removable parts of the state infrastructure. The threat that was to have been preempted proved illusory, and claims to humanitarian purposes were either disavowed or proved misleading.

The remainder of this book focuses on the *post bellum* criminal and collateral consequences unleashed by the preemptive war in Iraq. The preemptive policies of the Bush Doctrine unfolded along a path of criminal militarism and its fateful consequences. These consequences were even more fateful than the war itself, as the plan for a peaceful democratic transition included little more than the abrupt demobilization of the military and removal of skilled mid-level as well as top-level Ba'ath Party workers from essential government ministries.

The Arab Sunnis who were displaced from their former lives and livelihoods were especially hard hit. There was no plan for the rehabilitation and reintegration of the Arab Sunnis as productive citizens of the new Iraq. In the next chapter, we will see how the Arab Sunnis were in many ways disenfranchised and left with little alternative but to see the U.S.-led Coalition Provisional Authority and its accompanying interim governing council as illegitimate, unresponsive, and ineffectual – that is, the Arab Sunnis increasingly saw the new Iraq from the perspective of a defeated legal cynicism.

However, before we turn to the remainder of this story, it is important to briefly recognize that the choice to wage this preemptive war with all of its consequences coincided with a parallel decision *not* to undertake a humanitarian intervention in response to a genocide unfolding nearly simultaneously and in the "extremity of real time" in Sudan's Darfur region – a genocide that would enter the history books of mass atrocity alongside Iraq's Anfal genocide from years earlier.

DEMURRING ON DARFUR AND INVADING IRAQ

The choice to invade Iraq emerged alongside a fateful decision not to intervene in the Darfur region of Sudan. This was deeply and darkly ironic. The National Commission on Terrorist Attacks on the United States found that Iraq's Saddam Hussein did not cooperate with Osama bin Laden in planning the 9/11 attacks or otherwise. However, Sudan's leadership not only cooperated with bin Laden by hosting him and his entourage in Sudan, they also actively encouraged bin Laden to seek out Saddam's support. The result was that although bin Laden was allowed to stay in Sudan until 1996, and despite Sudan having encouraged his cooperation with Saddam, the United States nonetheless later covertly chose to nurture a relationship with this country that it hoped would yield useful cooperation and intelligence for its pursuit of al-Qaeda. As part of an ongoing relationship, in 2005 the United States flew the director of Sudan's security activities, General Gosh, to Washington for meetings at the Central Intelligence Agency (Hagan and Rymond-Richmond 2009:88).

As events in 2002 and 2003 led up to the invasion of Iraq, the United States often seemed to be doing its best to ignore the humanitarian emergency that was simultaneously building in the Darfur region of western Sudan. During the early months of 2003, Darfur was descending into genocidal chaos. The signing of a peace agreement in South Sudan, ending twenty years of genocidal violence in this part of the country, was given explicit priority by the United States over responding to Sudan's growing resort to repressive violence to the west in Darfur. Rebel groups in Darfur were frustrated that the peace agreement for the south did nothing to resolve their own neglect and mistreatment by Sudan's central government in Khartoum. The Darfur rebels were small in number, but they managed to stage several successful attacks on the government of Sudan's (GoS) military bases from February to April 2003.

The Sudanese government had in the past leveraged its government military forces with local Arab militias to overwhelm rebellious African indigenous groups. The government in Khartoum now rightly assumed that the United States would be too consumed with its invasion of Iraq to challenge a quick and brutal repression of the rebels in Darfur. Khartoum set up a special task force on Darfur and reapplied a strategy it had used previously in South Sudan.

In the early months of 2003, it was not difficult to foresee where this modeling on past militia-led violence in south and west Sudan would lead. Gerald Prunier writes:

> The GoS had clearly decided on a military solution to the crisis.... During May 2003 the New Task Force began seriously to explore the possibilities of formalizing the government's relationship with the already existing Janjaweed militias.... [T]hese rough armed bands had existed since the late 1980s in an indeterminate zone half-way between being bandits and government thugs. (2005:97)

Alex de Waal (2004), another long-time scholar of Sudan, called this strategic alliance "counter-insurgency on the cheap."

Prunier summarized the carnage that unfolded in Darfur simultaneously with the invasion and occupation of Iraq by observing that the Sudanese government "unleashed the Janjaweed on a grand scale" (2005:99). He noted that "There had been violence before, but by late July 2003 it had assumed a completely new scale and exploded." At least 300,000 ethnic Africans died and about 3 million were displaced from their homes and villages in Darfur in 2003 and 2004 (Hagan and Rymond-Richmond 2009).

The U.S. State Department documented this genocidal violence with detailed survey work among Darfurian refugees in neighboring camps in Chad, and it used the resulting evidence to declare the violence as genocide. It then tacitly supported (even though it formally abstained from) a UN Security Council resolution that allowed Sudan and its leadership to be referred for investigation to the International Criminal Court. Yet the United States demurred from undertaking a humanitarian intervention in Darfur that could have directly responded to the loss of hundreds of thousands of African lives. Instead, American eyes were focused on Iraq and the preemptive invasion designed to remove the perceived threat to the United States and its allies of Saddam's presumed hidden weapons of mass destruction.

This chapter has not minimized the cruelty of Saddam Hussein's barbaric regime. It has documented the atrocities of Saddam's reign of terror, as well as the vicious deceptions and brutality of the authoritarian practices his regime imposed through the legal and bureaucratic apparatus of its security agencies, courts, and prisons. There is dark irony in the fact that obviously malign legal authoritarian as well as apparently more benign legally cynical regimes can both resort to claims about judicial procedures and the rule of law to legitimize their practices, even when these regimes otherwise differ in fundamental ways.

For example, and perhaps most obviously, although U.S. policy elites are often compromised by moving back and forth between public sector military and private sector industrial positions, they also operate with varying amounts of autonomy in a comparatively more open, constitutionally embedded, and less pervasively and violently repressive political environment. This helps to explain how the United States was able to have both a relatively open and nonetheless fundamentally misleading debate about the contrived threat posed by Iraq to its homeland security and a resulting presumed need for a post-9/11 doctrine of preemptive war.

Among the lessons learned from this experience is the way a legally cynical yet relatively open and democratic society can operate in setting the predicate for a war of aggression. The simultaneously ongoing genocide in Darfur was essentially forgotten in the unfolding debate about the Iraq War. The result was a triumph of the legal cynicism of an aggressive criminal militarism over the responsibility to protect the victims of mass atrocity. Darfur was the path not taken. Iraq was the chosen war of aggression.

The American contrast between the willingness to invade Iraq and the unwillingness to intervene in Darfur illustrates the compounding ways legally cynical decisions can cascade in creating what the Nuremberg Tribunal called "the accumulation of evil." The silence that surrounded the simultaneity of these particular events and decisions may be unique, but silence itself may also be a distinctive feature of legal cynicism, especially when it is linked to patriotic calls for criminal militarism that are hostile to openly expressed doubts or objections. Thus *New York Times* public editor, Margaret Sullivan (2014), actually understates the facts when she reports that "The lead-up to the war in Iraq was not *The Times* finest hour. Some of the news reporting was flawed, driven by outside agendas and lacking in needed skepticism. Many Op-Ed columns promoted the idea of a war that turned out to be both unfounded and disastrous."

We rightly think of openness of discussion and debate as hallmark features of our democratic society. However, there can also be a discouragement of discussion and debate in a legally cynical democratic society that is symptomatic of a too little recognized kind of silencing, repression, and neglect in decisions about war, crime, and peace. This is a continuing theme of this book.

2

A Shadow of Hope

MIXED SIGNS

The U.S. invasion and occupation of Iraq began with its March 19, 2003 cruise missile and bunker-busting bomb attack on the group of homes and a restaurant near Baghdad where U.S. military intelligence mistakenly thought Saddam was meeting his sons. Exactly five months later, based on its own more accurate intelligence, al-Qaeda in Iraq undertook a more consequential attack. A flatbed truck packed with 1,000 pounds of explosives sped up an unguarded back road adjoining the UN headquarters and office of its chief envoy, Sergio Vieira de Mello.

De Mello was conducting a meeting with International Monetary Fund officials about the humanitarian costs of the war. Earlier he had helped draft a memo criticizing the coalition's recent shootings of civilians, a key problem that continued throughout the war and that is the focal point of the last chapters of this book. Samantha Power reports that de Mello's last words – "oh, shit" – were uttered "seemingly more in resignation than surprise," a split second after the explosion and the collapse of the building around him. De Mello bled to death under the rubble, one of twenty-one civilians killed in the blast (2008:4).

That same month, an important cleric and political figure, Ayatollah Baqir al-Hakim, was also killed by a massive bombing in Najaf. Within a year in this same center of religious leadership, U.S.-led forces would stage a brutal battle with Shia cleric Muqtada al-Sadr. This standoff, discussed in Chapter 4, would burnish al-Sadr's reputation as the head of the largest mass movement challenging the occupation. Violence was clearly rising. These increasingly violent attacks and counterattacks were turning points in a path-dependent process whose significance would become steadily more apparent in the months leading up to the end of the first year of the American presence in Iraq.

Sergio de Mello had arrived in Baghdad in May with a formal writ from the UN Security Council belatedly lending legal authority to the occupation, and bringing as well the legitimacy associated with his leadership of the UN High Commission on Human Rights and his experience with post-conflict reconstruction in a variety of settings. Soon after the attack on the UN headquarters in Baghdad, its entire staff would be withdrawn from Iraq. The law-like legitimacy that the United Nations had tried to belatedly give the U.S.-led coalition was losing out to mounting legal cynicism about the war.

Given that the United Nations had not authorized the invasion in the first place, and absent de Mello's UN backing and engagement, it would have been easy to surmise that there was never even a glimmer of hope for any better outcome than that which followed. Yet de Mello had begun with the hope that the United Nations could make a difference for the better in Iraq.

Samantha Power (2008) reports that de Mello began by trying to head off the threat of a wholesale power shift from the recently deposed Arab Sunnis to the newly enfranchised Shia majority. He saw the potential for the Sunnis to be marked as a group by the stigma of defeat and to choose active resistance rather than a passive resignation in response. De Mello urged Paul Bremer as head of the Coalition Provisional Authority (CPA) to reduce its reliance on ex-pat Ahmed Chalabi as the Iraqi leader apparent. Year earlier, members of the Shia Chalabi family had supported the British occupation before leaving Iraq when Ahmed was still a child. A precocious student, Ahmed Chalabi earned a doctorate in mathematics at the University of Chicago and set out to remake the family's fortune and reputation.

Chalabi was one of a number of ex-pats to whom Bremer and the CPA looked – in what would later be called an exclusive elite bargain (Dodge 2012) – as the new leadership for Iraq. Chalabi had been accused of defrauding Jordon's second largest bank. He consumed millions of dollars of unaccounted-for funds from the CIA to develop an Iraqi National Congress that never gained much grassroots support. Chalabi also proved a remarkably misleading source of intelligence, especially about weapons of mass destruction, in the lead-up to the American invasion. As we explain in Chapter 4, he later emerged as an ally of Muqtada al-Sadr, the Shia leader of the Mahdi Army that brutally seized control of Baghdad neighborhoods by displacing their former Sunni residents. The U.S. Army subsequently suspected both Chalabi and al-Sadr of colluding with Iran (Norland 2014; Bonin 2011).

The United States' early reliance on Chalabi was only one cause for concern. De Mello had further tried to get Bremer to understand the significance of a fatwa issued by Shia cleric al-Sistani insisting that an Iraqi constitution must be drafted by elected rather than appointed representatives. De Mello wanted Bremer to forestall the Sunnis falling into feelings of disenfranchise-ment by giving them a place at the table of governance. However, Samantha Power writes that:

> Bremer resisted implementing the UN's most important suggestions. Vieira de Mello had tried and failed to gain greater UN and Red Cross access to Iraqi detainees. He had tried and failed to persuade Bremer to devise con-crete timelines for a constitution, for elections, and for the exit of U.S. troops. And he had tried and failed to get the Coalition to rescind or scale back its two most destabilizing decrees – the wholesale de-Ba'athification of Iraqi institutions and the destabilizing of the Iraqi army. By July he had grown depressed. He told colleagues that Bremer and the Iraqis had stopped return-ing his phone calls. (2008:3)

Bremer proved a slow learner, only adopting many of de Mello's suggestions later – when it was too late.

Yet if de Mello had largely lost hope in his final days, it was not for lack of trying to make things work in the early months of the post-invasion period. In these efforts, he shared the early desperate hopes of many Iraqis. De Mello may have been Iraq's last best hope for a successful transition. Yet there was in this beginning an unmistakable – albeit anxious and ambivalent – shadow of hope for better possibilities.

ANXIETY AND AMBIVALENCE

The April 9, 2003 toppling of the statue of Saddam Hussein in Firdaus Square as American forces entered Baghdad foreshadowed much that followed in the months and years to come in Iraq. Arab-American journalist Anthony Shadid was in the square and called the toppling of the statue a "parable" of the rela-tionship between the Americans and Saddam (2005:147). His point was that despite Saddam's unpopularity, it took the world's greatest military power to tumble the statue and Saddam's residual grip on the country.

More specifically, it took a massive American M-88 tank recovery vehicle to bring down the statue. As they arrived in the square, the U.S. Marines hung an American flag over Saddam's head. A gathering crowd was audibly discomforted by this image, until an Iraqi flag was hung alongside, which generated greater approval. At least for the Americans, the symbolism of the moment demanded the toppling of the larger-than-life likeness of "the great leader." The M-88 was harnessed to the statue's base, which seemed to resist and stubbornly hold its ground against the powerful, straining machine. It wasn't until someone in the crowd suggested tying a cable to the neck of the thirty-nine-foot statue that the Marines were finally able to upend and wrestle Saddam's likeness to the ground.

Shidrak George, an Iraqi civilian, stood alongside Anthony Shadid in the crowd watching this spectacle, which was picked up by a live feed to CNN International and relayed back to a watching U.S. audience. The scene was more emotionally freighted and mixed in its meaning than the American audience could ever have appreciated. "It's a strong statue," Shidrak observed as Saddam's likeness resisted the pull of the M-88: "If Saddam was watching this scene, he would be laughing at us." Shadid, uniquely positioned beside Shidrak and probably the only Arab-American journalist in the square, recalled:

> In those few hours, I had heard glee at liberation, anger at an occupation … everything seemed *ghamidh*; it was all still mysterious and unclear. "We don't know what's next," he said. "They rid us of our repression, there's no question about that. But we want to know how it turns out. Are they here for our sake? They said they came to save us. Now they have to prove it."

Probably the best translation of the Arabic word *ghamidh* in this context is a sense of foreboding.

THE FACE OF THE INVASION AND OCCUPATION

Shadid already knew from his springtime 2003 vantage point in Firdaus Square what it would take the Bush administration a much longer time to realize: that Iraq was going to remain an American responsibility for a more extended period than optimistically imagined. In the early months, the American soldiers could still imagine that the Iraqi politeness they initially encountered on the streets of Baghdad meant that they were gratefully received by the larger population. "Everybody likes us," Spec. Stephen Harris told the *Washington Post*'s Tom Ricks. "I'd say ninety-five percent friendly" (Ricks 2006:177).

Ricks found a more ambivalent response when he spoke to Baghdad residents. He noted that the "residents gave different estimates – at best, 50-50, and at worst, a significant majority holding hostile views." The latter hostile voices expressed a nascent legal cynicism, questioning the legitimacy underwriting the legality of the invasion. Ricks ominously added that the "Sentiments often broke down along the religious cleavages that mark the country. Some Shiite residents hailed the Americans for ending Hussein's rule, which was particularly brutal toward their sect." But the Arab Sunnis were less persuaded. We more systematically assess Rick's anecdotal reading of the sectarian-inflected sentiments of the people of Baghdad later in this chapter.

First, it is important to understand what the Iraqi public was reacting to – the American face of the coalition invasion and occupation – which they must have doubted would be short-lived. This was despite the fact that the implicit if not explicit promise of the American plan for post-invasion Iraq was to be in and out of the country within six months, if not sooner. Being in the country longer than this would unacceptably imply "nation building," which the Bush administration had rejected as Clintonian. For Iraqis, it was an echo of the British occupation of the preceding century.

"Freedom" was the operative thematic enshrined in the Iraqi mission led by Defense Secretary Rumsfeld and Vice President Cheney. They interpreted the fact that the Iraqi army and police had vanished when the U.S.-led coalition forces arrived as evidence of the new freedom from authoritarian control. From their ideological vantage point, the post-invasion anarchy and looting that filled the vacuum and enveloped Iraq were rationalized as simply the first unstable steps toward democracy. Although the Ministry of Oil was uniquely protected as the American troops arrived in Baghdad, the Bush administration and its military did not view it as necessary to impose a curfew in the city, or do anything much more, such as declaring martial law. This was another path-dependent decision point.

The assumptions of the administration about the unrestrained benefits of freedom were a remarkable contradiction of more than a century of criminological theories about opportunity and social control. These theories cover a wide spectrum of criminological thought and juxtapose numerous competing predictions that generations of scholars and students have sought to competitively test and confirm. Despite significant differences, however, there is little disagreement in this writing and research (e.g., Gottfredson and Hirschi 1990; Nettler 1978; Hirschi 1969) that completely unfettered opportunities for crime combined with their uncontrolled pursuit leads to lawless results.

When the Coalition Provisional Authority tallied the costly consequences of the confirmation of this truth, the figure it calculated was $12 billion (Packer 2006:139). These, of course, were just the immediate domestic collateral costs to Iraq of the first weeks of the invasion. In Chapter 4, we calculate the longer-term domestic collateral costs and report a far higher figure.

THE SUIT

It was April 19, 2003 – exactly one month after the first attack of cruise missiles and bunker-busting bombs intended for Saddam – when an order was finally issued declaring that the U.S.-led coalition was the "military authority" in Iraq, thus assuming the legal responsibility required of an "occupier" by the Geneva Conventions. It was nearly another month before President Bush would appoint Paul Bremer as his presidential envoy and head of the Coalition Provisional Authority, replacing Jay Garner, the little-seen interim chief of the Office of Reconstruction and Humanitarian Assistance (ORHA).

Garner was a retired general previously credited with implementing the policy referenced in the previous chapter that saved many lives in northern Iraq following Saddam's repression of the post–Gulf War Kurdish rebellion. However, in his several months as chief of ORHA, Garner was never able to establish a presence in Baghdad. Garner didn't even arrive in Baghdad until April 21, and within a few weeks he was gone. Paul Bremer would next try to fill the void.

Bremer was the handsome prep school diplomat – always neatly dressed for public appearances in his perma-press Brooks Brothers suit and combat boots. Within several weeks of his arrival in May, Bremer undertook a set of bold and misguided decisions that would undermine the remainder of his thirteen months in the country and firmly entrench the path dependency of later outcomes.

Bremer's (2006) thinking about Iraq was premised on an historical analogy to de-Nazification in post–World War II Germany. This led to his conclusion that de-Ba'athification was essential in post-Saddam Iraq. Within days of his arrival in Baghdad, Bremer dissolved Garner's ORHA into the CPA and locked horns with Garner over his de-Ba'athification plans. Bremer's first executive order was to ban government employment of individuals from the top four membership levels of the Ba'ath Party. This led to a sweeping wave of dismissals from the essential governing institutions of Iraq. It was a headlong leap into a deregulated void destined to produce criminality and chaos.

For all their other failings, and even though they were Sunni dominated, the military and government ministries had been the major inter-sectarian institutions designed to bring some non-Sunni diversity into Iraq governance and control. To enforce and grant limited exceptions to the Ba'ath Party ban, Bremer established a de-Ba'athification commission with Ahmed Chalabi as its head (Chandrasekaran 2006: chapter 4). The Shia Dawa Party politician and eventual prime minister, Nouri al-Maliki, was also later named to this commission. These exiles from Saddam's ruthless regime were far more inclined to ensure enforcement than to grant exceptions to the ban against their former enemies.

Eleven days after his arrival, Bremer issued his second executive order, which dissolved the army, the navy, the Ministry of Defense, and the Iraqi

Intelligence Service. The combined effect of his first two executive orders within weeks of his arrival in Iraq was to aggravate a swelling mood of cynical anger against Bremer and his CPA. More specifically, these legal dictates created a pool of more than a half million educated and angry unemployed persons – mainly Arab Sunnis – with little incentive but to at first cynically and silently, and then more militantly, support an insurgency against the American occupation. The unemployment rate in Iraq was already over 40 percent, and the ban and dissolution added to this number with well-educated and highly experienced Sunni bureaucrats and generals. Some called Bremer a "control freak" and others credited him with singlehandedly creating a violently angry insurgency.

Thus Bremer's de-Ba'athification program added the hostility of humiliating dismissal and unemployment to the anarchic conditions of freedom that had already unleashed the looting of the Iraqi government and infrastructure. The situation was anomic. It was as if a cynical conspiracy had united the major causal forces identified in all the classic theories of crime – weakened informal and formal social constraints, perceptions of injustice and illegitimate denial of opportunity, and oppositional group identification – with the intent to create maximum conditions for the lawless expression of legal cynicism.

To this, Paul Bremer added another fateful decision, the creation of an interim governing council (IRC). This decision may have been less significant for what it did – because Bremer made clear that this was not an actual governing structure and that he alone would remain primarily in control – than for what it symbolized. Especially to the Arab Sunnis, it symbolized the CPA's skepticism about their potential involvement in Iraq's new governance.

Thus the council was not only an interim transitional entity rather than the beginning of inclusive self-rule, it was also calibrated with its twenty-five-member composition to signal the influence of the newly recognized Shia majority. Thirteen of the members were Shia, five Sunni Arabs, five ethnic Kurds, and one ethnic Turkman. The final member was Christian. Men outnumbered women members by twenty-two to three. Nine of the members were exiles who had not been in Iraq for years. Bremer himself expected to remain in control for several years, but this proved an optimistic assessment. He would be gone in just over a year.

By the summer of 2003, the emerging consequences of the legally cynical, dubiously preemptive, U.S.-led invasion were apparent: violence against American forces was increasing in Baghdad and elsewhere in Iraq. When Donald Rumsfeld met the press for a briefing on June 19, he confronted the fact that forty-two soldiers had been killed in the previous six weeks – the date when President Bush had declared that the war was over. Rumsfeld's explanation was a misleading attempt at comparative criminology:

> Look, you've got to remember that if Washington, D.C. were the size of Baghdad, we would be having something like 215 murders a month. There's going to be violence in a big city. It's five and a half million people.

Of course, the number of killings that included civilians in Baghdad was likely much larger than 215 during the comparable period, and Rumsfeld was speaking as if only the deaths of the forty-two American soldiers "counted" (Ricks 2006:170).

In addition to the lack of planning and misjudgment about how to control crime after the invasion and during the occupation, perhaps the most legally cynical aspect of the CPA's early involvement in Iraq was its approach to developing a follow-up solution to the problem of security and policing. Baghdad had been known as a "safe" city before the invasion, largely because Saddam's security agencies had responded with such bureaucratic efficiency to any kind of criminal violence other than their own. However, Iraq's key legal authoritarian institutions – the Iraqi military and police – had melted away after the invasion, and this combined with de-Ba'athification and demobilization to leave the public feeling insecure and unsafe – that is, as the theory of legal cynicism predicts: unprotected. The theory of legal cynicism warns that a system of law enforcement that cannot keep the population it patrols safe is at great risk of being seen as illegitimate – and therefore dismissively regarded with cynicism and disdain.

The U.S. Justice Department sent a team of experts to assess the situation. Seeing the growing violence in Baghdad and beyond, the expert consultants recommended bringing in thousands of foreign policing advisors. The Bush administration rejected this advice. The administration instead sent New York City police commissioner Bernie Kerik, who had gained celebrity status for his media display of authority during the 9/11 emergency.

With his shaved head, sound-bite commentary, and rugged Rambo demeanor, Bernie Kerik was Mayor Rudolph Giuliani's handpicked "top cop" in New York City. In early May, Giuliani convinced a willing President Bush to make Bernie Kerik his point man on policing in Iraq. Those who knew more than the public image of Kerik recognized this appointment as a perilous choice.

As Rajiv Chandrasekaran caustically put it, Kerik was not a "criminal justice theoretician" (2006:96). It was apparent as soon as he arrived that his approach was in sync with Rumsfeld's perspective and primarily theatrically driven. He explained that "I'm here to bring more media attention to the good work [of the] police because the situation is probably not as bad as people think" (2006:97). In the weeks that followed, Kerik made numerous media appearances to communicate his assurance that law and order was returning to Iraq. He had Paul Bremer's enthusiastic support.

Kerik's job was to reestablish the police in Iraq under the administration of the Ministry of Interior. However, this ministry had been emptied out by Bremer's de-Ba'athification order. Kerik on his own initiative sought out a former police commander from Saddam Hussein's regime – mixing the old legal authoritarianism with an imported legal cynicism – and reinstalled him in Baghdad. Throughout his time in Iraq, Kerik was best known for participating personally in police raids with South African mercenaries in Baghdad and for supervising at long distance his home renovations back in New Jersey (Packer 2006:241).

Although Kerik was tasked with reequipping the Iraqi police, when he left Iraq less than four months after arriving, his single acquisition was 50,000 Glock pistols at what General Ricardo Sanchez (2008:250) regarded as suspiciously "exorbitant prices." Sanchez reported that "Bremer had adamantly refused to give up or share responsibility for building the new security and police forces, and with that came control over contracting. Unfortunately, the entire process failed miserably" (2009:251).

Kerik was subsequently convicted in the United States of various misdemeanors and felonies, including lying to White House officials, and he was sentenced to four years in prison. Kerik was emblematic of an arrogant ignorance of accepted tenets of criminological theory and criminal justice practice during the invasion and occupation of Iraq.

BEGINNING TO MEASURE THE SOCIAL CONSEQUENCES

One could well imagine dismay if not anger among the Iraqi public about much that we have described about the invasion and occupation of Iraq. Rajiv Chandrasekaran reported that "Every Iraqi I knew either had been a victim of a violent crime or knew someone who was" (2006:95). His description of Baghdad in the first months following the invasion was terrifying:

> The Iraqi police were almost nonexistent. They had fled their stations as American troops converged on Baghdad. Most were at home. Some had even joined the orgy of looting. The few who had reported back to work were too scared to enforce the law. They had pistols. The criminals had AK-47s. (2006:95)

However, there is also another useful perspective on this early period.

Charles Tripp (2007 [2010]) is the most noted historian of Iraq. Tripp located the initial response of the Iraqi public to the American-led invasion in the historical context of earlier convulsions in this nation's politics and governance. He drew a comparison to the period during and following the overthrow of the British-supported monarchy in the military coup d'état of July 1958. He concluded that the American presence now posed a clear and present danger of repeating all the failings of the British involvement in Iraq.

Yet, as then, Tripp argued there was a shadow of hope in the initial Iraqi response to the American invasion and occupation and all that followed, saying that "As in 1958, that other year when many possible futures stood before Iraq after decades of repressive rule, so in 2003 there were those who saw the collapse of the old regime as a golden opportunity to recapture some of what Iraq might have been" (2010:278).

Tripp was most impressed with the potential for a new political freedom driven by an emerging media and civically engaged organizations: "The array of new media, the possibilities offered for NGO (nongovernmental organizations) and trade union activities, as well as the novel freedom to communicate and debate, were avidly seized upon, bringing a host of new and original Iraqi voices to the fore" (2010:278).

Tripp's insights into sources of hopefulness among Iraqis during the first months of the invasion and occupation add another dimension to the accounts of lawlessness by journalists in the country during this period. We noted earlier that Tom Ricks (2006) indicated a contrast in the perceptions of U.S. soldiers and Iraqi citizens, emphasizing that the soldiers had a far too rosy view of what Iraqis were thinking, but observing that the mood of the public was difficult to discern. Anthony Shadid (2005), with his description of the toppling of Saddam's statue, offered a nuanced sense of how ambivalent and anxious the Iraqis he interviewed were.

It is therefore difficult to get a clear sense from these "first drafts of history" about the public mood during the early months. We have used two sources of more extensive interviews to further explore the disposition of Iraqis during this period. The first source is an extension of the Iraq History Project (IHP) introduced in the prior chapter. The extension of this ambitious project was called the Current Violations Initiative (CVI).

Our introductory use of the CVI portion of IHP in this chapter focuses on the interviews conducted with displaced and non-displaced Iraqis who experienced humanitarian and human rights crimes during the invasion and early occupation. The United Kingdom's Foreign and Commonwealth Office and the Soros Open Society Institute funded the survey interviews. We use pseudonyms to personalize excerpts that we quote from the interviews. The representativeness of this data set is discussed in further detail in Chapter 4. We were surprised to find evidence expressed in the interviews of initial hope and even optimism, albeit often fleeting, about the early post-invasion period.

Mixed Hopes

Manal spoke of an unexpectedly improved security situation for Kurds soon after the invasion, which initially raised her hopes about the end of the old regime's legal authoritarianism, although this relief proved brief:

> Until 2003, our life was difficult, but safe. When the war started we were all afraid of what would happen. After the war between US and Iraqi forces was over, the regime had fallen. Everyone was happy that the government was gone. We were pleased because we thought that with the end of the dictator's tyranny, Kurds would live a safe and prosperous life. My sons' work was going well. Everyone in the area liked them because they were polite and respectful to others. They were popular with our neighbors and friends. They were God-fearing, hard-working young men who took good care of me and their sister. Then the situation in Baghdad began to get worse. There was a sharp increase in bombings, kidnappings, death threats and looting. Thieves came to steal from homes in broad daylight.

Some respondents were more hopeful than others. Nazir hoped for a return for normality after the initial looting, but in time he also was disappointed. A skepticism or legal cynicism about the criminality of public institutions began to overtake his more optimistic expectations:

> In the first days after the fall of the past government, things started to deteriorate. Anarchy prevailed in the country.... Thieves and looters took everything. They stole from government offices, universities, schools and banks. They even looted from offices that provided basic services like electricity and water. It was painful to see this happening. But nevertheless, I hoped that eventually things would get back to normal, especially after they appointed a new mayor. Contrary to my expectations, the looting and theft only became organized. It affected non-governmental organizations, private business and even laboratories. To safeguard my belongings, I moved all my equipment from the clinic to my home.

Qutaiba recalled that things went from bad to better and then back to bad; but in between, he saw his earnings improve because of the new money in dollars he was receiving in contracts with the coalition forces:

My work went on until 2003, when the war began, and Saddam's regime was toppled. Then, the looting and plundering began. Americans filled the streets. All work came to a stand-still. There was no electricity, and no fuel. We just sat there waiting to see what would happen to us and Iraq. Two to three months after the regime fell, life began to reemerge in a new form. There were huge amounts of money that had been stolen by people who didn't know what to do with it or how to spend it. There were many gangs because there was no rule of law. Despite all that, work was possible until Dr. Iyad Allawi became Prime Minister. During that time, I used to get good contracts with the Coalition forces. I did well, even better than before, because then I was earning money in dollars.

Rayan also understood his experience as changing over time and as directly linked to the behavior of the American-led forces in a largely negative way. A rising sense of skepticism and legal cynicism about a U.S.-led criminal militarism was reflected in his observations of the increasing randomness of raids and arrests by American forces:

At the beginning, they behaved normally. They were cooperative and got along well with us. But, after six months or so, exactly at the beginning of 2004, the Americans began to change their ways. Then, they started random raids of people's homes and began arresting people, especially men.

For some, like Sroor, the problem was that the opportunities of working with the American forces began with benefits and ended with threats:

In the beginning, the situation changed for the better, especially for us because my husband's specialization was translation. My husband would go to work with the foreigners every day. He was happy with his work.... Our situation improved, but I didn't know that my husband's job would bring me a lifetime of misery. In the beginning of 2004 ... the situation grew more dangerous. That was when the kidnapping started, especially against those who worked with the Americans.

Zahour's story continued the theme of a renewal of hope followed by a descent into a dangerous and ultimately fatal despair embedded in cynicism about the prospects for protection that the American forces' "rule of law" could bring:

We were really happy when the regime fell. We had finally gotten rid of the surveillance, the censorship, and the interrogations. The Da'wa party came back to Iraq and opened up offices in every governorate. That same year my son Ahad graduated from the University of Baghdad and

> decided to follow the footsteps of his father. I didn't want this to happen
> because it was politics and political parties that had taken their father
> away from me.... My daughter Layla graduated from pharmacy school
> in 2004 and started working at Ibn al-Nafees Hospital.... I worried about
> her every day until she got home. Then, the security situation began to
> get worse. There were more car bombs and the explosive devices.
>
> Zahour saw her worst fears realized. She lost her daughter to a car
> bomb and her son was kidnapped from her own home by a group of
> masked intruders and never found. "Now, I am tired of my life," she
> concluded in despair, asking, "What is life worth after you have lost the
> ones you love?"

Several of these interviews mark 2004 as a year of fateful change. Prior to this, many of those interviewed recalled a sense of hopefulness, despite the looting and lawlessness that followed immediately after the invasion. Of course, this hopefulness was far from universal and it was not randomly distributed. A Gallup Poll (GP) undertaken in Baghdad the week after Sergio de Mello was killed in the UN headquarters located on the outskirts of the city provides an opportunity to unpack the extent and sources of the initial hopefulness that many Iraqis first felt.

BAGHDAD AFTER THE INVASION

The Gallup organization began work on an Iraq post-invasion survey before the United States even entered the country, starting preparations for the survey interviews in Baghdad just two months after the invasion. Gallup finished its work in the beginning of September – a little less than six months after the invasion began – having completed nearly 1,200 interviews. The survey used a mixture of closed and open-ended items, with respondents answering in considerable detail.

The consequences of the invasion were initially played out in terms of respondents' reports about many of the most prosaic demands of negotiating everyday life in Baghdad. Figure 2.1 presents a summary of the responses in the Gallup survey for the nearly six months since the invasion and in the last month before the survey. Of course, the responses are larger for the longer period, and we focus on these. Regardless, there is little evidence despite the widespread looting of public institutions that personal criminal victimization was yet a significant problem for Baghdad residents.

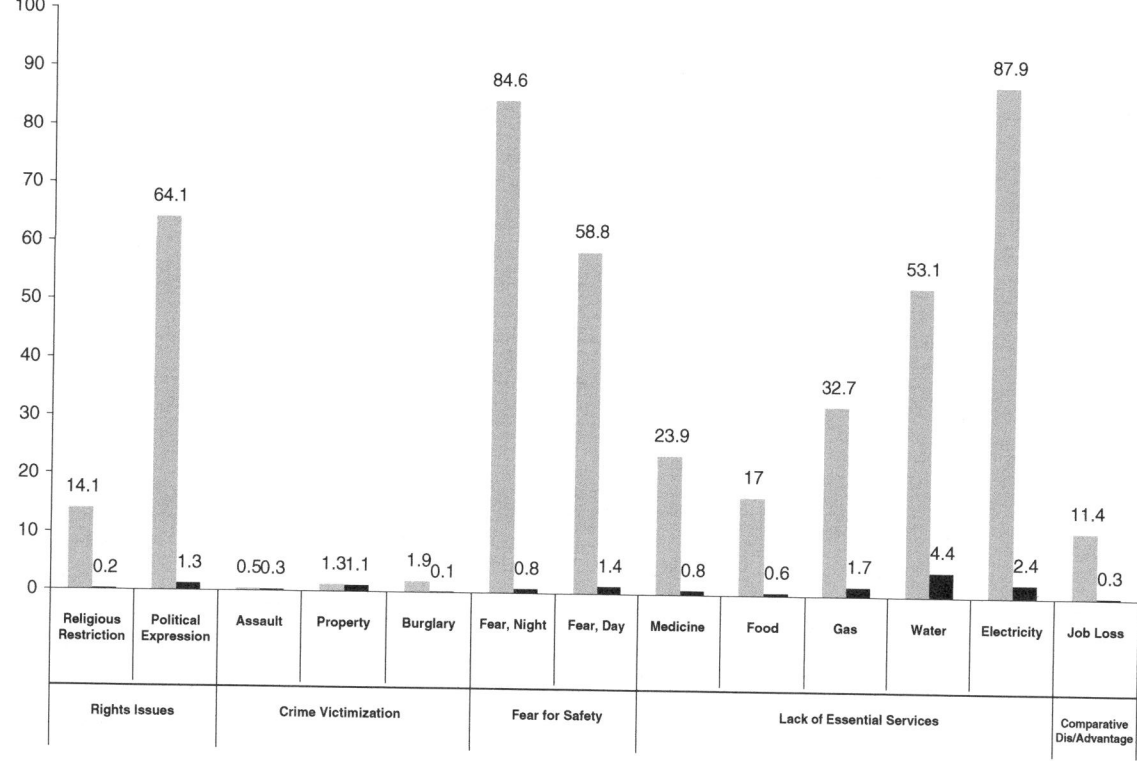

FIGURE 2.1. Experiences since the Invasion (six months) and in Previous Four Weeks (one month), Baghdad circa August/September 2003

The largest report of crime was of burglaries, but less than 2 percent (1.9%) of residents reported one or more burglaries in the half year since the invasion. On the other hand, since the invasion, the majority of residents of Baghdad recalled being fearful about going outside their homes at night (84.6%) and even during the day (58.8%). This is evidence of the kind of ambivalence and anxiety that Anthony Shadid (2005) reported. Anxiety about personal and family safety and lack of confidence in the capacity of military or security forces to effectively respond to it was a likely source of growing legal cynicism in Iraq.

The largest problems Baghdad residents reported were, in the following order, getting electricity (87.9%), water (53.1%), gas (32.7%), medicine (23.9%), and food (17%). Although the CPA achieved some success in improving these essential services during the summer of 2003, including electricity, by fall the advance had stalled. Herring and Rangwala (2006:73) similarly conclude that "The water and electricity sectors indicate how the state did not establish itself in the role of a service provider, a key method of cooptation for the modern state."

Problems were also severe in the employment sector. More than 10 percent (11.4%) of the residents of Baghdad reported losing a job in the six months after the invasion. The overall unemployment rate was about 40 percent. We have noted that the de-Ba'athification policy aggravated this problem. Here Herring and Rangwala observe in understatement that "the CPA began its rule of Iraq with a programme to dismantle organizations that were also some of Iraq's biggest employers prior to the invasion, and its reputation suffered accordingly" (2006: 274).

The brightest spot in the survey's report involved freeness of political expression. As Tripp suggested, the early period after the invasion included a vast array of new media outlets and NGO activity (2010:278). Nearly two-thirds (64.1%) of the respondents reported experiencing this new freeness of political expression soon after the invasion. However, as Tripp also noted, "they faced a hard struggle trying to carve out a secure space in which to enjoy these freedoms."

Given the range of problems the public perceived and experienced in Iraq – especially the fears for neighborhood safety, the scarcity of public services, and the persistent unemployment – it is hard to imagine that six months after the invasion Iraqis would still be hopeful about their national fate. This might seem particularly true in Baghdad, where many of the problems were acute and highly concentrated, especially in the immediate aftermath of the explosion that killed Sergio de Mello and twenty-one others at the UN headquarters.

TABLE 2.1. *Scale measures of perceived legitimacy of U.S./coalition invasion of Iraq*

Taking everything into consideration, do you think the coalition invasion of Iraq has done more harm (35.5%) than good (27.2%)?

In your opinion, is Iraq much better off (3.1%), somewhat better off (29.1%), or much worse off (14.9%) than before the U.S. and British invasion?

How about you and your family, would you say you are much better off (4.3%), somewhat better off (28.3%), somewhat worse off (22.5%), or much worse off (11.7%) than you were before the U.S. and British invasion?

Right now, do you think that economic conditions in Baghdad as a whole are getting better (48.2%) or getting worse (22.8%)?

Do you expect that at this time next year you and your family will be better off (61.1%) than now or financially worse off (11.0%) than now?

Thinking about any hardships you might have suffered since the U.S. and British invasion, do you personally think that ousting Saddam Hussein was worth it (61.7%) or not (30.1%)?

Responses do not add up to 100 percent because all responses recorded are not included in survey prompts.
Alpha reliability coefficient for scale is 0.7.

It would seem quite unlikely that in this context the U.S.-led invasion of Iraq would have been very widely perceived as legitimate. We have noted that perceived illegitimacy is a key source of legal cynicism. We expected that a mood of skepticism and incipient illegitimacy would already be apparent about the war and all it brought. Recall that we adopted Kirk and Papachristos's (2011) definition of legal cynicism as a cultural frame or orientation in which legal institutions are viewed as illegitimate, as well as unresponsive and ineffectual in providing public safety.

We were able to use the Baghdad Gallup Poll to construct a six-item scale reported in Table 2.1 (with a relatively high reliability score) that involves the legitimation aspect of legal cynicism six months after the invasion. The focus of this scale is on effects on the residents of Baghdad and resulting perceptions of the legitimacy of the invasion and occupation.

The bottom three items in the table could be taken as revealing perhaps surprising support for the legitimacy of the invasion. Nearly half (48.2%) of the Baghdad respondents said they thought things were getting better, while almost two-thirds (61.1%) thought their own families would be better off financially within a year, and almost two-thirds (61.7%) said they thought ousting Saddam Hussein was "worth it."

In contrast, the first item in the table provides the strongest indication of illegitimacy, with more than a third (35.5%) of respondents saying they

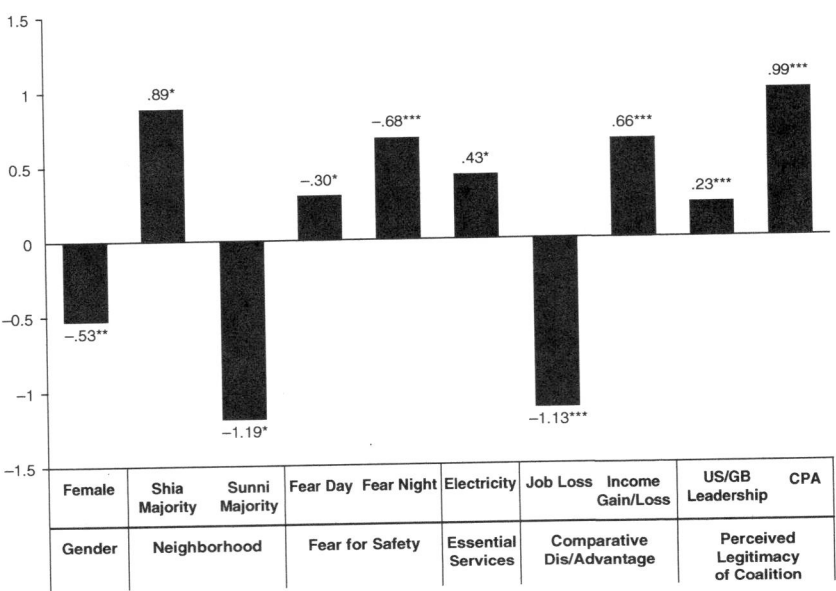

FIGURE 2.2. Net Unstandardized Effects of Post-Invasion Conditions in Baghdad on Perceived Legitimacy of Iraq Invasion, August/September 2003

thought the invasion had done more harm than good, while just over a quarter (27.2%) took the opposite view that more good was done (i.e., the remainder were uncertain or in between these positions). The last pair of items at the top half of Table 2.1 indicates more favorable than cynical views of the invasion, although not as strongly positive as the items in the lower half of the table. Still, six months after the arrival of the U.S.-led coalition forces, Baghdad respondents seemed surprisingly hopeful.

The question that remains is what factors account – apart from the earliness of this evaluation – for the positive and negative reactions of Baghdad residents to the invasion. The results of our prediction models are presented in the Appendix in Tables 2.2–2.3, and the graph presented in Figure 2.2. This figure uses a bar graph to represent factors that can be understood as positively and negatively influencing the respondents' perceptions of the legitimacy of the U.S.-led invasion. All of the effects summarized in this figure are statistically significant. The factors with negative coefficients would be most likely to predict legal cynicism about the U.S. invasion and occupation.

We see first in Figure 2.2 that males were more favorable in responding to the invasion than females. Although the survey did not ask the ethnic identity of the respondents, we have been able to use information on the majority composition of the respondents' neighborhoods to anticipate this influence. Shia-majority neighborhoods perceived the invasion more positively than Sunni-majority neighborhoods, which were more cynical in their assessments. It is notable that the negative response from the Sunni-majority neighborhoods is the strongest effect indicated in Figure 2.2. This effect is an early empirical sign of a salient source of legal cynicism that would lead to militant opposition among Iraq's Sunni population to the CPA and its successor institutions of governance in Iraq.

Residents' fears about going outside in the neighborhood at night and during the day also negatively influenced the perceived legitimacy of the invasion. This fear about safety and security is a likely reflection of legal cynicism about the capacity of American military or Iraqi army, police, or other institutions to provide effective protection from criminal and other threats to personal and collective well-being. We have emphasized that the perceived inability and failure of law enforcement institutions to provide security goes to the core of the meaning of legal cynicism.

The most unexpected finding in the analysis is that problems with electricity positively influenced perceptions of the invasion. Our only explanation of this counterintuitive finding is that neighborhoods that had the greatest post-invasion electrical problems also experienced the greatest gains in service during the summer months of 2003. More predictably, job loss negatively impacted while income gain positively influenced perceptions of the legitimacy of the invasion. Most predictably, positive attitudes toward the U.S. and Great Britain's leaders (i.e., Bush and Blair) and toward the CPA enhanced the perceived legitimacy of the invasion. The latter variables were included in the analysis to control for their expected effects, and all the effects reported in Figure 2.2 are net of the influence of the latter variables.

Finally, as a way of confirming the link between the CPA and the Shia neighborhoods' support for the invasion (versus Sunni neighborhoods' cynicism), we tested whether CPA support and Shia neighborhood residence together had a multiplier effect in increasing the perceived legitimacy of the invasion (see Table 2.3 in the Appendix). We again found that the relationship between support for the CPA and the invasion was stronger in Baghdad Shia-majority neighborhoods than in Sunni-majority neighborhoods, with residents especially likely to see the invasion as legitimate if they both approved of the CPA and lived in Shia-majority neighborhoods.

On the other hand, residents of Sunni-majority neighborhoods were likely a growing sectarian source of legal cynicism about the invasion and occupation.

From the outset, Iraq's Arab Sunni population was pessimistic about its fate in the new Iraq. Ultimately, our interest is in whether measures in later and more comprehensive surveys analyzed in following chapters coincide in predicting heightened levels of legal cynicism, and whether this cynicism in turn will have led to support of Arab Sunni militancy and to support of the Arab Sunni insurgency in Iraq.

HOPE FADES

Hope and fear were the contradictory emotions engendered by the U.S.-led invasion of Iraq. As we have seen, these hopes and fears were not uniformly experienced. The residents of Shia neighborhoods in Baghdad who had greater confidence in the CPA were the most hopeful, while there was also already counter-sentiment by 2004 that conditions were worsening in Iraq, especially from Arab Sunnis who were cynical about the CPA. English scholar Charles Tripp holds the United States and its allies – including the British, whose own past colonial experience with Iraq should have provided foresight – accountable for ignoring lessons of the history of imperial militarism. Tripp writes, "the western allies whose military intervention gave many Iraqis hope for a radical break in their history often failed to recognize how much they were part of this same history and thus ran the risk once more of succumbing to its baneful logic" (2010:317).

This chapter provides early post-invasion evidence about the double and linked macro- and micro-level structural dimensions of the theory of legal cynicism. In the Iraqi context, this theory includes attention to macro-level sources of cynicism about the U.S. and Iraqi political, military, and legal elites who were directing the war (especially the newly empowered Shia governing elite), and the micro-level cynical attitudes produced by the perceived actions of these elites among those groups who felt they were being ignored and excluded (especially Arab Sunnis).

Thus the consequences of the military occupation were already taking their toll by early 2004. The government de-Ba'athification and military demobilization were breeding a sense of disenfranchisement and disbelief among the Arab Sunnis that were early markers of a rising cynicism about the new legal framework designed for Iraq by Paul Bremer and the American-led Coalition Provisional Authority. The absence of governing structures that were broadly perceived as legitimate combined with the lack of planning for the protection of newly vulnerable places and people, planting the seeds of a Sunni cynicism that would later build into a full-fledged fear of and opposition to the new Shia-dominated regime.

At the peak of the occupation, there were over 170,000 U.S. troops in Iraq. From 2003 through 2010, over one half million U.S. soldiers served in Iraq. U.S. and other coalition forces were a constant presence in many regions of the country. Patrols stormed through city streets on a regular, often daily basis – in heavy tanks, fighting vehicles, and armored Humvees. There were signs from the outset that this presence would be a source of legal cynicism about the war and its consequences.

In many urban areas, such as Baghdad, Ramadi, and Bakuba, shootouts were common. Coalition soldiers sometimes working with Iraqi security forces searched tens of thousands of Iraqi homes – often in the middle of the night. They detained large numbers of Iraqis, some for short periods of time, and others for years. In many regions of the country, virtually every Sunni Iraqi knew of a detained friend or family member. The U.S. troop presence was therefore more likely to have been perceived, especially in Arab Sunni neighborhoods, as a source of insecurity and danger rather than security and protection. These experiences were sources of legal cynicism about the war and the U.S.-led criminal militarism that it brought to Iraq.

A First Person Report

The period of the occupation is often described in the American media in a vague or abstract way that loses the intensity and brutality of the experience. First hand accounts make the costs of the occupation for the people of Iraq more visceral. Harev described for a CVI interviewer the harrowing experiences involving his family in Ramadi:

> We lived a quiet life in Ramadi. We had no problems. We had everything we needed. There were many jobs in the city. We never had to leave our loved ones or the city to make ends meet.
>
> After the regime fell it was terrible for us in Ramadi to see the American occupation with their tanks running over our Iraqi soil. However, life stayed normal for about a year after the occupation began. Then there were no clashes between the resistance and the occupation army but the occupation stayed and there was no real Iraqi government. The Americans started to offend the Iraqis. This made many Iraqi youth join the resistance.
>
> I saw one of these attacks with my own eyes before I left the city. It was an attack by the Americans on our neighbor Abu Ibrahim and

his family in July 2004. It was about midnight. There was no electricity because of a power outage in the area. They were in their house. Abu Ibrahim's second son, Raid, and his wife and son were sleeping in their garden. He carried a lantern in his hand so his wife could see while she laid out the bedding on the ground. An American tank was watching their house from the top of a hill. All of a sudden without any particular reason and without prior warning the tank shot at the poor family and killed Raid's young wife and son in front of him. When Raid's mother heard the shooting she hurried to her grandson in the garden and carried him outside the house.

She ran to our house and banged on the door like a mad woman carrying the child in her arms. We opened the door and invited her in. She was shaking from fear. She told us what happened. She didn't know if her daughter-in-law was alive or dead or what had happened to her son Raid and his brother Ibrahim.

She stayed overnight. She kept crying and asking us to let her go home. However we wouldn't let her go. We tried to calm her down. We were afraid of what might happen if she returned to the house. None of us could sleep that night. We stayed awake with her. After the dawn prayer when it got light so we could see we went to Abu Ibrahim's house.

We entered the garden and saw Raid's poor wife lying with blood all over her. Murdered. On the other side of the garden a few meters away Ibrahim was also lying there. Murdered. His blood was everywhere.

We went inside the house. We found Raid in a corner of a back room hysterical. He was crying and couldn't move. Abu Ibrahim was in another corner. He wasn't in any better shape than his son.

In this way the poor family lost a son, a grandson and a daughter-in-law in a moment for no apparent reason. We saw the tank still sitting there as if it hadn't committed such a barbaric crime....

A few months after this accident, I decided to leave Ramadi for Sulaymaniyyah. The security situation was getting worse and the Americans were committing many acts of violence. In addition, the financial situation in Ramadi was very bad; there were no jobs. So I went to Sulaymaniyyah in September 2005 – from then on I went back every 6 months to Ramadi for 2 or 3 days and then returned to Sulaymaniyyah. I often asked myself, is my life normal? Am I a normal person? Should I have to go through this hardship? Is a young man supposed to spend his youth sleeping on reed mats and half built buildings surrounded by cement and sand in the summer, in winter?

Harev was not alone in enduring such abuse. His experiences are among numerous CVI reports of human rights violations at the hands of American soldiers.

Even Iraqis who were initially somewhat hopeful about the possibilities for a better future often were overwhelmed by the sweeping skepticism and cynicism that followed from the unfolding consequences of the American war in Iraq.

3

Judging Torture in Iraq

With Gabrielle Ferrales and Guillermina Jasso

James Harding (Financial Times): "Mr. President, I want to return to the question of torture. What we've learned from these memos this week is that the Department of Justice lawyers and the Pentagon lawyers have essentially worked out a way that United States officials can torture detainees without running afoul of the law. So when you say you want the United States to adhere to international and United States laws, that's not very comforting. This is a moral question: Is torture ever justified?"

President Bush: "Look, I'm going to say it one more time.... Maybe I can be more clear. The instructions went out to our people to adhere to law. That ought to comfort you. We're a nation of law. We adhere to laws. We have laws on the books. You might look at these laws, and that might provide comfort for you. And those were the instructions ... from me to the government."

– News conference, Sea Island, Georgia, June 10, 2004

RULE OF LAW BY TORTURE

In the months following the invasion, President George W. Bush began to emphasize bringing democracy and the rule of law to Iraq instead of preempting the threat of Saddam Hussein's never found weapons of mass destruction. In a speech given to the National Endowment for Democracy (Bush 2003), the president insisted that democratic societies "protect freedom with the consistent and impartial rule of law."

However, within a year of the invasion, Americans were shocked to find their military charged with torturing prisoners in violation of international rules of law in the very same Abu Ghraib prison where Saddam's regime practiced some of its most notorious human rights abuses. As we saw in Chapter 1, Saddam's use of torture was not a secret and instead was a legal authoritarian resource openly used to terrorize would-be threats to the regime.

The American use of torture by law was something different. Its use of torture was unknown to the public until the famous photos made it impossible for Americans to ignore. The "whole world watching" nature of the video loop of photos and commentary on Al Jazeera made the issue of torture in Iraq impossible to avoid. However, it was perhaps not so much surprise about the torture as it was its flagrant contradiction of Bush administration claims to be bringing the rule of law to Iraq that began to awaken Americans to the consequences of this war.

The United States now was charged with covering up and failing to meaningfully prosecute and punish its own use of torture. The majority of Iraqis held in prisons like Abu Ghraib were Arab Sunnis swept up by dragnet military tactics that seldom led to provable charges. Legal cynicism about the methods of American militarism – now at least to some a transparently criminal militarism – emerged as a less ignorable part of the dynamic of the American war in Iraq. Was it plausible for knowledgeable Iraqis or Americans to expect that the Arab Sunnis would not militantly resist these practices? The double and linked macro- and micro-dimensions of the legally cynical practices and perceptions were too visibly coupled to easily ignore – at least among those who were watching. Cynicism about American law enforcement practices had taken on a global dimension.

Yet notwithstanding the torture scandal, two years after the invasion, President Bush (2005) was anxious to report success in nurturing the rule of law and the political independence of Iraq's judiciary as part of his new *National Strategy for Victory in Iraq*. He observed that "hundreds of judges have been trained" and concluded that "as Iraq's political institutions mature, its judicial system has become an independent branch, better able to promote the rule of law."

At the time of this optimistic assessment, intended to provide a new validation of the war, this claim seemed beyond any kind of objective or reliable evaluation. The optimistic claim was clearly at odds with classical conflict theories and a political sociology of crime and law that disputes the capacity and success of powerful government figures or bureaucracies to monitor and evaluate their own policies and practices, especially when imposed in contexts of military invasion and occupation (Turk 1982).

The claim that Iraq's judges had become an independent branch of government enforcing the rule of law was also at odds with the legal cynicism surrounding a series of dubious judicial decisions. Political interference with judicial decision making did not improve with time, and included an August 2013 decision of Iraq's top court that overturned a term limit prohibition that by law would have disallowed Prime Minister Maliki from seeking a third term in 2014. We argue in this chapter that the roots of failure to achieve political independence for Iraq's judiciary were already apparent during the early period of occupation.

AN UNEXPECTED INVITATION

Unexpectedly, in 2004, we received an invitation from a European legal institute (which we must leave unidentified) to evaluate a program titled "Judging in a Democratic Society" developed by the U.S. State Department to provide legal education for Iraqi judges. The institute invited successive groups of forty to sixty Iraqi judges to attend two-week programs taught mainly by U.S. judges and lawyers. Instruction highlighted the role of judges in democracies, emphasizing the importance of judicial independence, legitimacy in the rule of law (with a focus on international human rights and humanitarian law), ethics, and leadership.

This program was a highly valued part of the State Department's efforts to establish the rule of law during the occupation of Iraq. The invitation was a rare opportunity. There are few in-depth studies of how local actors respond to efforts by outside agents to forcefully introduce law reforms in previously legal authoritarian regimes. We know of no such studies in the Arab countries of the Middle East.

The question was whether the U.S./coalition could actually instill new standards of judicial independence in this traumatized nation. We developed a sentencing experiment to address these issues. During the closing sessions of the institute program in 2004 and 2005, we asked groups of Iraqi judges to make sentencing decisions in a survey experiment based on hypothetical cases of torture of suspected terrorists. The study focused on patterns of judicial collaboration with and resistance to the U.S.-led coalition, and its practices of criminal militarism, in decision making about the sentencing of convicted torturers.

Testimonies of Torture Victims

> Two interviews from the Iraq History Project convey a sense of how torture by American forces became intertwined as "standard operating procedure" in the everyday post-invasion lives of Iraqis. Rayan reported:
>
> > On April 4, 2004, at three in the morning, the American forces broke into our house. There were almost twenty soldiers. They pointed their guns at the men, women, and children inside the house....
> >
> > They took my father with them. They also broke into my uncles' home which was next door to our house. They arrested four of my uncles and took them all away.

The Americans didn't find anything suspicious in our house, but still they took my father and uncles. They took them for no reason.... Then the mayor came and asked about my father and uncles. He told us that they were at the military base in Habbaniya.

After seventeen days, the Americans released my uncle, Jamal. He told us that the others were still being held at the military base in Habbaniya. My uncle also told us that the soldiers had tortured and insulted my father and uncles. He said, "They tied our hands to a metal column for eleven days. We couldn't sleep well. We would only sleep for an hour or less. Whenever we fell asleep, the soldiers would come and pour water on our heads, and in such cold weather."

He also said, "They gave only one packet of biscuits and one bottle of water each day. They tortured us by forcing us to stand continually for eleven days. This caused our legs and feet to swell. They interrogated us every day." ... Twenty days after the Americans released my uncle Jamal, we heard that they had released my father and my other uncles, except my uncle Hameed.

Before releasing them, the Americans moved my father and uncles to Haswa. Then, they put them in an American military vehicle to take them back to Ramadi. A bomb exploded beneath the vehicle which held my father and uncles. The terrorists thought that the car was full of Americans because it was covered with a military canopy. My uncle Saleemm was killed. My uncle Rashid lost his left hand.

A second interview involves a period of detention at Abu Ghraib prison, which, interestingly, is described as involving better treatment than other American prisons. Hamad reports:

On April 3, 2004, I went to visit my relative in Ramadi. I stayed with my cousin Sa'ad in his house.

The next day at midnight, the American forces came into the area.... They broke into the house in a terrifying way. They threw a stun grenade inside. I can't describe the panic that we felt. It was terrifying.

They entered very quickly and pointed their guns at me and my cousin Sa'ad.

We could hear the screaming and crying of the children and Sa'ad's mother and wife in the next room.

I thought I was going to be killed.

After that they put black hoods, one on my head and [one] on Sa'ad's head. They handcuffed each of us and forced us to go with them without beating us.

They put us in their military cars. I felt as though there were other detainees with us in the car, maybe nearly ten.

They drove us to the 8th Brigade located at the outskirts of the city. When we arrived there, they took us out of the car, one after the other, and imprisoned each of us alone in a small room.

Then, they untied the handcuffs from our hands and removed the hoods from our heads.

There was a big window in the room but the room didn't have a bed or mattresses. So, we used to sleep on the floor. That caused me chronic pains on my left hip and muscle spasms in my legs and back.

I was there for eighteen days. They used to give us different MREs, but I only ate the biscuits from these ready meals. I was afraid that the meals might include pork or things that could affect our health. We were always suspicious of the policies and intentions of the Americans.

They used to take us one by one to the interrogation room every day. When they did this they handcuffed us and put hoods on our heads.

Every time, two or three Americans used to take me, in the same way they might act if they'd arrested Bin laden.

When we go to the interrogation room, they'd untie my handcuffs and remove the hood. There I saw the American officer dressed in military uniform with an Arab translator. I think he was Lebanese.

That American officer interrogated me about an incident where the Americans were attacked in the Khaldiya neighborhood.

I told him that I didn't do anything. I tried my best to explain to him that I am not from Ramadi, but that I just came from Baghdad to visit my relatives. But, it was no use. The American tried his best to force me to confess to the crime.

Then, he ordered them to bring in a guard dog that seemed trained to frighten prisoners. The dog tore off our clothes, but didn't wound us.

I was very afraid that the dog might attack me. Whenever they brought the dog, I worried that they would use it to kill me. The same thing happened every day and the interrogation generally lasted around two hours. I grew bored with their questions.

Sometimes, the American officer would not allow me to stand before him, face to face. He would order me to turn toward the wall, spread my legs apart, and raise my hands. It was very annoying because I had to stand like that for two or more hours.

... I was released on June 25, 2004 along with around one hundred other prisoners.

THE TORTURE SCANDAL

The American public was stunned in the spring of 2004 when photographic evidence appeared in the media of the abuse of Iraqi prisoners by U.S. soldiers at Abu Ghraib prison. A fifty-three-page document completed earlier in February by Major General Antonio M. Taguba (2004) was leaked to Seymour Hersh (2004) of the *New Yorker* magazine. The report indicated numerous instances of "sadistic, blatant, and wanton criminal abuses" that were perpetrated between October and December 2003 on detainees at Abu Ghraib prison by U.S. soldiers of the 372nd Military Police Company and by members of the American intelligence community.

These abuses included breaking chemical lights and pouring the phosphoric liquid they contained on detainees; pouring cold water on naked detainees; beating detainees with a broom handle and a chair; threatening male detainees with rape; allowing a military police guard to stitch without anesthetic the gaping wound of a detainee who was injured after being slammed against the wall in his cell; sodomizing a detainee with a chemical light and perhaps a broom stick; using military working dogs to frighten and intimidate detainees with threats of attack; and in one instance biting a detainee.

As noted earlier, not only did the American media broadcast the degrading and sexually explicit photographic evidence of this torture, but perhaps more significantly these photos appeared all over the Middle East, including in Iraq, in the press and on Al Jazeera and other Arab satellite television channels. The torture of detainees accused of terrorism at Abu Ghraib prison caused shock and outrage around the world, confirming impressions among critics that torture tactics were a standard operating procedure of American criminal militarism.

Defense Secretary Donald Rumsfeld apologized for the treatment of prisoners at Abu Ghraib and promised prosecutions and to "make changes as needed to see that it doesn't happen again." Yet following the mass release of military communications by WikiLeaks, the Bureau of Investigative Journalism (Stickler 2011) culled 303 claims of alleged abuse by coalition forces in Iraq that were reported to the American military authorities. The majority of the reported incidents occurred during arrests or transfers to detention centers rather than in American-run prisons. The same communications revealed that U.S. soldiers witnessed, or were told about, more than 1,300 cases of detainee abuse during the same period by Iraqi authorities. However, U.S. military personnel were explicitly instructed not to investigate these cases unless coalition forces were involved (Stickler and Woods 2011).

Further outrage had followed from the reporting (Priest 2005) that CIA interrogators at other overseas secret prison sites were using "harsh interrogation methods" on al-Qaeda detainees. These "enhanced interrogation techniques" again included noise, stress positions, and isolation, as well as waterboarding. Videotapes showing the use of these interrogation techniques by CIA personnel on top operatives of al-Qaeda were destroyed by CIA officials in November 2005 (Mazzetti and Johnston 2007).

Before and after this, charges and commentary about use of these techniques on al-Qaeda detainees again were heard all over the Middle East and in Iraq on Al Jazeera and other Arab satellite television channels, adding to the international outrage and encouraging the view that these policies and practices of criminal militarism were based on policies imposed from top levels downward through the chain of command of the U.S. government (Hersh 2004). The charges seemed to support some of the worst fears about wars of aggression, as well as more prosaic legal cynicism about the American war in Iraq.

AN EXPERIMENT INVOLVING THE INDETERMINACY OF LAW

Our research moved beyond the immediate perpetrators and victims of this torture. We were concerned with the broader radiating effects on important legal decision makers – such as Iraq's judges – of the highly publicized interpretations of torture law by the Bush administration. In particular, we were concerned about the impact of the indeterminacy of American interpretations of torture law on the thinking of Iraqi judges about the meaning and acceptability of torture.

As noted, these judges were among the primary targets of American efforts to bring the rule of law to Iraq. The issue of torture was an important arena in which Iraqi judges formed early impressions about the application of the rule of law in a modern democratic nation. These judges were confronted with the prospect of resisting or collaborating with official interpretations of torture law promulgated during the American occupation of Iraq.

The legal cynicism of the administration made it doubtful that a meaningful set of legal norms existed about human rights violations such as the torture of prisoners in post-Ba'athist Iraq. In the aftermath of Abu Ghraib and the torture of terrorism suspects in clandestine prisons around the world, it became reasonable to specifically question whether Iraqi judges would collaborate with or resist the cynical interpretations of the Bush administration about forceful interrogation, for example, in punishing coalition soldiers for torturing suspected al-Qaeda terrorists. Could the Iraq judges be expected to act independently of the example and influence of the U.S.-led coalition?

Throughout the Iraq War, U.S. soldiers were immune from prosecution and punishment in Iraq's courts. When the Status of Forces Agreement that granted this immunity lapsed at the end of 2010, Iraqi authorities insisted that if U.S. forces remained in the country they must be liable to prosecution in the Iraqi justice system. It therefore made sense to inquire during the occupation how Iraqi judges would have actually decided cases about the use of torture, if they were assigned to try them. Furthermore, if we are to learn from the experiences of Iraq and beyond, we need to understand how our export of rule of law ideas impacts those we wish to influence – such as Iraqi judges. Specifically, should we expect judges in such circumstances to cynically collaborate or independently resist the importation of dubious American legal norms?

Following an initial visit by fifty leading Iraqi jurists to the European institute, our study included eighty-two additional Iraqi judges randomly chosen and flown in several groups to the institute for the training program. We analyzed the sentencing decisions of each judge in hypothetical torture cases. The hypothetical decisions by the Iraqi judiciary in their decisions brought to light major issues associated with the Bush administration's interpretations of torture law.

H. L. A. Hart anticipated what has become a core principle of a conflict or critical legal theory of law: namely, that law is indeterminate (see also, for example, Matsuda 1987). By this, Hart meant that "[i]n every legal system a large and important field is left open for the exercise of discretion by courts and other officials in rendering initially vague standards determinate, in resolving the uncertainties of statutes, or in developing and qualifying rules only broadly communicated by authoritative precedents" (Hart 1961:132). This principle of critical legal theory plays a central role in the unfolding of our research design, because vague standards offer important opportunities for the development of legally cynical policies and practices by authorities.

Critical legal theory shares many features in common with conflict theories of crime and punishment. Critical legal scholars have vigorously advanced the thesis that legal doctrine lacks determinacy (Tushnet 1983:781, 819). According to strong statements of the indeterminacy thesis, laws, regulations, and court decisions allow a judge to justify almost any specific outcome she or he wishes in any particular case. The implication is that "a competent adjudicator can square almost any decision in favor of either side in any given legal dispute" (Solum 1987:462, 502). This indeterminacy is a fertile breeding ground for legal cynicism about criminal militarism.

Of course, the assertion of indeterminacy, like the claims of legal cynicism, can be overstated. The overview of legal cynicism presented in the prologue of this book emphasizes a combination of constraint-possibility and cause-effect applications. The former application of a legal cynicism perspective, for example, in generating possibilities, is less determinate in its implications.

Mark Tushnet reprises a similar issue in the brief but controversial trajectory of critical legal theory.

> [B]old and overstated claims that *all* results were underdetermined were replaced by more defensible ones, to the effect that many results were underdetermined, or that results in many interesting cases were, or . . . that enough results were underdetermined to matter. One or another of these revised versions of the indeterminacy argument is, I think, accepted by nearly every serious legal scholar in the United States. (2005:13)

Beyond this, Tushnet suggests that "major components of critical legal studies have become the common sense of the legal academy, acknowledged to be accurate by many who would never think of identifying themselves as critical legal scholars" (2005:99). The implication is that legal cynicism is common, albeit not omnipresent or necessarily well recognized, making it important to persuasively document where and how this concept appropriately applies.

We draw from a critical legal perspective to guide our understanding of the indeterminacy of torture law and sentencing in the context of occupied Iraq, but our data analysis further reveals that a more nuanced explanation of the sentencing behavior of Iraqi judges is required. Like the conflict theorists in criminology, in addition to the indeterminacy thesis, critical legal scholars also have maintained the widely accepted and related thesis that legal discourse and decisions conceal and reinforce relations of power and domination (e.g., Turk 1982).

The implication is that, through indeterminacy, the legal system can reinforce relations of social and economic domination, while retaining the appearance of neutrality and autonomy. That is, indeterminacy can free legal actors from the apparent constraints imposed by existing rules through use of "legitimized" legal arguments. Critical theory therefore does not assume that the indeterminacy of law is simply random, but that resulting legal outcomes are expressions of power and domination, and threats to the existing social order that are facilitated by legal cynicism and enabled by the indeterminacy of law.

In this chapter, we examine why and how the U.S. effort to introduce democracy with a legally cynical and indeterminate rule of law produced inconsistency – patterns that we interpret as instances of collaboration and resistance – in the projected decisions of the Iraqi judges we studied. The projections are the sentencing decisions imposed by the judges in hypothetical case scenarios that describe guards convicted of torturing prisoners suspected of terrorism. The hypothetical fact patterns operational-ize the indeterminate effect of torture law by experimentally manipulating the national/military affiliations of the guards and prisoners in the scenarios, with a particular focus on coalition soldiers whose power derives from their association with the U.S. military force, and al-Qaeda prisoners whose pro-tected status is undermined by indeterminate interpretations of the Geneva Conventions.

"JUDGES' SCHOOL"

Rehabilitating the Iraqi judiciary became an important symbolic task for the occupation and its belatedly expressed goals of bringing democracy and the rule of law to Iraq. As a first gesture toward protecting the Iraqi judiciary from bribes and financial corruption, the Coalition Provisional Authority increased the salaries of judges from approximately 100 to 1,000 dollars per month. Yet the judges were still thought to need what the professional American bar calls "continuing legal education." For example, given three decades of judicial participation in a system of legal authoritarian Ba'athist rule that mandated extensive use of torture, Iraqi judges were still believed to require reform and reeducation. The idea quickly emerged of what in less professionally sensitive circumstances might have been called a "judges' school."

Thus our research opportunity to observe Iraqi judges followed a post-invasion introductory meeting initiated by American and British law-yers in August 2003 in Baghdad between the leadership of the Iraqi bar and representatives of coalition countries. Tragically, this meeting ended in the chaos of the August 19 al-Qaeda bombing of the UN headquarters described in Chapter 2 that killed Sergio de Mello, the UN high representative to Iraq, among a score of others. The UK-based international legal association pro-posed in the aftermath to assemble groups of Iraqi judges with judges and lawyers from the coalition countries at a legal training institute located in a more secure setting.

A legal institute was already in operation in a central European capital, training judges and lawyers from the postcommunist states of eastern and central Europe. With the support of the U.S. State Department, the insti-tute brought more than 100 judges from all over Iraq (see Figure 3.1) to this institute. We were invited to attend and assess these two-week courses with an evaluation methodology of our choice. We decided to build our experimental design around the issue of legal cynicism and indeterminacy in the develop-ment of U.S.-led policies and practices of torture in Iraq.

FIGURE 3.1. Jurisdictional Locations of Sample Judges

A CYNICALLY INDETERMINATE INTERPRETATION OF TORTURE LAW

On August 1, 2002, in response to a request from White House Counsel Alberto Gonzales, the Office of Legal Counsel (OLC) issued a memorandum entitled Standards of Conduct for Interrogation, now commonly known as the "Torture Memo." This memo was written by a Berkeley law professor then working in the OLC, John Yoo, and signed by his superior at the OLC (Bybee 2002). As a legal matter, the purposes of an OLC memo are to advise the president as to the state of the law and to serve as a binding legal interpretation (Moss 2000).

The Bush administration had now declared its "Global War on Terror" and techniques for interrogation of suspects and prisoners had quickly become subjects of intense discussion at the highest levels of the administration. Because of the importance then attributed to al-Qaeda in Iraq in the War on Terror, the administration requested legal advice about the methods CIA interrogators could use with suspected al-Qaeda detainees. White House Counsel Alberto Gonzales requested that Assistant Attorney General Jay Bybee and John Yoo provide a guiding OLC opinion about the restrictions imposed by the Convention against Torture and Other Cruel, Inhuman, or Degrading Treatment (CAT).

In the memo, Yoo argued:

> 18 U.S.C. section 2340A does not prohibit as "torture" merely cruel and inhuman interrogation techniques, but only those interrogation techniques that inflict pain akin in severity to death or organ failure.... But if we are wrong, to the extent 18 U.S.C. section 2340A prohibits interrogation techniques the President approved, the law would violate the American Constitution. This is because it is inherent in the Presidential office to determine what interrogation techniques shall be used, and neither Congress nor the Supreme Court has a greater power than the President on the subject.... However, if the President's commands were found subject to 18 U.S.C. section 2340A without violating the Constitution, then, nevertheless, the President's endorsement of such interrogation techniques could still be justified as a matter of necessity and self-defense, being the moral choice of a lesser evil: harming an individual enemy combatant in order to prevent further al-Qaeda attacks upon the United States.

Writing in the aftermath of the September 11 attack on the United States, Yoo was asserting that there was a legal distinction between torture and "merely" or "extremely" cruel and inhuman interrogation practices.

This distinction dated to a decision by the Reagan administration not to specifically ask for Senate ratification of the "cruel and inhuman" language of CAT. Instead, "undefined torture" was the presumed basis of the treaty ratification.

Torture, the Yoo memo therefore reasoned, referred only to those interrogation techniques that it specified as causing "pain similar to death or organ failure." According to Yoo, although CAT prohibits "cruel, degrading, and inhumane treatment" as well as extreme torture, there is a distinction between the two. Yoo claimed that the Senate ratification of CAT explicitly prohibited only torture, saying that "certain acts may be cruel, inhuman, or degrading, but still not produce enough pain and suffering of the requisite intensity to fall within section 2430(A)'s proscription against torture."

Yoo further claimed that the president of the United States had constitutional authority to determine which interrogation techniques shall be used as a matter of national necessity and self-defense against further al-Qaeda attacks.

Finally, Yoo argued for a legal distinction between protected prisoners of war and unlawful enemy combatants to justify the use of torture. He claimed that Taliban and al-Qaeda prisoners were not entitled to prisoner-of-war status under the Geneva Conventions, which protected U.S. officials from prosecution under the War Crimes Act.

The importance of the Torture Memo is that it made the indeterminacy of the U.S. ratification of CAT explicit. The United States used this memo as the foundation for the use of coercive interrogations in the "Global War on Terror." As the short history of the Torture Memo illustrates, in the space following from uncertainty, the government's own interpretation can become de facto law (Cover 1986). Following September 11, coercive interrogation techniques were authorized at the highest levels of the administration, legally certified by attorneys in the White House and the Department of Justice, conveyed to the Pentagon and the Central Intelligence Agency, and apparently communicated down the chain of command to prison guards and interrogators.

Jack Goldsmith, Yoo's successor at OLC, writes that:

> The message of the August 2, 2002, OLC opinion was indeed clear: violent acts aren't necessarily torture; if you do torture, you probably have a defense; and even if you don't have a defense, the torture law doesn't apply if you act under the cover of presidential authority. CIA interrogators and their supervisors, under pressure to get information about the next attack, viewed the opinion as a golden shield, as one CIA official later called it, that provided enormous comfort. (Goldsmith 2007:144)

It is difficult to read this "golden shield" reference without thinking that it represented rationalization as much as or more than rationality, and of a legally cynical form.

While a former White House lawyer (Hatfield 2006) has suggested that "if you line up 1,000 law professors, only six or seven would sign up to [the Torture Memo's viewpoint]," a number of well-recognized scholars such as Eric Posner (2004), Michael Ignatieff (2004), and Alan Dershowitz (2002) argued that there was merit in the reasoning of the Torture Memo. Our reading of the Yoo memo is that it tendentiously used indeterminacy in the U.S. ratification of the UN Convention against Torture to justify legally cynical policy and criminal military practice.

The impact of this memo probably cannot be overstated. It was the basis for the use of coercive techniques noted earlier against several high-ranking detainees (Johnston and Risen 2004). In January 2003, Secretary of Defense Donald Rumsfeld formed a working group to study interrogation techniques. Much of the language of the Torture Memo was incorporated in its report (see Greenberg and Dratel 2005). Rumsfeld subsequently promulgated a list of aggressive interrogation procedures to be used at Guantanamo Bay, and use of these techniques in turn migrated to Iraq.

While the Bush administration continued to debate internally which interrogation methods were protected under what grounds by the Geneva Conventions, Iraqi judges confronted a cynical and indeterminate legal understanding of the laws of torture. On the one hand, articles of the UN International Covenant on Civil and Political Rights, which Iraq and the United States both ratified, specifically prohibit the torture of prisoners of war. Articles 127[1] and 333[2] of the Iraqi Code of Criminal Procedure also specifically criminalize the use of torture by any public servant. Yet Yoo's memo undermined the legal scope and force of the Geneva Conventions and cynically placed the final authority in the hands of the U.S. president to determine what torture meant more broadly, and specifically in the context of suspected al-Qaeda members in Iraq.

Descriptions of disagreements within the executive branch continued to reveal the indeterminacy of torture law in the Bush administration. Jack Goldsmith, when he served as head of the Office of Legal Counsel, took the highly unusual step of withdrawing the Torture Memo after the Abu Ghraib scandal emerged in 2004. Based on interviews with Goldsmith, Jeffrey Rosen writes that:

> Goldsmith says he believed at the time, and still does, that this extreme conclusion would call into question the constitutionality of the federal laws that limit interrogation, like the War Crimes Act of 1996, which prohibits grave breeches of the Geneva Conventions, and the Uniform Code of Military Justice, which prohibits cruelty and maltreatment. He also found the tone of both opinions tendentious rather than cautious and feared that they might be interpreted as an attempt to immunize government officials for genuinely bad acts. (2007a: 40–3)

It is precisely this "attempt to immunize government officials for genuinely bad acts" that we regard as a useful illustration of legally cynical justification by elites of criminal militarism. Goldsmith felt so strongly about the torture issue that he resigned from the Office of Legal Counsel simultaneously with his withdrawal of the Torture Memo.

However, subsequent opinions by the new head of the Office of Legal Counsel, Daniel Levin, reaffirmed the interpretations of Yoo's earlier memo. This encouraged Yoo to maintain that subsequent memos and statutes continued to provide that:

> The legal meaning of "torture" is not as all inclusive as some people would like it to be. Legally, we are not required to treat captured terrorists engaged in war against us as if they were suspects held at an American police station.... Unpleasant as it is, our government has a responsibility to do what is reasonably necessary in self-defense. (2006:226)

Yoo's reference to "an American police station" clearly reflects a more optimistic vision of American criminal justice than suggested by the Chicago research of Kirk and Papachristos (2011). It is the contradiction between this optimistically idealistic vision and what Yoo regards as acceptable in international conflict zones that is central to the perspective of legal cynicism.

Yoo's perspective is asserted notwithstanding the decision of the Supreme Court in the 2006 *Hamdan v. Rumsfeld* case that legal protections of the Geneva Conventions apply to al-Qaeda. Thus torture law in Iraq during the period of our research in 2004 and 2005 remained remarkably indeterminate. As our experimental data presented later in this chapter demonstrate, this indeterminacy, and we submit the legal cynicism of policies of criminal militarism, had direct implications for practicing judges in Iraq.

THREE TESTABLE HYPOTHESES

We anticipated that indeterminacy in torture law could produce three patterns of sentencing by Iraqi judges that we treat as competing hypotheses.

Hypothesis 1: *Uniform Lenient Sentencing.* We first predicted that the indeterminate interpretation of torture law reflected in the Bush administration memos, and the absence of any challenge or critical reaction to it in the institute training program, would create a "climate of leniency" in which Iraqi judges would impose short sentences for guards convicted of torturing prisoners in Iraq. By the beginning of 2002, John Yoo publicly opined that "treaties do not protect al-Qaeda"[3]; Donald Rumsfeld stated that "unlawful combatants do not have any rights under the Geneva Convention"[4]; and Alberto Gonzales observed that "this new paradigm renders obsolete Geneva's strict limitations."[5]

The Iraqi judges were living through a period in which the U.S. military courts were treating torture in Iraq leniently. Thus the expectation of leniency was consistent with the limited punishment imposed by U.S. military courts for the torture that occurred at Abu Ghraib. Only about a dozen soldiers were convicted of charges related to the torture at Abu Ghraib, and most of them received minor sentences. Specialist Charles Graner was convicted and sentenced most severely to ten years in federal prison. However, the highest-ranking officer, Lieutenant Colonel Steven Jordan, was acquitted of all charges of prisoner maltreatment against him and received only a technical reprimand. The Final Report of an Independent Panel for the Department of Defense absolved all senior U.S. military and political leadership of responsibility, concluding that "the Panel finds no evidence that organizations above the 800th MP Brigade or the 205th MI Brigade-level were directly involved in the incidents at Abu Ghraib."[6]

The first photographic evidence of U.S. guards torturing detainees at Abu Ghraib prison appeared on CBS News four months before the first Iraqi judge training program in the spring of 2004. Interestingly, neither the photos nor torture law were openly discussed at the institute. However, we hypothesized that the American presence (i.e., both in the institute program and in Iraq) and the silence in the program about U.S. involvement in the use of torture would produce a collaborative atmosphere of uniform lenience in prescribing sentences for the case vignettes described later in this chapter. That is, we expected that Iraqi judges would assign lenient sentences to prison guards convicted of torture and thereby express their collaborative orientation to the occupation and its use of torture.

Hypothesis 2: *Selectively Lenient Sentencing*. Alternatively, we hypothesized that the pattern of lenient sentencing of torture might selectively be reserved for a particular combination of guards and prisoners. Coalition soldiers obviously held unique positions of power that derived from their association with the U.S. military in Iraq, and we therefore hypothesized that Iraqi judges would collaborate with the coalition authorities by imposing lenient sentences on *coalition* guards who tortured al-Qaeda prisoners.

A critical legal perspective emphasizes the role of power in shaping judicial decision making and explains how law is used selectively to protect the powerful (Dezalay and Garth 2002). The former head of the Office of Legal Counsel quoted earlier, Jack Goldsmith, candidly calls the interpretation of torture law "an exercise of sheer power" (2007:39). We concur and add that the interpretation was a legally cynical legitimation of this power.

Lawyer-sociologist David Garland (1990) calls groups such as al-Qaeda who threaten the powerful "problem populations." Judges in Iraq likely found torture convictions involving interrogations by coalition forces of al-Qaeda prisoners especially "troublesome" or "hard cases." Anthropologist Sally Merry notes that "it is at these moments of trouble that the systems of law that regulate social life are laid bare, raised into the domain of the explicit" (1998:15). Group membership is a frequent source of what classical anthropologists and legal scholars, such as Llewellyn and Hoebel (1941), cite as "trouble cases."

Al-Qaeda in Iraq claimed responsibility for as many as 1,700 attacks on coalition and Iraqi forces in a three-month period in the city of Mosul alone.[7] The law of torture became a legal vehicle through which the power of the coalition forces was unleashed in responding to the threat posed by al-Qaeda in Iraq. At the time of our study, concern about al-Qaeda in Iraq was at a high level.[8] Our second hypothesis is, therefore, that Iraqi judges would specifically collaborate with the occupying coalition forces by imposing selectively lenient sentences in the troublesome cases involving *coalition guards torturing al-Qaeda prisoners.*

Hypothesis 3: *Polarized Lenient and Severe Sentencing.* Finally, we noted that it was possible that the aforementioned type of hypothesis could be regarded as too simple in its application of a critical legal perspective. Indeterminacy in the law of torture left open an opportunity for severity as well as leniency in sentencing convicted torturers. Of course, severe sentencing of coalition guards for torturing al-Qaeda prisoners would mean resisting the Bush administration's implementation of harsh interrogation methods, for example, against suspected al-Qaeda terrorists at Abu Ghraib. Yet, if these harsh interrogation methods were ineffective or even counterproductive, or seen as unjust or illegal, some judges might resist the adoption of these harsh methods and impose severe punishment for their use. In our third hypothesis, we therefore predicted a polarized sentencing pattern in which *some judges collaborated* with the authorities by imposing lenient sentences for coalition guards convicted of torturing al-Qaeda, while *other judges resisted* and imposed severe sentences for the same exact fact pattern. This third hypothesis was more nuanced and contingent than the preceding two hypotheses in that it predicted differing responses of collaboration and resistance among the Iraqi judges.

The further importance of this third hypothesis was that it predicted a split among the judges, with some choosing a more legally cynical path of collaboration with the U.S.-led coalition, and others opting for a more independent path of resistance against the coalition's extension of Saddam Hussein's legal authoritarian use of torture with the compliance of Iraq's judiciary described in Chapter 1.

THE EXPERIMENTAL VIGNETTES

Our challenge was to understand the sentencing decisions that Iraqi judges would make during the occupation of their country. We used the factorial survey method developed by Peter Rossi (1974), which has been called "the methodological gold standard" for the study of decision-making situations (Seron et al. 2006). In our study, each Iraqi judge was asked to respond to hypothetical cases or vignettes by assigning prison sentences to prison guards accused of torturing prisoners who were suspected terrorists.

The vignettes contained fact patterns that were randomly varied in an experimental fashion. As illustrated in this chapter, the random assignment allowed factual elements of the cases to be examined independently of one another. This allowed us to assess the independent effects of characteristics of the defendant (e.g., a coalition guard) and the victim (e.g., an al-Qaeda prisoner) on judges' punishments (e.g., sentence length) of particular behaviors (e.g., torture), removing the "veil" that critical legal scholars indicate often obscures judicial decision making.

An important feature of the vignette method is that the randomization of the fact patterns in the hypothetical cases diminishes confounding correlations among the case characteristics, or the possibility of strong systematic associations among the facts. In practical terms, this means that after we identify the important case facts in the multivariate analyses briefly summarized later in this chapter, we can then use simpler bar graphs to display the influence of specific factors.

To illustrate, we next introduce from our study results the influence of the degree of injury resulting from torture, measured in terms of days of required hospitalization in a simple bar graph of sentence length, with days in the hospital on the horizontal axis and sentence length on a vertical axis. Thus Figure 3.2 indicates with the data we introduce further later that injuries leading to one to two weeks of hospitalization result in average sentences in the range of two to four years in prison, that injuries leading from three weeks to more than eight months of hospitalization result in average sentences of nearly seven years, while injuries causing death result in sentences of about fifteen years in prison. As a result of the randomization, this effect is net of other influences, such as the identity of the prison guard or prisoner.[9]

In this study, the vignette methodology can be thought of as allowing an examination of the reasoning of the judges as they assign sentences to the hypothetical cases. As we noted at the outset, because U.S. soldiers were immune from prosecution in Iraqi courts, our design cannot represent actual sentencing practices by Iraqi judges. There were a number of cases whose facts

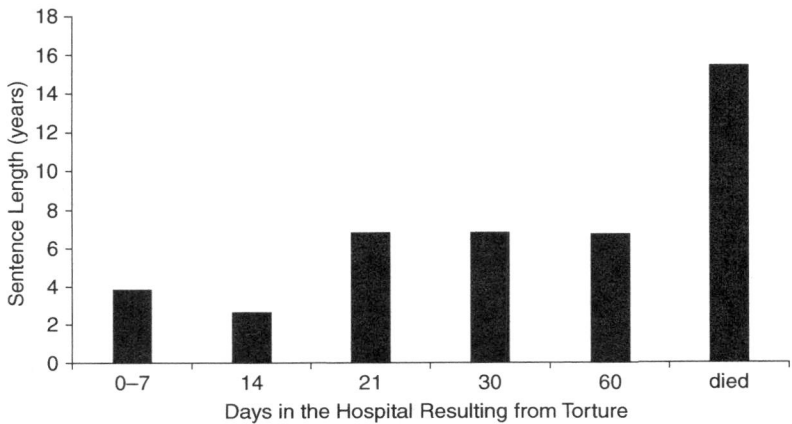

FIGURE 3.2. Mean Iraqi Judge Prison Sentences by Days of Hospitalization Required for Tortured Prisoner

pressed the boundaries of U.S. immunity (Lewis 2006; Moss 2006). However, because the United States never actually allowed any coalition soldiers to be prosecuted in Iraqi courts, our hypothetical case approach represented the only means we are aware of to have analyzed sentencing decisions by Iraqi judges involving coalition forces and al-Qaeda in Iraq. Our vignette experiment is likely unique in the way it captured the historical experience of challenges to the rule of law and judicial independence in occupied Iraq.

THE HYPOTHETICAL TORTURE CASES

August 2004: The pilot phase of our research involved an initial meeting with fifty of the highest-ranking judges from Iraq, one of whom was subsequently selected to preside over, and later resigned from, the trial of Saddam Hussein. Our study's first challenge was to demonstrate that the vignettes would work with these Iraqi judges who spoke little English. We developed an instrument that was translated and printed in Arabic for use with the following groups. These groups included eighty-three further Iraqi judges who attended subsequent training courses in November 2004 and April 2005. This group represented about 10 percent of the approximately 700 judges in Iraq. Three of the only seven women judges in Iraq were included. Following the pilot phase, judges were selected in Iraq at random to attend the institute.

November 2004: The Arabic translation of the instrument consumed much of our time prior to the next meeting three months later. Yet compared to the events enveloping the judges and their courts in Iraq, our problems were mundane. Several of the judges who took part in institute sessions were subsequently assassinated. Security was a constant concern in the transportation and housing of the judges for the programs. Further security issues emerged when the head of the Coalition Provisional Authority, Paul Bremer, and the deputy secretary of state, Richard Armitage, paid courtesy visits to the institute program.

Media coverage of the issue of torture at Abu Ghraib prison continued from early 2004 throughout the institute programs. The writing, rescinding, and rewriting of memos by Yoo, Goldsmith, and Levin also continued through the period of our research. Just prior to and during the November 2004 program at the institute, coalition forces mounted the major counteroffensive producing heavy loss of life in the city of Fallujah. In January 2005, voters in Iraq selected representatives to the Transitional National Assembly to write Iraq's constitution.

Iraq was not yet experiencing the level of sectarian violence verging on civil war in late 2006 discussed in the following chapter. Nonetheless, Iraq was already the most violent country in the region, not only in terms of war casualties and related terrorist attacks, but also escalating assassinations, murders, rapes, and property destruction and theft. Felony case dispositions, including torture, were rising rapidly, for example, increasing by 40 percent between November 2003 and November 2004 (O'Hanlon and Unikewicz 2005). These background conditions gave face validity to the vignettes used in our research.

As compensation for their involvement in the study, the judges each received a phone card with about $20 in credit for phone calls from the institute to Iraq. This proved a powerful inducement, as the judges were anxious about the safety of their families and the institute could not provide phone assistance.

In November 2004, all forty-three Iraqi judges attending the institute program were asked to impose hypothetical sentences on prison guards accused of torturing imprisoned suspected terrorists. At this program session, both the prison guard and the prisoner were described in our vignettes as Iraqi. This meant the statuses of the torturer and terrorist were held constant and, more specifically, that the power and conflict dynamics involved in coalition forces torturing al-Qaeda were excluded from this stage of the design.

We return later to this crucial design decision, but already this decision makes clear that the inclusion of variable characteristics of the situations in the vignette template was a key consideration. Each dimension (e.g., length of hospitalization resulting from torture) contains levels or categories. We developed a vignette template based on descriptions of torture situations discussed in human rights reports, the media, and actual military cases.

The vignettes vary considerably but are systematic in evaluating how situational or mitigating factors (noted later in this chapter) affect the judges' responses to the cases, as measured by the question, "What do you believe is a just sentence for this case?" The judges were instructed to assign a sentence in number of months or years of incarceration, or assign a sentence of "zero" if they believed no prison time was warranted. A sample vignette from the November 2004 administration reads as follows in English:

> The offender, a PRISON GUARD, was convicted of ordering the torture of a PRISONER in violation of the International Covenant on Civil and Political Rights. At the time of the offense, the state had declared a public emergency because of terrorist activities, including a string of bombings in major cities. The PRISONER and GUARD are from different ethnic groups. The PRISONER was also a known low-ranking terrorist. The offending PRISON GUARD is female; the PRISONER is male. At the time of the offense, the offending PRISON GUARD was forty years old; the PRISONER was thirty years old. The offending PRISON GUARD was married with no children; the PRISONER was also married with no children. The PRISONER required hospitalization for three weeks as a result of his injuries. Prior to this offense, the offending PRISON GUARD had no prior record of misconduct involving prisoners.

Case characteristics were systematically varied in the November 2004 design, as described more fully in Table 3.1: the guards' age, gender, command responsibility, family background, and prior record; the prisoners' age, gender, family background, injury, and terrorist involvement; and whether the guard and prisoner were from the same or different ethnic groups.

April 2005: Our decision to make both the prison guard and the prisoner Iraqi in our November 2004 factorial survey made sense as a means of initially holding constant the national statuses of the torturer and terrorist. Yet this omitted the more complicated and provocative power dynamics involved in the now worldwide awareness that U.S.-led coalition forces were torturing suspected al-Qaeda in Iraq members along with other prisoners. Experimental designs may often sacrifice external for internal validity in this way, but this also had the unintended effect of eclipsing the critical legal reality of the Iraqi occupation and insurgency that was of international concern.

After our study, the daily average of interethnic attacks increased fifteen fold (Kamp et al. 2006:A2). At this earlier juncture in the conflict, it was already becoming apparent that we needed to make the operative exogenous power dynamics of coalition, al-Qaeda, and other national/military affiliations

TABLE 3.1. *Descriptions of variables used in hypothetical cases*

Independent variables	Variable description
Age of Prison Guard & Prisoner	Eight Levels, in increments of five years (18, 20, 25, 30, 35, 40, 45, 50).
Ethnicity of Prison Guard & Prisoner	Prison Guard & Prisoner from "the same ethnic group" or from "different ethnic groups"
Prison Guard & Prisoner's Family Background	Single, Married with no children, or Married
Command Responsibility	Prison Guard was "ordered to commit offense" or "not ordered to commit the offense" or "ordered commission of the offense only"
Prison Guard's Prior Record	The offender has "a prior record of misconduct involving prisoners" or "no prior record of misconduct involving prisoners."
Injury to Prisoner	The victim was "released from the hospital the same day"; or "required hospitalization" for one, three, five, or seven days; or for two weeks, three weeks, one month, or two months; or the victim "died as a result of the offense."
Gender of the Prison Guard & Prisoner	Prison Guard: Prisoner (1) Male: Female (2) Female: Male (3) Male: Male (4) Female: Female
Group Affiliation of the Prison Guard & Prisoner (Included only for April Group 2)	Prisoner: Prison Guard (1) Coalition: Iraqi (2) Iraqi: Coalition (3) Coalition: Coalition (4) Iraqi: Iraqi (5) Al-Qaeda: Iraqi (6) Iraqi: Al-Qaeda (7) Al-Qaeda: Coalition (8) Coalition: Al-Qaeda
Terrorist Information	(1) "The prisoner is a suspected terrorist." (2) "The prisoner is a known high-ranking terrorist." (3) "The prisoner is a known low-ranking terrorist." (4) "The prisoner is not a terrorist."

explicit in our design. A critical legal perspective was becoming increasingly salient in our understanding of these events and we could no longer ignore its obvious implications.

We addressed the issue of external validity in April 2005, when another group of thirty-nine Iraqi judges came to the institute and participated in the study. We modified the design by dividing the judges into two groups, one each of twenty and nineteen judges, and conducting an experiment within the vignette design. The first group engaged in essentially the same exercise as the earlier group of judges in November. The second group of judges in April was asked to engage in identical sentencing tasks as the first group, with the exception that the case characteristics now further included the nationality/military group affiliations of the guards and their prisoners, including the coalition forces and suspected al-Qaeda. This procedurally simple but theoretically salient modification involved inserting into the vignette this sentence: "The PRISON GUARD is a member of ——— while the offending PRISONER is ——— ," with the guard/prisoner blanks filled in with the alternative categories indicated in Table 3.1.

Recall that legal indeterminacy in the definition of torture widened the opening for decisions based on the influences of power. The Yoo Torture Memo expressed an official U.S. government interpretation of the indeterminacy of torture law that it resolved in favor of allowing "harsh" interrogation techniques and asserting their special necessity in response to a fear and perceived need for protection from al-Qaeda. The number of "foreign fighters" in Iraq was said to have nearly doubled between November 2004 and November 2006 (Kamp 2006). The indeterminacy of the law of torture gave the Iraqi judges the latitude to respond with varying degrees of punishment to the power of the occupying coalition forces and to fears of al-Qaeda.

THE RESULTS

As noted earlier, the factorial surveys with the Iraqi judges were conducted with one group of forty-three judges in November 2004 and two groups, one each of twenty and nineteen judges, in April 2005. We first examine differences in average sentences across the three groups. Next we consider sentencing decisions of the individual judges. Finally, we focus in greater detail on the second group of April judges who sentenced cases that included the experimental variation in the nationality/military affiliations of guards accused of torturing suspected terrorists. We focus particularly on cases of coalition forces torturing al-Qaeda in Iraq.

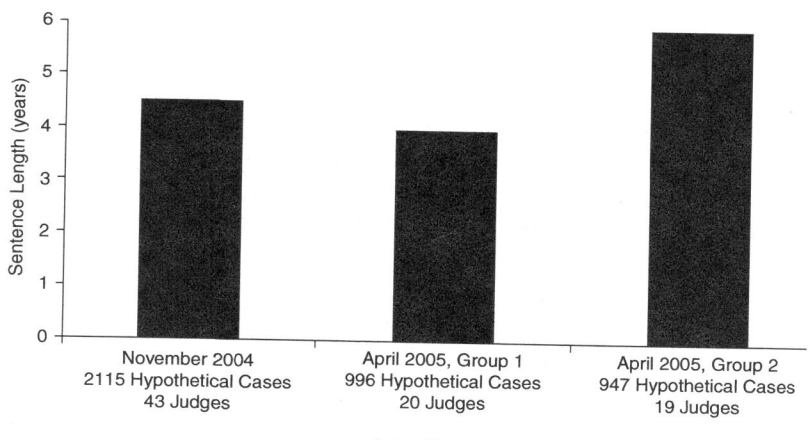

FIGURE 3.3. Mean Sentence Length for Iraqi Judge Groups

Table 3.1 describes the case facts randomly assigned in the vignettes or hypothetical cases considered by all eighty-two judges. For example, this table describes ten different levels of the "injury to prisoner" variable already considered in Figure 3.2. This table also includes the national/military affiliation that is introduced as the experimental variable in the second April group. Overall, the Iraqi judges were asked to sentence a total of 4,150 hypothetical cases.

The average sentences imposed by judges in each of the three groups are indicated in Figure 3.3. Of course, overall averages can conceal great variation. Nonetheless, a notable preliminary finding in Figure 3.3 is that in contrast with our first hypothesis, the *average* sentences were more than four years in prison, which is *not* lenient. Furthermore, even though the average sentence length in Figure 3.3 modestly declined after the elections and the accompanying upsurge in violence between November 2004 and April 2005, the decrease was only from 4.51 to 4.01 years. These are still rather severe average sentences. The Bush administration memo and the presence of the American judges in the institute program apparently did not lead *all* the Iraqi judges to leniently sentence convicted torturers. This is why we examine with greater specificity the distribution of severity and leniency in these sentences.

Even more striking in Figure 3.3 is the sharply increased average sentence for the second group of Iraqi judges in April 2005, from 4.01 to 5.95 years. Recall that the only change in the vignettes presented to the second group of judges in April is the inclusion of added information on the nationality/ military group affiliations – including coalition forces and al-Qaeda – of the prison guards and prisoners. This means that when the specific affiliations of the respective combatant parties were included in the hypotheticals in our second April experimental group, the Iraqi judges on average became notably more severe. This abrupt change is consistent with our second hypothesis that torture convictions involving coalition forces and al-Qaeda suspects represent "troublesome" or "hard cases" for these Iraqi judges, but the resulting change is again inconsistent with the expectation of leniency.

For our purposes, the results thus far underline the importance of introducing the apparently crucial information about the nationality/military group affiliations of the guards and prisoners. We therefore next concentrated our attention on the second April experimental group and further investigated the results for each of the nineteen individual judges in this group. Although our results were further confirmed with extensive multivariate regression analyses, we are able to take advantage of the randomization involved in our experimental design to summarize the results with much more easily interpreted bar graphs.

Thus the results are summarized with several additional graphs that highlight for comparative attention the second April experimental group. First we present in Figure 3.4 the two April groups of Iraqi judges: the comparison group and the experimental group. Well over half of the judges in the April experimental group are either more lenient or more severe than the least and most severe judges in the comparison group. [Note: The comparison group consists of one more judge than the experimental group.] As suggested by the relative group means in Figure 3.3, the greatest change is in the direction of sentence severity. There is an approximate 50 percent increase from four to nearly six years in sentence length. Nonetheless, Figure 3.4 further indicates that there is an overall polarization – including leniency as well as severity – that results from the experimental introduction of the military/national affiliations in the second April experimental group. We demonstrate next in Figure 3.5 how the *same fact patterns* – specifying coalition guards torturing either al-Qaeda or Iraqi suspected terrorists – simultaneously produced both the most severe and most lenient sentences in the experimental group of judges.

We focus in Figure 3.5 on only the nineteen judges in the second experimental April group. This figure focuses on the specific effects of the previously listed guard-prisoner combinations. Figure 3.5 reveals that nine of the judges gave shorter sentences to coalition guards for torturing al-Qaeda prisoners than to coalition guards for torturing Iraqi prisoners. As illustrated in Figure 3.6, these Iraqi judges treated this group of coalition torturers of al-Qaeda as if they were guilty of misdemeanors. As noted earlier in this chapter, the U.S. military tribunals imposed similarly mild punishment on officers

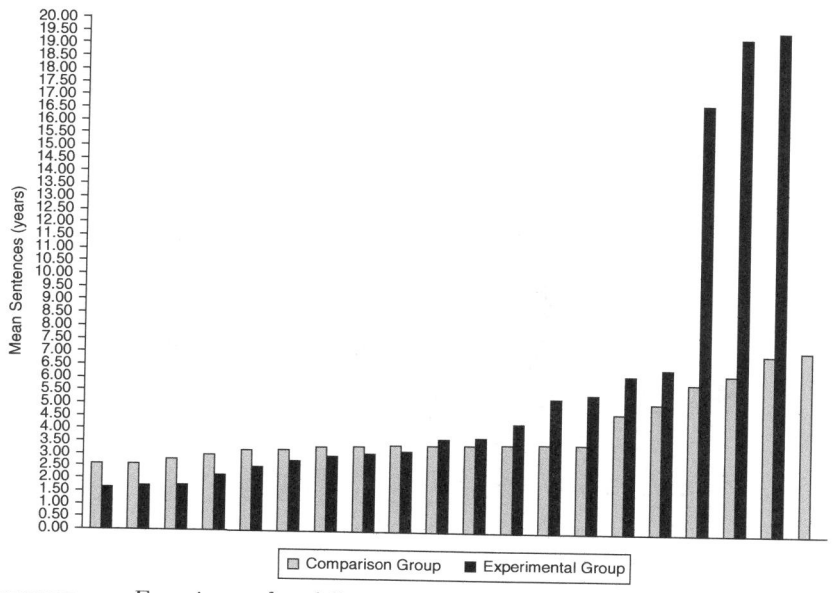

FIGURE 3.4. Experimental and Comparison Groups of Iraqi Judges, April 2005

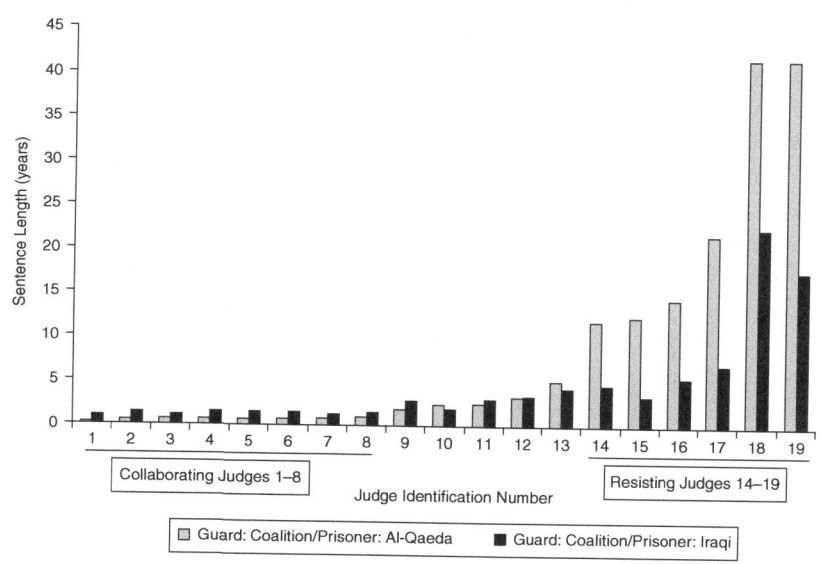

FIGURE 3.5. Mean Iraqi Judge Prison Sentences by Guard-Prisoner Combinations, Experimental Group (all judges), April 2005

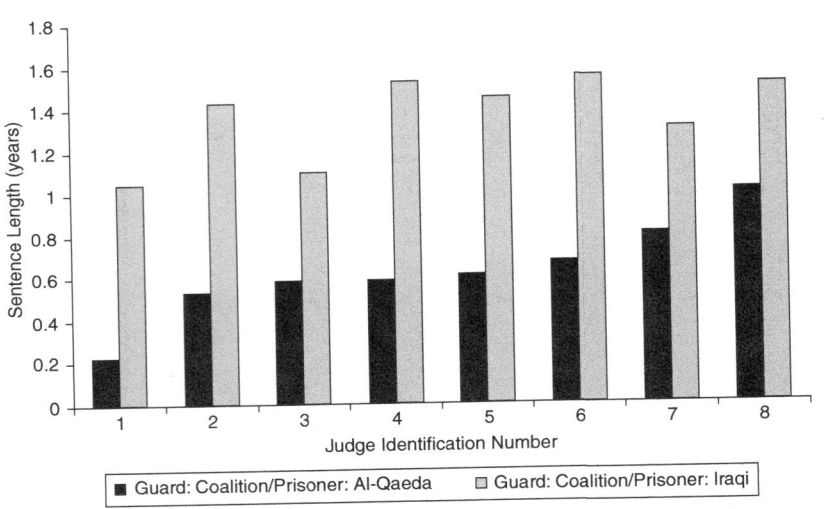

FIGURE 3.6. Mean Lenient Iraqi Judge Prison Sentences by Guard-Prisoner Combinations, Experimental Group (collaborating judges), April 2005

associated with torture at Abu Ghraib. In this experiment, nine of the Iraqi judges in the experimental group collaborated with the Bush administration's permissive and lenient attitude toward torture.

However, in stark contrast to this pattern of leniency, the last seven judges in Figure 3.5 gave longer average sentences in general, and specifically to coalition guards who tortured al-Qaeda prisoners. The sentences of six of these judges ranged from ten to more than forty years, and as noted, with the most severe sentences imposed on coalition guards who tortured al-Qaeda prisoners. These judges strongly resisted the example of the Bush administration's permissive and lenient interpretation of torture law. Figure 3.5 therefore reveals how disparate and polarized the judges were in their decisions when sentencing the trouble cases involving coalition guards and al-Qaeda prisoners.

Finally, Figure 3.6 magnifies the scale of the lower end of the sentence length scale to better illuminate the lenient sentences given by the first eight collaborating judges in Figure 3.5.

All eight of the judges in Figure 3.6 gave shorter sentences to coalition guards for torturing al-Qaeda rather than Iraqi prisoners, assigning sentences from about one to one and one half years in length in these cases. The misdemeanor length of these sentences – especially in the cases of coalition guards convicted of torturing al-Qaeda prisoners – is an empirical indication of normative judicial collaboration with the Bush administration's permissive interpretation of torture law.

These results clearly reveal inadequacies in our first and second hypotheses and unequivocally support our third hypothesis. Rather than simple uniform or selective leniency, the pattern of sentences in the experimental group of judges indicates a polarized pattern of lenience *and* severity reflecting both collaboration and resistance in relation to the Bush administration's interpretation of torture law.

INTERPRETING THE JUDGMENTS OF IRAQI JUDGES

Supreme Court Chief Justice John Roberts remarked in his confirmation hearing that "Judges wear black robes because it doesn't matter who they are.... That's not going to shape their decisions" (cited in Rosen 2007b:27). This "blank slate" view of judicial thought processes is completely at odds with more critical traditions of legal thought. We suggest that it is actually a view that is so naïve as to raise suspicion of legal cynicism on Roberts's part. A critical legal perspective further highlights how indeterminacy in the rule of law permits abuses of power. In Iraq, indigenous legal actors were confronted with choices about collaborating or resisting abuses in response to the indeterminate law surrounding torture. Our research provided a rare opportunity to advance a critical legal understanding of processes of collaboration and resistance in a methodologically unique way: through a systematic analysis of a judicial sentencing experiment.

Overall, we found little support for a naïve or idealized conception of the independent rule of law in occupied Iraq. The Bush administration's post-9/11 memos exported indeterminate and permissive interpretations of torture law to Iraq. The former head of the Office of Legal Counsel, Jack Goldsmith (2007), candidly called the interpretation of torture law a manifestation of "sheer power." We added that the Yoo memo was a tendentiously reasoned and legally cynical legitimation of this power.

Iraq's judges had lived through a brutal legal authoritarian regime in which torture was routine. Yet Iraq, like the United States, also had ratified the Geneva Conventions on torture and had passed its own law banning torture. The Bush administration's new interpretations of torture law presented a dilemma for Iraqi judges. They could cynically collaborate with U.S. criminal militarism or independently resist its normative imperatives.

To understand the response of Iraq's judges to a new era of torture associated with the occupation, we designed a sentencing experiment that included consideration of the indeterminacy of torture law and the hierarchical position of coalition prison guards in relation to convicted al-Qaeda suspects. It is important that we were able to conduct the experiment at a critical historical moment: soon after the media disseminated graphic images around the world of torture by coalition forces at Abu Ghraib prison.

We first hypothesized that Iraqi judges would simply collaborate with the new American-dominated Coalition Provisional Authority by uniformly treating torture leniently. Alternatively, we hypothesized that the disparity in power between coalition forces and al-Qaeda would result in Iraqi judges more selectively collaborating by imposing lenient sentences in these "trouble" cases, specifically, coalition guards convicted of torturing al-Qaeda prisoners. Finally, we alternatively hypothesized a polarized sentencing pattern in which some judges would collaborate with the authorities through lenient sentences of coalition guards for torturing al-Qaeda prisoners, while other judges would resist and impose severe sentences on the same combination of guards and prisoners.

There was little support for our first hypothesis of a "pervasive climate of leniency" in the punishment of torture. Overall, the judges imposed relatively long average sentences, with mean sentences ranging from four to six years. Nonetheless, some of the judges imposed short sentences, partially supporting our second hypothesis. Closer examination further revealed that the sentences were highly polarized, as predicted in our third hypothesis, resulting in both short and long sentences for coalition guards specifically convicted of torturing al-Qaeda prisoners.

This variability in sentencing reflects the indeterminacy of the law in Bush administration advisory memos on torture. As noted, the judges responded with a polarized variability. Our findings indicate that while nearly half of the Iraqi judges in our experimental group sentenced coalition guards to less than a year in prison for torturing al-Qaeda prisoners, about a third severely sentenced coalition guards to more than ten years in prison in the same kinds of cases. The polarized variation in sentencing severity in itself is confirmation of important effects anticipated by a critical legal perspective on the indeterminacy of law. We argue that the lenient sentencing reflected a cynical collaborative attitude toward the American occupation of Iraq, while severe sentencing indicated a more independent pattern of resistance.

It bears note that the Iraqi judges did not completely abandon conventional sentencing norms. Their sentencing decisions sustained a semblance of formal rational commitment to the rule of law, for example, by responding to the degree of injury and harm indicated by days in the hospital resulting from the torture of suspects. Still, we found convincing evidence that indeterminacy of the law and the hierarchical position of the occupying forces were the sources of selectively severe and lenient sentencing of cases involving coalition torture of al-Qaeda suspects.

The Iraqi judges who sentenced coalition guards severely for torturing al-Qaeda prisoners exercised a degree of judicial autonomy in resisting the occupying powers' permissive interpretations of torture law that we did not fully anticipate. On the other hand, the contrasting Iraqi judges who sentenced these same cases leniently accommodated the coalition leadership and collaborated with its position that the way to drive the presumed foreign threat of al-Qaeda from Iraq was to torture al-Qaeda prisoners into leaving and informing on their peers. Even if the latter judges did not fully condone the torture of al-Qaeda members, they expressed a tolerance for its use by punishing the coalition torturers less severely. They were more inclined to accommodate and collaborate with the powerful coalition occupiers, perhaps in hopes of professional career advancement.

There was little or no evidence in our findings that the January 2005 election in Iraq influenced sentencing decisions. The occurrence of this election between the November 2004 and April 2005 visits by the judges did not seem to notably influence sentencing outcomes. Our design also provided generic consideration of interethnic conflict with the inclusion of a variable indicating whether the torturer and suspected terrorist were from the same or different ethnic groups (i.e., reflecting a sectarian split). The effect of ethnic variation between the torturer and the suspect was actually in the unexpected direction of lenience, although this effect was never statistically significant. However, we think it is still likely that the results of this study involving al-Qaeda prisoners reflect the judges' engagement with the Sunni-Shia divide.

As noted earlier in this chapter, al-Qaeda in Iraq is a Sunni organization, and while the proportion of the Sunni insurgency estimated during the period of this experiment to be composed of foreign al-Qaeda fighters never exceeded 5 to 10 percent, President Bush blurred the lines between these groups when attempting to stimulate public support. He consistently referred to the growing Sunni insurgency and attacks in Iraq as the work of al-Qaeda. The president used al-Qaeda as a generic label, which implicitly invoked discredited links between Iraq and the 9/11 attacks. The military dragnets that swept many Sunni men into jails in Iraq justified their detainment by calling them al-Qaeda suspects.

The Islamic State of Iraq and Syria (ISIS) was founded at the peak of the Iraq War in 2006 and by 2012 eclipsed al-Qaeda in Iraq as a dominant insurgent force. ISIS made a point of being more extreme in its violent methods and split off from al-Qaeda. ISIS used U.S.-run detention facilities as key sites for indoctrination, and it turned prison breaks freeing Sunni detainees into a recruitment strategy for expanding its forces. Abu Bakr al-Baghdadi, who emerged as the successful leader of ISIS, spent time in U.S. detention.

ISIS shortened its name to the "Islamic State" when it claimed in 2014 to establish a caliphate in the territory overlapping the borders of Syria and Iraq. The cross-border activity of ISIS increased the level of foreign involvement in Iraq, which had been less common during the period of our judicial experiment and the earlier and continuing sweeps and detentions intended to deter foreign involvement in Iraq by groups like al-Qaeda and ISIS. The deterrent effect of detentions focused on Arab Sunnis seems not to have worked as intended.

Ahmed al-Dulaymi is a thirty-one-year-old Arab Sunni who escaped from Abu Ghraib prison with about 500 other detainees in 2013. He explained the link between al-Qaeda and the Sunni insurgency in a way that also applies to ISIS. He argued that al-Qaeda and ISIS links with the Sunni insurgency formed in reaction to the brutal and unjustified way other young men like him were imprisoned following security sweeps and held for long periods as suspects without charges or evidence. Although Ahmed returned to farm work and did not join al-Qaeda or ISIS, he explained that "Many of my friends were good people, but because of the government's actions, my friends have become dangerous people and leaders in al-Qaeda." Adopting the logic of legal cynicism, he concluded that "Injustice is what gives birth to al-Qaeda" (Arango and Schmitt 2014:A4; also Arango, Fahim, and Hubbard 2014).

The detention experience described by Ahmed al-Dulaymi and the recruitment strategy of ISIS adds another point of path dependency to the double and linked macro- and micro-level dimensions of the theory of legal cynicism and its consequences discussed in earlier chapters. As noted earlier in this chapter, the detention and torture policies migrated from the top macro-level of the Bush administration down through intelligence and defense channels to Quantanamo, and on to the detention facilities in Iraq. Al-Dulaymi's account illustrates how the macro-level policy sources of cynicism about U.S. and Iraqi political, military, and legal elites were linked to the micro-level cynical attitudes of those who perceived that they were being targeted as a group – namely the Arab Sunnis.

Thus judges in our study likely regarded most of the prisoners labeled as al-Qaeda in our experiment as Arab Sunnis. This is likely true of both the judges who lightly and severely sentenced coalition guards for torturing al-Qaeda prisoners, that is, for both the judges we have called collaborators and resisters. An implication is that the resisting judges probably were expressing a support that was increasingly extended in Sunni communities to their male members who were being detained if not tortured in U.S.- and Iraq-operated jails. Like the Sunni respondents in the Gallup Poll analyzed in the previous chapter who were less hopeful about the effects of the invasion and occupation, the resisting judges in this chapter likely reflected a growing sentiment in their communities that increasingly supported an organized militant opposition to the U.S.-led occupation.

We have found that judges who might have expected to experience political independence instead experienced encouragement to collaborate with a torture policy of their American advisors that was not sufficiently different from that of the prior Ba'athist regime. This didn't just portend a conflicted judiciary, but also a judiciary that could later be cynically turned to the purposes of a new Shia-dominated government that despite its constitutional and democratic features reproduced authoritarian practices of the past.

4

Night Falls on Baghdad

The thesis of this chapter is that the U.S. invasion of Iraq unleashed a self-reinforcing, self-reproducing, and self-fulfilling prophecy of fear, amplifying a brutal process of death and displacement that reconfigured a previously Sunni-dominated Baghdad into a Shia-controlled city. Recall that in addition to skepticism about the legitimacy of state and non-state actors and actions, fear about personal and family safety is a central component of the theory of legal cynicism. There was much to be cynically fearful about in post-invasion Baghdad.

Sunni and Shia militias posed dangerous and growing threats. Al-Qaeda, which was unwelcome under Saddam, gained a foothold with the most militant elements of the Sunni insurgency known as al-Qaeda in Iraq (AQI). At about the same time, a well-armed Mahdi Army emerged from the Shia-based Sadrist movement led by rising cleric Muqtada al-Sadr.

Many in Iraq believed that the U.S./coalition forces provoked the Sunni insurgents and the Shia Sadrists more than they protected the civilian population. Our thesis is that a rising fear in the civilian population became a further amplifying force and source of displacement of the Arab Sunnis from entire neighborhoods of Iraq's most populous city. The result was a new sectarian demography of Baghdad with radically cynical, exclusionary, and disadvantaging consequences for Arab Sunnis. Fear of this massive displacement and replacement, especially among Arab Sunnis, was not publicly acknowledged and was more generally denied by Bush administration policy makers – either as a result of their irresponsible ignorance or willful neglect of the sectarian realities of Iraq.

This ignorance/neglect is retrospectively and legally probative with regard to the charge of U.S. aggressive war. However, it is obviously important to also emphasize that it was al-Sadr's Mahdi Army that organized and enacted the displacement of Arab Sunni residents from Baghdad neighborhoods in a coordinated program of ethnic cleansing and crimes against humanity. Andrew Bell-Fialkoff explains that "ethnic cleansing can be understood as the expulsion of an 'undesirable' population from a given territory due to religious or ethnic discrimination, political, strategic or ideological considerations, or a combination of these" (1996:110). In the 1990s, the term was used by Serbian leaders in the former Yugoslavia to describe their systematic displacement of Muslim Bosnians (see Hagan 2010:182–3; Burns 1992). The UN General Assembly subsequently identified ethnic cleansing as a violation of international humanitarian law.[1]

It is crucial in establishing that ethnic cleansing has occurred to demonstrate that the "systematic elimination and removal" of a population has taken place. A mixture of the kind of social-scientific criminological and legal evidence presented in this chapter is essential to documenting and explaining ethnic cleansing.

BAGHDAD IN CONTEXT

As noted in Chapter 1, the Ba'ath Party first seized power in Iraq in 1963. It then lost control for several years before retaking power in 1968, with Saddam assuming complete control of the party in 1979. He systematically imposed his own brutal form of nationalist and militaristic autocratic rule on Iraq. Saddam's militarism was organized in response to perceived foreign threats and suspected ethnic-religious insurgencies. The most significant conflicts emerged from the division between Sunni and Shia adherents of Islam and the non-Arab Kurds, although many other groups were involved.

Beyond this, Iraqi society was significantly structured by complex tribal affiliations that still define social and political relations to this day (Tripp 2010; Hashim 2006; Dodge 2005). The complex divisions between these groups have periodically been contested through political violence, for example, as evidenced by the near-constant Kurdish struggles for independence from the central government. This diversity has long been a challenge to the construction of an inclusive, modern nation-state.

U.S. policy makers supporting the 2003 invasion based their strategic decisions on a limited understanding of Iraqi society – as exemplified by the failure to engage the intricate relations and contestations that define ethnic, tribal, and religious identities (Jabar 2004). Much of the reality of Iraq was glossed over by U.S. policy makers, with devastating consequences. These consequences were prominently manifested in Baghdad.

Baghdad is the country's capital, home to over 7 million people, representing as much as a quarter of the nation's population. Traditionally, it has hosted a population that mirrored the nation's diversity, including significant populations of Arab Shia, Arab Sunni, Kurds, Jews, and multiple Christian groups. However, by the U.S. invasion, the most acute and politically relevant sectarian divisions in Baghdad were between Arab Shia and Sunni groups, with some neighborhoods defined as largely Shia, largely Sunni, and mixed Sunni and Shia.[2]

The regime of Saddam Hussein managed these religious/ethnic divisions with its brutal autocratic and legal authoritarian rule, seeking to create a unifying national identity while targeting groups that sought greater autonomy or questioned Saddam's authoritarian ideology. As described in Chapter 1, the government engaged in ongoing military and political efforts to control the Kurds in the north as well as multiple, shifting policies to manage its majority Shia population concentrated in the south. Although many of these violent campaigns responded to separatist Kurdish movements or antigovernment Arab Shia challenges, the scope of the violent repression was brutal and often indiscriminate – involving the systematic torture, massacre, institutionalized rape, and forced relocation described in Chapter 1. While some of these practices have been investigated, others – including the sectarian rape and sexual violence documented in Chapter 1 – remain largely under researched.

Although the government of Saddam Hussein and the Ba'ath Party plunged the nation into its devastating war with Iran in the 1980s, isolating the country from the international community and engaging in policies leading to years of crushing sanctions, the state nonetheless remained the central organizing force for the economy and social order. And the Hussein government kept order in Baghdad, albeit with increasing difficulty following the onset of the sanctions era, yet maintaining a city in which conventional crime was rare and where there was only one social force with significant power: the state. With the fall of the government of Saddam Hussein, the vast administrative structure of Iraq's centrally managed society collapsed, leaving Iraqis understandably fearful about what would come next.

However, beyond anecdotal descriptions by journalists and others, there is little empirical exploration of *how* this fear was socially constructed and the *mechanisms* by which this fear profoundly changed the composition of Baghdad's neighborhoods – in path-dependent ways unanticipated through ignorance or neglect when the Bush administration preemptively invaded Iraq. The thesis of this chapter is that fear, born of the potential for sectarian strife, amplified by historical context, and provoked by the invasion and its chaotic aftermath, propelled a self-reinforcing and self-fulfilling process that would change the sectarian face of Baghdad and Iraq for the foreseeable future.

NIGHT DRAWS NEAR

The Bush administration cynically misled journalists during the lead-up to the invasion of Iraq. A widely cited front-page *New York Times* story by Judith Miller (2001) claimed that there were "secret facilities for biological, chemical and nuclear weapons [located] in underground wells, private villas and under Saddam Hussein Hospital in Baghdad." This kind of story mistakenly corroborated fears of Saddam Hussein's "unwillingness to stop making weapons of mass destruction." The leaks that sparked these misleading stories were eventually traced back to the U.S. vice president and an administration eagerly seeking public support.

Such reporting is suggestive of Merton's useful distinction between the present and future path-dependent consequences that follow from the "imperious immediacy of interest": when a decision maker is so absorbed with the intended goals of an action that the unintended consequences are purposefully ignored (1936:901). The Bush administration's goals – of thwarting a false threat of weapons of mass destruction and overcoming a perceived Vietnam War syndrome – eclipsed a proportionate consideration of the human and social consequences of its preemptive war.

Linked to Merton's attention to intended and unintended consequences are the extraordinary failures of the U.S.-led invasion to carefully consider the basic structure of Iraqi society – particularly its latent ethnic and religious divides. Given the fact that the conflict is estimated to have led to thousands of U.S. and coalition military deaths (Fischer 2010), to have cost the United States trillions of dollars (Stiglitz and Bilmes 2008) while causing hundreds of thousands of Iraqi deaths (Burkle and Garfield 2013), and heretofore un-estimated Iraqi economic costs that are considered later in this chapter – there is a pressing need for serious reflection on what occurred.

Despite the dominance of a pro-invasion perspective within the media – the *New York Times*, the *Washington Post*, and others later issued apologies for their imbalanced coverage[3] – there were important countervailing voices early in the process. One distinctively critical voice was the Arab-American journalist introduced in Chapter 2, Anthony Shadid, who wrote about ordinary Iraqis. As we earlier noted, Shadid used the Arabic word *ghamidh* to express a mood of apprehension, metaphorically remarking that "Night always seemed to be drawing near in Iraq, and now [in the first years of the occupation] the chaos and the sense of the unknown seemed to generate their own momentum" (2005:425).

Shadid described this momentum as driven by "a logic of violence, ruled by men with guns" (2005:426). What is fascinating about Shadid's work is that it chronicles the extraordinary uncertainty and fear that Iraqis felt in 2003 and 2004, before the country fell into a state of devastating violence from 2005 through 2008. Shadid documented ordinary Iraqis' worries about a future characterized by the absence of a strong, unifying state, combined with the easy and widespread availability of arms, in a highly contested region (two neighboring nations had been invaded by Iraq), and occupied by a foreign army that precipitously dismantled local systems of control. *Within this context, Iraqis inevitably wondered, wouldn't a multiplicity of dangerously violent forces emerge to compete for power?*

As we explain in this chapter, the anticipation of conflict for control between rival armed groups in Iraq is suggestive of Tilly's (2003; 1985) theory of state making as organized crime, and Cloward and Ohlin's (1960) opportunity theory of crime. These theories direct attention to foreseeable consequences of collective criminal behavior grounded in legal cynicism and involving both opportunistic and coordinated violence. We apply concepts drawn from these theories of state making and crime to particularly analyze – through a case study – one key element of the sectarian violence that emerged in post-invasion Iraq: the rise of Shia-on-Sunni organized violence and the particular role of Muqtada al-Sadr and the Mahdi Army in a sequence of harassment and threats that led, especially during the 2006 peak in violence, to a widespread and systematic ethnic cleansing of previously Sunni and mixed neighborhoods during what we term the battle for Baghdad.

Our case study assesses a Mertonian hypothesis about unanticipated consequences, namely that ordinary Iraqis were victims of an amplifying "self-fulfilling prophecy of fear" that we conceptualize and test as a driving source of displacement in Baghdad. We show how this fear had predictable, *neighborhood-specific*, self-reinforcing consequences in Baghdad that American decision makers either failed to anticipate or chose to ignore.

ORGANIZED, OPPORTUNISTIC, AND COORDINATED CRIME

Regime change in Iraq required an unmaking and remaking of the state. Charles Tilly's (2003; 1985) key insight is that state making is often the product of organized criminal activity. He argues that state creation frequently involves "coercive entrepreneurship" based on organized criminal elements of threat and protection. He explains that state makers often create and facilitate threats and then provide protection from them to build power and capital. This entrepreneurial initiative uses "opportunistic violence" and "coordinated destruction" to expand and control territory, which Tilly calls "boundary activation." State making, therefore, is often initiated and advanced through collectively organized crime.

Tilly's perspective parallels Cloward and Ohlin's opportunity theory of crime, with organized crime as a linking theme. Cloward and Ohlin (1960) wrote in an era when many Americans had an exaggerated fear of organized crime that they worried would lead to the *Theft of a Nation* (Cressey 1979). Cloward and Ohlin articulated the ways organized criminals could infiltrate state law-enforcement organizations and connect legitimate and illegitimate opportunity structures to facilitate state-protected criminal enterprise. They explained how groups lacking legitimate opportunities might respond to their sense of injustice, or legal cynicism, by seeking out opportunities for state-protected organized crime.

In this chapter, we indirectly assess Tilly and Cloward and Ohlin's ideas about state making and opportunity structures with a case study that traces the rise of a particular faction of Arab Shia religious-political activity, the collection of forces known as the Mahdi Army. This militant organization was founded by Muqtada al-Sadr, a young cleric whose unique sectarian expression of legal cynicism and injustice about both Saddam's Ba'athist regime and the U.S.-led invasion and occupation became the foundation of a rapidly expanding social movement and militia. This Sadrist movement and Mahdi Army were centrally involved in the chaos and uncertainty linked to the ethnic cleansing of neighborhoods they conducted in the post-invasion context.

The Mahdi Army was a well-armed, militant wing of the Sadrist social movement. The latter developed a large following among an increasingly urban poor Shia population, while providing social services and giving voice to the Arab Shia sense of victimhood and associated political concerns. The Mahdi Army wing of the movement ultimately adopted the violent tactics of non-state criminal militarism, including threats, harassment, extortion, and kidnapping as well as killing and rape that led to mass forced displacement and ethnic cleansing of Arab Sunnis and non-Shia groups from Baghdad neighborhoods. The Mahdi Army's crimes provided material benefits as well as a form of employment for Arab Shia youth lacking noncriminal economic opportunities (Hashim 2006; International Crisis Group 2006).

The Sadrist movement and the figure of Muqtada al-Sadr ultimately extended their reach to take on a substantive role in legitimate political activities. This later phase in al-Sadr's rise to influence included the appointment and later election of his key allies to Iraq's new government. Most significantly, this movement into politics allowed the "coercive entrepreneur" al-Sadr to gain control of the key Ministry of Security and its national Iraqi Police (International Crisis Group 2008). This allowed his Mahdi Army to populate the Iraqi Police and, with a change in uniforms, to extend and consolidate their ethnic cleansing and control of newly Shia-dominated Baghdad neighborhoods.

We directly assess with interview-based data the mechanisms of this neighborhood transformation. We observe how the use of harassment and threats by the Mahdi Army against the Sunnis and other households led the victims to flee their neighborhoods, simultaneously serving the boundary-expanding territorial goals of a collective movement and providing opportunities for economic gain by the perpetrators. Green and Ward call this "dual purpose violence" (2009:3).

It is important to note that other armed groups engaged in similar tactics of brutal violence. However, focusing on the case of the Mahdi Army provides an especially dramatic means of documenting and analyzing the complex relations between fear, violence, criminal activity, and the restructuring of politics in post-invasion Iraq.

Cloward and Ohlin's theory describes the perceived legal and economic injustice that can motivate and organize such criminal tactics, while Tilly's theory predicts how such criminal mechanisms can be used for purposes of boundary activation involved in accomplishing collectively organized goals. We will see how the targeted harassment and threats anticipated in these theories and used by the Shia-populated Mahdi Army against Sunnis and other non-Shia victims in Baghdad played an essential mediating role in amplifying a consequential, Mertonian self-fulfilling prophecy of fear with effects that were anticipated by apprehensive Iraqis and ignored or neglected by the invading and occupying Americans.

THE SHIA–SUNNI CONFLICT IN HISTORICAL CONTEXT

As noted in Chapter 1, building on the country's long-standing challenge of creating a unified national identity out of diverse and competing groups, the government of Saddam Hussein and the Ba'ath Party directed substantial resources toward the creation of an intricately interwoven, brutally repressive security state. This process ultimately resulted in a highly bureaucratic legal authoritarian regime built around an extensive security agency apparatus that was legitimated through and in collaboration with the Iraqi judiciary and courts. We saw in the previous chapter that when the U.S.-led coalition brought its own use of torture tactics to Iraq, the consequence was to reproduce a willingness among many of Iraq's judges to collaborate in a new state regime with familiar legal authoritarian traits.

Haddad (2011; see also Jabr 2003) explains how a rising sense of Shia victimhood formed the background for the evolution of a new regime with authoritarian traits. Haddad calls sectarianism Iraq's "skeleton in the closet," while also emphasizing that the terms *Shia* and *Sunni* were seldom publicly used in Iraq before the 1990s. He argues that events in the 1990s and following the first Gulf War provoked a growing sense of victimization among the Sunnis that paralleled an intense sense of victimhood among the Shia. The growing sense of Shia victimhood followed brutal repression by the Ba'athist regime and generated new expressions of religious and ultimately political identity among the Shia, while Sunnis increasingly felt victimized by the intensifying international sanctions that followed the first Gulf War and that devastated civilian life in Saddam's state-based command economy. The feelings of victimization among the Sunnis and victimhood among the Shia contributed to an "us" versus "them" polarization and sectarian split between these two important groups.

American strategists had little or no understanding of the deep feelings of legal cynicism and political volatility that were emerging among the Arab Shia who constituted the majority of the nation's population. One of the most important examples of U.S. strategic ignorance or neglect involved the rapid and unexpected rise – anchored in a restive and rebellious social movement – of Muqtada al-Sadr.

Al-Sadr rose from a position of relative obscurity. The American-led coalition underestimated the significance of al-Sadr's leadership of the Sadrist movement – the only truly new mass movement in post-invasion Iraq – and the development of his Mahdi Army (Cockburn 2008:13). As we further explain later in this chapter, in Tilly's terms, Muqtada al-Sadr evolved as an effective coercive entrepreneur. Al-Sadr gave religious force and direction to an underlying mood of moral and legal cynicism.

Muqtada al-Sadr was born to an influential family of respected Shia clerics, including his father, Ayatollah Muhammad Muhammad Sadiq al-Sadr, and his father's cousin Ayatollah Muhammad Baqir al-Sadr. Muhammad Baqir, in particular, played a key role in developing a politically oriented expression of Shia faith that was viewed as profoundly challenging by the government of Saddam Hussein. Muhammad Baqir was killed with hundreds of his supporters in 1980, after the revolution in Iran.

Muhammad Sadiq's preaching gained new importance and he became a key Shia religious and political leader after the systematic brutal repression of the unsuccessful uprising in the south following the first Gulf War. Muhammad

Sadiq developed an effective rhetorical response in his preaching to the repression that silenced other key Shia leaders, many of whom were killed or fled to Iran. In 1999, Muhammad Sadiq was assassinated by Iraqi government agents along with two of his sons, the older brothers of Muqtada al-Sadr, leading to mass protests (Cochrane 2008; Cockburn 2008; International Crisis Group 2006; Cole 2003).

The followers of the Sadrist movement – those inspired by Ayatollah Muhammad Baqir al-Sadr, Ayatollah Muhammad Muhammad Sadiq al-Sadr, and, later, by Muqtada al-Sadr – were young, uneducated, and intensely religious, with the kinds of socioeconomic grievances and feelings of injustice emphasized by Cloward and Ohlin. Of course, the state-based source of these feelings of injustice was the vicious repression by the Ba'athist regime of Saddam Hussein.

Given the brutal repression of the Shia, U.S. policy makers might have hoped the aggrieved followers of al-Sadr as well as other Shia leaders to support the American vision of rebuilding Iraq following the 2003 invasion. However, this assumption underestimated the acute sense of betrayal among virtually all Shia movements dating from the 1991 Gulf War and described in Chapter 1 when President George H. W. Bush encouraged a broad-based uprising in southern Iraq and then withheld the critical support of U.S. forces.

After the Shia insurgency failed, Saddam Hussein engaged in ongoing and systematic repression of all Shia movements. When Muqtada al-Sadr's father and brothers were assassinated, he inherited an angry, underground, and youth-dominated Shia movement that was subjected to constant surveillance and ongoing brutal reprisals by Saddam's security agencies. While the leaders of some other Shia movements – such as SCIRI and the Dawa Party – mostly fled to Iran, al-Sadr and his inner circle remained in Iraq. The result was an acute sense of legal cynicism among the Shia Sadrists who stayed.

The appeal of al-Sadr was distinct and at times in conflict with other more dominant Shia religious and political movements, including the teachings and leadership of Grand Ayatollah Ali al-Husayni al-Sistani. Al-Sistani was the primary established Shia spiritual leader in Iraq and was linked to the development of the Supreme Council for the Islamic Revolution in Iraq (SCIRI – later ISCI, when in 2007 it removed the term *revolution* from its name). SCIRI had its own armed group, the Badr Brigade (later the Badr Organization) (Hashim 2004).

As the invasion and occupation unfolded, it became apparent that SCIRI and the Dawa Party were willing to work with the U.S.-led coalition, while Muqtada al-Sadr instead opposed the American occupation. During the year following the invasion, Paul Bremer and President Bush began referring to al-Sadr as an "outlaw." The brewing confrontation involved a kind of stigmatization process that is central to criminology's labeling theory (Lemert 1967; Becker 1963; Garfinkel 1956). The essence of this theory is that stigmatic labeling often stimulates rather than deters the behavior it seeks to restrain.

As if to offer testimonial evidence for labeling theory, al-Sadr delivered a response to the U.S. authorities steeped in legal cynicism, saying, "If Bremer means that I am an outlaw according to the American legal code, then I take pride in it" (cited in Cockburn 2008:147). The Shia Sadrists were scornful of the prospect that the U.S./coalition forces that invaded Iraq in 2003 would be a source of security and protection for them. At the same time, the Sunnis also had reason to fear that they would be dismissed and disenfranchised for their presumed guilt by association with Saddam's Ba'athist regime. And as we have seen, these fears were confirmed by the disdainful and dismissive attitude of the Bush administration's Coalition Provisional Authority and Paul Bremer. The Shia Sadrists and the Arab Sunnis composed two large, albeit opposed groups with abundant reason to share legally cynical attitudes about the occupying U.S./coalition forces.

NIGHT FALLS AND CHAOS FOLLOWS

Kalyvas and Kocher emphasize that key decisions made during and soon after the U.S.-led coalition's invasion explain why sectarian conflict in Iraq emerged so violently (2007:185). As noted in Chapter 2 and earlier in this chapter, the coalition's early decisions gave special influence to formerly exiled Shia opposition groups and leaders, while deconstructing Iraq's last remaining national and somewhat ethnically inclusive institutions – the government ministries, the army, and the Ba'ath Party. The U.S. preference for exiled and often Western-educated Shia leaders notably overlooked and excluded Muqtada al-Sadr and his Sadrist movement while also disregarding the Arab Sunnis. Al-Sadr and his followers had gone from being targets of the overt repression of Saddam's brutal authoritarian regime to being objects of neglect, suspicion, and outright hostility from the new U.S.-led coalition. This kind of official rejection and neglect intensified Sadrist as well as Arab Sunni legal cynicism about post-invasion Iraqi governance.

Iraq was in a state of chaos following the U.S. invasion. Few institutions essential to social order, from banks to hospitals to schools, functioned. Daily life was filled with uncertainty and Iraqis watched with shock and horror as many in this previously tightly controlled society took to the streets and looted every state building that was not under armed guard, even stealing mass amounts of weaponry. The Sadrists organized for self-protection during this period, while Arab Sunni groups went underground.

The U.S. failure to provide even the most basic provisions for public security and safety led some of the most militant Sunni-led groups to align with al-Qaeda and to engage in multiple attacks on Shia mosques and markets. This intensified the Sadrists' cynicism and anger, while reinforcing that their safety, protection, and political viability required marshaling their own resources, including the Mahdi Army. After a U.S. helicopter knocked over a religious banner in Sadr City in August 2003, and then again when AQI bombed Shia mosques in Karbala and Kadhimiya in March 2004, the Sadrist movement grew with a momentum that amplified fears of ordinary Iraqis (Rosen 2010; Cochrane 2008; Cockburn 2008; International Crisis Group 2006).

Muqtada al-Sadr had announced the formation of the Mahdi Army in July 2003, and he soon claimed more than 10,000 recruits with an established base in the slums of Baghdad's Sadr City (Rosen 2010; Cockburn 2008). Shadid reports that by 2004 the Mahdi Army began "to shed its makeshift quality and take on the air of a fighting force with an elaborate hierarchy and formidable organization" (2005:435). Rosen similarly observes that "the Mahdi Army began forming into divisions and became more organized and hierarchical" (2010:65). As is common with organized crime groups, there is skepticism about just how well-organized and disciplined the Mahdi Army actually was, and there is little question that later on substantial parts of the Mahdi Army became highly decentralized and violently undisciplined (Cochrane 2008; International Crisis Group 2008).

Nonetheless, from Cloward and Ohlin's perspective, the Mahdi Army was emerging as an organized, illegitimate opportunity structure for young increasingly cynical and underemployed Shia men. As noted previously, the Mahdi Army also infiltrated the security ministry and formed alliances with the national and local police forces operating in Baghdad (Allawi 2007:422). From Cloward and Ohlin's perspective, this represented a linking of the legitimate and illegitimate opportunity structures that also fits with Tilly's depiction of state making as organized crime.

It is important to again emphasize that the Mahdi Army was one among numerous armed ethno-sectarian groups in post-invasion Iraq, the majority of which were structured along key power divides among Shia groups, multiple Sunni groups, and the relatively stable Kurdish parties in the north. Despite underlying tensions, the Patriotic Union of Kurdistan(PUK) and the Kurdistan Democratic Party (KDP) worked closely together following years of independence from the central government and were backed by the Peshmurga, their capable military forces. Other populations – Christians, Yazidis, Sabean

Mandeans, and so forth – lacked armed backing. Beyond the Mahdi Army, the other primary Shia armed group was the previously noted SCIRI-backed Badr Corps (later the Badr Organization). Many of its leaders were trained in Iran. Yet, in contrast with the Mahdi Army, from 2003 they aligned themselves with the U.S. occupation and for the following decade supported the U.S.-backed Iraqi government.

Some have attributed these opposing alignments to class differences between al-Sadr's followers and those of the Badr Corps (Dodge 2012). While al-Sadr's followers were the "poorest of the poor the *mustazafin* (dispossessed) ... who had stayed in Iraq and bore the brunt of Saddam's megalomania and brutal tactics" (Hashim 2006: 267), many within the Badr Corps were drawn from the Shia commercial middle class who had managed to go into safe exile in Iran until the U.S.-led invasion. The Badr Corps had less reason to feel the intense sense of injustice and legal cynicism that characterized al-Sadr's followers in the Mahdi Army.

Over time, the units of the Mahdi Army grew increasingly aggressive: Shadid reported that the militia began to act as "the long dreaded arm of the movement," sending out death threats and intimidating neighborhood residents (2005:437). By 2005, the Sadrists and the Mahdi Army had initiated an ethnic cleansing of the Sunni and mixed neighborhoods of Baghdad. They established checkpoints in neighborhoods to display their power, openly carrying weapons in defiance of the U.S. military, and harassing Sunni residents. They addressed letters threatening households with demands for protection money and warning of violent reprisals. Tilly's boundary-activation process set in and the dominant demography of Baghdad's neighborhoods began shifting from Sunni to Shia.

THE BATTLE FOR BAGHDAD

By 2005, efforts to rebuild the Iraqi state's security forces were largely being controlled by the Shia political parties who recruited young Shia men into their ranks. The International Crisis Group (2007) reported that "poor Shiites filled the ranks of the security forces and – even as they operated under SCIRI-appointed commanders – often expressed loyalty to Muqtada al-Sadr." Rosen explained that "the interior ministry had been given to Shiites ... Most poor young Shiite men supported Muqtada, so it followed that the security forces fell under the control of Sadrists and their Mahdi Army" (2010:60). While the American military wanted to see 2006 as the year of a politically independent national police, Rosen reported that "[i]nstead it was the year the police and the Mahdi Army became one" (2010:234).

The 2006 AQI attack on the religiously important al-Askari Shia shrine in Samarra drove the violence to its peak. Most believed that AQI attacked the shrine to provoke and escalate Shia Mahdi Army counterattacks on the Sunnis. The Sunnis had no confidence that U.S./coalition forces would defend their neighborhoods from the Mahdi Army, and they were correct in this fear. General Casey was committed at this point to a "leave to win strategy" – holding his forces in check, and pulling them back into their bases, in anticipation of drawdowns in combat troops and the phasing of combat forces out of Iraq.

Cockburn observed, "A pervasive sense of terror settled over Baghdad" (2008:181). Nouri al-Maliki was selected as prime minister by a U.S.-led process during the 2006 peak in violence.[4] Maliki was the Shia leader of the formerly exiled Dawa Party. He had risen through the de-Ba'athification commission established by the coalition and was seen by Arab Sunnis as a menacing threat.

A Family Caught in the Spiral of Violence

A CVI interview with "Ahmed" from the post-invasion part of the Iraq History Project captures the spiral of violence that engulfed Baghdad's neighborhoods in 2005 and 2006. Ahmed was Sunni and reported that things changed dramatically for the worse in 2005 when Shia, former Dawa Party politician Ibrahim al-Jaa'fari was selected as prime minister. He recalled, "That's when the militias started to appear as if they were 'sleeper cells.'" Because of the electricity shortages, the situation was literally as well as metaphorically dark, and the Mahdi Army was the source of fear: "The Mahdi Army caused us many problems. They were at war with the Sunnis and still are today":

One night in April 2005 after midnight, the electricity was out. It was pitch black. Everyone was asleep. We woke up to the sound of a loud, strange knocking at the front door. We got out of bed. We were all terrified about what might happen.

My father refused to let any of us go out. He went to the front door and asked in a trembling voice, "Who is it?"

"Open the door. Don't be afraid," they answered, "If you don't open the door, we'll break it down!"

My father refused to open the door. He was afraid for our safety.

Around five minutes later, they started to break the door down. There were six men armed with Kalashnikov rifles. They were terrifying. They wore all black with black masks. They carried flashlights. They started saying anti-Sunni slogans.

They put us together in one room. One of them was large, tall and spoke with an angry voice.

He asked, "Which one of you refused to open the door?"

"It was me," answered my father.

Then, the man hit my father in the face and knocked him down. My father was old and couldn't take those kinds of blows. My mother, my brother's wife, and my sisters all started screaming out of fear. Then, the man pulled my little sister by her hair, took out a knife and placed it against her neck. He threatened to kill her if they didn't stop crying.

It was a terrible thing to witness. Sitting there was very difficult.

My poor sister was trembling in his arms out of fear for her life. She was so scared that she peed.

My mother couldn't handle what was going on. She started screaming in a trembling voice and tried to stop Karrar from tying up my brother. She began cursing them and striking herself in the face.

The man threatened her and told her to keep quiet. She continued to cry. He began yelling at her. She spit in his face. Suddenly, he let go of my little sister, took a gun from his belt and pointed it at my mother.

Then he went through with it.

He shot her in the head.

She dropped to the floor.

I lost control at that moment and began hitting him. I was shaking from how intense it all was.

It was a terrible situation. My father was unconscious and lying on the floor. My mother had been murdered. And, there they were, trying to take my brother away.

Two men grabbed me and then the leader started beating me. After a few minutes, I lost consciousness.

When I opened my eyes, I was in a hospital. I was unable to move my right hand or either of my legs.

I saw my brother Mohammed and my sister Haifa standing near me. Tears were streaming from her eyes. My brother looked sad.

"What's wrong with me?"

He said, "God protected you. But, both your legs and your right arm are broken."

I asked him about my mother.

With tears streaming down his face, he said, "They took her to be buried. Father, thank God, regained consciousness but his nose is broken."

To this day when I tell my story, I want to take revenge on those criminals. Yet, I feel powerless because, sad to say, I don't know who they are. Hopefully, one day I will find out who they are. Then I will get my revenge.

I asked him about my brother Husam.

He said, "They took him away. We don't know what's happened to him." ...

The next day they released me from the hospital.

I returned home broken, unable to do anything. We were so sad over what had happened to my mother and brother. We lost two members of our family in a single night and my father was in bad shape from the shock of the beating.

Our financial situation was also quite poor. We didn't have enough money for a memorial service. So, we sat at home and our relatives and neighbors came to offer their condolences.

Five days after my mother was killed there was a knock at the front door. My sister went out to see who it was. She screamed loudly and then fainted. I was sitting in a wheelchair that one of the neighbors had given me. I tried to wheel towards her but I couldn't. ... Then, my father and brother also started yelling. Everyone was wailing and slapping themselves in the face.

I asked them what was wrong and my brother said, crying and screaming, "They sent Husam's head to us. They slaughtered him."

Imagine our situation.

How was this possible? What was our crime? Just being Sunni? We'd lived in the neighborhood for many years. We were like brothers to our neighbors. We helped them. We attended their family events and they attended ours.

What had happened?

Should we now start hating Shia? I don't know.

After hearing the screaming and crying, our neighbors came over. They took my brother's head, which was in a plastic bag, and buried it next to my mother.

My elderly father decided that we couldn't stay in our home and that we needed to protect what was left of our family. We sold our furniture for a fourth of its value, locked up the house, and went to an uncle's house in the Salahaddin governorate. We stayed with them for a while since we had very little money and were unable to rent a house. Then

> we went to one of the villages and rented a house for 100,000 dinars a month. . . .
>
> We don't know our fate. Will we have to live forever like this?
>
> Al-Sadr's loss of control over the Mahdi Army, illustrated by the attack on Ahmed's family, may have resulted in part from the difficulties of focusing his forces on fighting the U.S. and coalition forces. During this period, al-Qaeda Sunnis launched a relentless anti-Shia bombing campaign that spurred recruitment into the Mahdi Army and strengthened Sadrist communal relations more broadly.

Initially, al-Maliki seemed to see al-Sadr and the Mahdi Army as useful to his Shia-dominated new government, although he may also have simply feared the capacity of al-Sadr to undermine his hold on power. Regardless of reason, al-Maliki for several years restrained the U.S./coalition forces from targeting the Mahdi Army and insisted on prioritizing the pursuit of the Sunni insurgency that was gaining ground especially in Anbar province. The Mahdi Army was now also evolving into a dispersed force that was imposing a toll on the Sunni and mixed neighborhoods in Baghdad that escalated beyond even al-Sadr's effective control.

The Mahdi Army's role in sectarian violence had now shifted from its 2004 so-called intifadat al-Mahdi against coalition forces, and a brief alliance with the Sunni insurgency during the U.S.-led fight for Fallujah, to attacks predominately aimed by 2006 at the ethnic cleansing of Sunni neighborhoods in Baghdad. The Arab Sunnis and Shia were entering a period of sectarian civil war.

The turn from anti-U.S./coalition attacks to the internal, sectarian-driven violence was not immediate but gradual. Adding to the complexity, the Mahdi Army cooperated with the Badr militia forces in the battle for Baghdad in 2006, only to fight against them in 2007. The Mahdi Army benefited from government protection and immunity in 2006 and 2007, but finally became targets of joined U.S./coalition and Iraqi Army attacks during the surge in 2008. However, by the time of the latter attacks on the Mahdi Army, they had already redrawn the ethnically cleansed neighborhood map of Baghdad.

In international criminal law terms, the actions of the Mahdi Army constituted widespread and systematic repression and laid the groundwork for crimes against humanity and the ethnic cleansing of civilian Sunni neighborhood populations.[5] This was criminal militarism perpetrated by non-state actors. And by the end of 2007, the Mahdi Army had prevailed in the battle for Baghdad's neighborhoods; it had gained sectarian dominance over the previously advantaged Sunnis in many parts of the capital city.

Thus the majority of Baghdad's neighborhoods were mixed in 2003, but by 2008 these neighborhoods were "unmixed" and Shia occupied (see discussion of Figure 4.1). Yet al-Sadr's legitimacy and control over his forces were simultaneously diminished. Bodies were piling up on the streets of Baghdad, and even supporters of the Sadrists now feared the Mahdi Army. In late August 2007, whether in response to having successfully ethnically cleansed much of Baghdad, losing control of his forces, the peaking of the U.S. surge of forces, a counterproductive clash between the Mahdi Army and the Badr Corps in Karbala, or simple exhaustion of his military possibilities, al-Sadr declared a six-month *tajmid* – or freeze – on operations of the Mahdi Army (Farrell 2007).

Al-Sadr's ceasefire and the beginning of the drawdown of U.S. surge troops largely left the recently reconfigured neighborhoods of Baghdad in place. Cockburn reports, "At least ten neighborhoods that had been mixed a year earlier were entirely Shia" (2008:177). The local and federal governments were in Shia hands, and now the neighborhoods increasingly were too. Figure 4.1 shows the increase in Shia neighborhoods from 2003 to 2008.

The four maps in Figure 4.1 are reconfigured from the work of Michael Izady (http://gulf2000.columbia.edu/maps.shtml). The upper left and lower right maps most clearly show that while the majority of Baghdad's neighborhoods were mixed in 2003, by 2008 these neighborhoods were "unmixed" and Shia occupied. The Shia now controlled the great majority of the neighborhoods east of the Tigris River and a large share of the neighborhoods to the west.

Using data described and explored more fully later in this chapter, the upper right and lower left maps show concentrations of harassment and threats with dots, and a quartile ranking of the neighborhoods with bigger circles indicating where the largest numbers of displacements occurred. Amos (2010) called the outcome of the battle for Baghdad the "eclipse of the Sunnis," while Nasr (2006) now called Iraq "the first Arab Shia State." The Mahdi Army's ethnic cleansing had played a major role in changing the balance of power and demography in Baghdad.

ANTICIPATION AND AMPLIFICATION OF THE SHIA–SUNNI CONFLICT

We have noted that there was a polarizing sense of victimization and victimhood following the first Gulf War that contributed to the mood Anthony Shadid described as fearful foreboding during and after the invasion. Hadad

FIGURE 4.1. Sectarian Make-up of Baghdad

observes that in the later 1990s Mohammad Sadiq al-Sadr had fueled this kind of fearful cycle through his preaching, noting that "Sadr propelled Shia identity into assertive sectarianism ... fostering a sense of threat ... [and] thereby feeding the cycle" (2011:113). He adds that it does not take many participants to launch such a cycle, and that the result can be a "spiraling series of assertions of antagonistic group identities" (184) in which "views toward the mass come to dominate perceptions of the other at the expense of the more favorable" (192).

The uncertainty created by the invasion and the ensuing chaos further intensified these fears, and the chaos and fear began to feed on themselves in a self-reinforcing cycle. The question we now address in this chapter is whether there was a neighborhood-specific anticipation and amplification of this fearful sense of foreboding and chaos that led to the escalation of the displacement and ethnic cleansing of individuals and families from their neighborhoods during the battle for Baghdad.

The journalistic coverage of the war in Baghdad characteristically included references to the neighborhoods where the reported violence occurred. Yet little more is revealed in this reporting about these neighborhoods. Our hypothesis is that citizens of Baghdad's Sunni and mixed neighborhoods were victims of threats and harassment by al-Sadr's Mahdi Army, which aggravated a Mertonian "self-fulfilling prophecy of fear." In this process, a Sunni class-based fear of the "Shia hordes" became increasingly prominent, which in turn intensified displacement and ethnic cleansing, ultimately changing the demography of the city.

We hypothesize that this prophecy involved fearful anticipations of civil strife that compounded in self-amplifying cycles of violence (Brubaker and Laitin 1998). Quillian and Pager (2011; 2012) make an important parallel point about the American sociological literature on the fear of crime. They note that this literature often overlaps and conflates objective risks of being a victim of crime with intensified subjectively perceived consequences of victimization (see also Rountree and Land 1996; Bursik and Grasmick 1993; Warr and Stafford 1983). Subjective perceptions that extrapolate beyond actual experiences can provoke amplified expectations of victimization. We empirically investigated these fearful processes in post-invasion Baghdad by distinguishing an objective anticipation of violent victimization from the subjective amplification of this victimization risk. Both objective and subjective anticipations contributed to ethnic cleaning in Baghdad.

Our use of the concepts of anticipation and amplification builds from research by Quillian and Pager (2010) on statistical discrimination and stereotype amplification in American neighborhoods. Quillian and Pager use

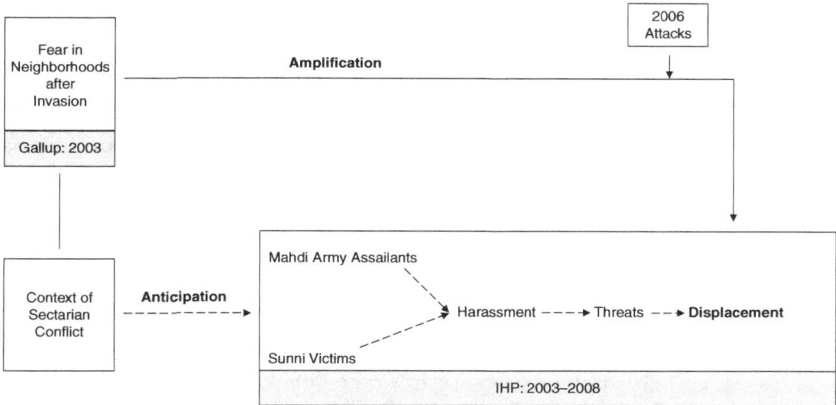

FIGURE 4.2. Anticipation and Amplification of Fear in Iraq, circa 2003–8

the term *statistical discrimination* to conceptualize how relationships between social conditions such as poverty and crime are invoked to justify police and public responses to American minority neighborhoods based on anticipated high risks of crime victimization. *Stereotype amplification* refers to the further cultural processes that can contagiously inflate the calculation of these victimization risks.

We refer in Iraq to related neighborhood processes of anticipation and amplification. We use the term *anticipation* to refer to the process by which ordinary Iraqis accurately foresaw looming conflicts in neighborhoods where they perceived victimization risks would be highest. Given the growing uncertainty and chaos in Baghdad, and based on their knowledge and observations of the places where they lived, ordinary Iraqis gauged for their own neighborhoods the potential for dangerously violent problems to occur.

Quillian and Pager's argument is that the accuracy of such empirically based predictions further feeds into cognitive processes that cause *amplification of* fearful responses. The importance of this perspective, which we simply summarize with the concepts of cognitive anticipation and amplification, is the implication that the latter process adds a self-fulfilling momentum to fearful perceptions of risk.

We summarize in Figure 4.2 the hypothesized processes of anticipation and amplification that emerged within neighborhoods during the battle for Baghdad. The model presented in Figure 4.2 includes anticipation as an arrow at the center left, indicating the initiation of an indirect, neighborhood-specific process leading to household displacement. This indirect process is represented as flowing through experiences of Sunni respondents being victimized by Mahdi Army perpetrators with harassment and threats, leading to displacement from their neighborhoods. In addition, the model includes a horizontal arrow at the top of the figure, indicating a further neighborhood-specific direct effect. This direct effect is net of all other variables in the model and is interpreted as indicating amplified expectations involved in a self-fulfilling prophecy of fear that intensified the process of neighborhood displacement.

Finally, the arrow at the top right of Figure 4.2 indicates an expected peak in the effects of 2003 post-invasion neighborhood-specific fears on displacement three years later, following the 2006 attack on the al-Askari Mosque in Samarra. This is the period when ethnic cleansing peaked in Baghdad.

This was certainly not the first time in which attacks on symbolically important cultural sites were used as an instrument to advance ethnic cleansing. Mosques all over Bosnia were destroyed in the 1990s as part of the ethnic cleansing of the former Yugoslavia, and legal protection of cultural property in the context of war dates to the American Civil War. These protections were institutionalized internationally in the 1954 Convention for the Protection of Cultural Property, and were extended in 1977 to include "any acts of hostility directed against the historic monuments, works of art or places of worship which constitute the cultural or spiritual heritage of peoples." Cultural war crimes were prosecuted at Nuremberg, where Nazi officials received the death penalty for crimes that included the destruction of cultural property.[6]

The effects of anticipation and amplification in the model presented in Figure 4.2 combine to create a Mertonian self-fulfilling prophecy of fear, leading to widespread and systematic displacement and ethnic cleansing of individuals and families from their homes and neighborhoods. In the sociological terms of Tilly and Cloward and Ohlin, the harassment and threats leading directly and indirectly to displacement were organized crime tactics that created and amplified fear with the goal of changing the demography and control of the neighborhoods of Baghdad.

MODELING ETHNIC CLEANSING AND DISPLACEMENT IN BAGHDAD

The ethnic cleansing and displacement model we have presented begins with the everyday fearful anticipations of ordinary Iraqis in their neighborhoods following the invasion in 2003. In the beginning, these fears were real but inchoate, as suggested by the title of Shadid's book, *Night Draws Near*, and as reflected in his reference to *ghamidh*.

The American-led invasion of Iraq began in March 2003, and six months later the Gallup Poll (GP) conducted its post-invasion survey introduced in

Chapter 2. Shadid (2005) observes that already by May 2003, post-Saddam Baghdad was edgy and unsettled. The removal of the Sunni-led regime ended a period of Ba'ath Party domination, and Shadid writes, "There was a growing apprehension and anxiety over the fate of a [Sunni] minority that, by virtue of its wealth, its education, and the favoritism of overlords, had ruled Iraq ... through colonialism and coups, dictatorship and war" (2006:23). Now a new and contested political reality included the prospect of Shia rule, with the likelihood that long-standing resentments and growing legal cynicism would fuel sectarian violence between the Shia and Sunnis. This is the foundation of what we have called the anticipation of neighborhood-specific violence leading to ethnic cleansing and displacement.

Using a measure that invokes the ominous metaphor of Shadid's book title, Gallup asked respondents to report fear about going out at night in their neighborhoods during the previous months since the invasion (March 2003), as well as before the invasion. We created measures from the responses and aggregated them by neighborhood to indicate variation in pre- and post-invasion fear across Baghdad.

Only 6 percent of the GP respondents reported being fearful of going out in their own neighborhoods at night before the invasion, which is consistent with Chehab's observation that "[h]owever vicious and murderous Saddam's regime was, under his iron rule there was virtually no crime – no burglaries, no rapes, no murders" (2005:98). This observation is especially true of the period before the 1990s. In any case, fear radically increased after the invasion. Figure 4.3 shows the sharp jump in fear after the invasion. Many more respondents were fearful at some point since the invasion, with more than two-thirds being fearful in the neighborhoods during the day and more than 90 percent being fearful at night.

We assess the remainder of the model presented in Figure 4.2 by linking the neighborhood measures drawn from GP to measures included in the Iraq History Project Current Violations Initiative (CVI) conducted in 2007 and 2008. This survey asked respondents to report if and when since the invasion they had experienced human rights violations and crimes, including harassment and threats leading to displacement. CVI interviews were conducted with self-identified Iraqi victims of human rights and humanitarian violations in 2003–2008, more than half of whom were from Baghdad and are the focus of this analysis.

The majority of the CVI victims were displaced and therefore, by definition, unrepresented in GP because of its residential household sampling frame. CVI sampled these displaced victims through contacts with community and national groups (e.g., political prisoners' associations), local NGOs,

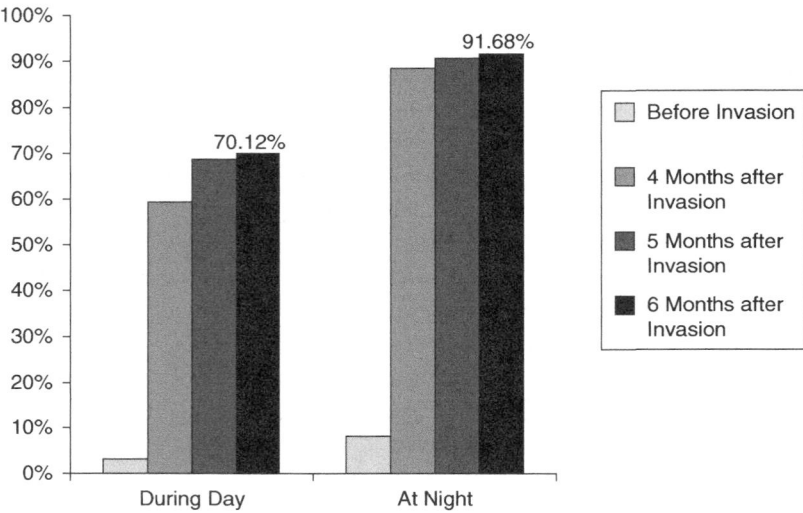

FIGURE 4.3. Fear of Going Outside in Baghdad Neighborhood, Before and After the Invasion

displacement camps, and interviewers' tribal and family affiliations. CVI uniquely addresses the full range of human rights crimes in post-invasion Iraq – such as displacement, killings, assassinations, indiscriminant attacks, abductions, torture, threats, detentions, and other abuses – by a variety of armed factions, including U.S.-led coalition forces, Iraqi government forces, al-Qaeda, and various Sunni, Shia, and other militias.

Although non-random, CVI's sampling approach was essential to representing victims of human rights crimes during a violent and chaotic period in Baghdad. The challenge was to join the respective methodological strengths of GP and CVI for our analytic purposes. We have elsewhere more fully described and demonstrated the overlapping representative qualities of the GP and CVI surveys (Hagan et al. 2012; 2015; see also Appendix Table 4.2).

ANTICIPATED CONSEQUENCES IN BAGHDAD

More than three-quarters (81.28%) of CVI respondents from Baghdad had been displaced since the invasion, which is consistent with evidence that displacement was many orders of magnitude more common than killings (Tripp 2010). The CVI interviews (described in Appendix Table 4.3) charted the processes leading to displacement summarized in Figure 4.2, including dating when the violations began.

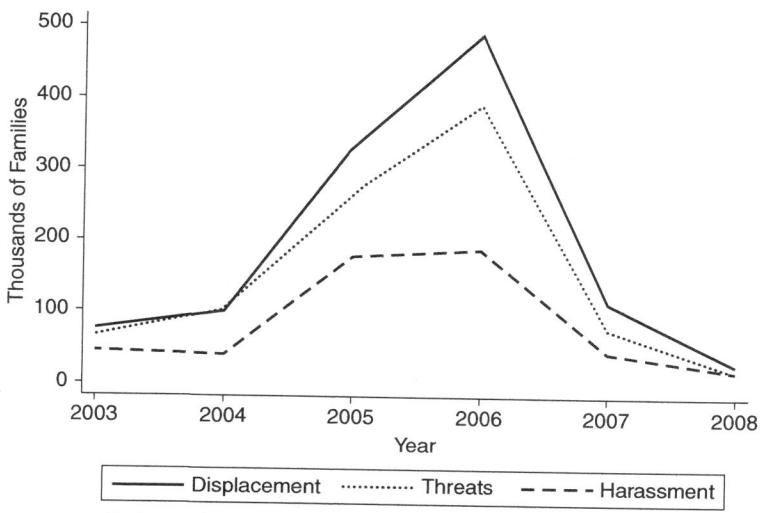

FIGURE 4.4. Estimated Displacement, Harassment, and Threats in Baghdad, circa 2003–2008

Respondents identified themselves as members of Shia (36%), Sunni (40%), and other groups (24%), and they often identified perpetrators in these attacks, which most frequently involved Mahdi Army assailants (33%), and next most often AQI (13%) and U.S. military forces (10%). They described harassment (35%), which frequently involved indiscriminant stops as well as detentions, and threats (59%), which commonly involved demands delivered in writing for protection money to prevent assaults, blackmail, and killings.

The process diagramed in the interior box of Figure 4.2 unfolded over the five-year period (2003–8) addressed by the interviews. As expected, reports of harassment, threats, and displacements are shown in Figure 4.4 as peaking in 2006, the year widely recognized as the peak of violence (35% of the reported displacements occurred in 2006). To the extent that the displacement process is anticipated in the early post-invasion neighborhood-specific fears and ensuing experiences of harassment and threats by ordinary Iraqis reported in our analysis of the GP and CVI data, we will refer to it as the collective cognitive product of an objective neighborhood-based process of anticipation. To the extent that there is a net direct effect of the early post-invasion, neighborhood-specific fear that exceeds the indirect harassment and threat process that links these fears to later displacement in Figure 4.2, we will refer to it as the collective, cognitive product of neighborhood-based amplification leading to the self-fulfilling prophecy of fear. We present our findings on the neighborhood-based process of anticipation in this section, and the finding for these neighborhoods regarding amplification in the following section.

Neighborhood-level measures were drawn from several sources and displayed earlier in Figure 4.1. The 2003 sectarian identification of the Baghdad neighborhoods is derived from the maps developed by Michael Izady.[7] The majority of neighborhoods were mixed in sectarian identity before they were "unmixed" by ethnic cleansing and displacement following the invasion. In 2003, about a fifth of the neighborhoods were clearly majority Sunni, more than three-quarters were mixed, and just over 10 percent were Shia. The Mahdi Army dramatically changed the demography of Baghdad between 2003 and 2008, from a majority of neighborhoods being mixed to a majority being predominately Shia.

We aggregated the CVI reports of killings, harassment, and threats at the neighborhood level to indicate how these were linked to displacement and how the demographic shift was imposed. As noted earlier, the maps on the top right to lower left diagonal in Figure 4.1 show how the incidents of harassment and threats (indicated with dots) were linked to the level of displacement that is ranked in quartiles (with smaller to larger circles).

A table presented in the Appendix (Table 4.5) confirms the anticipated patterns of perpetration and victimization that we have described as occurring across Baghdad neighborhoods. Thus the first model in this table indicates that – as also reflected in Figure 4.2 – it is the Sunni and mixed neighborhoods where displacement was most common. The second model reveals that these were the neighborhoods in which respondents were most likely to fear going out at night, which is consistent with an accurate anticipation of the danger of violence. The third model confirms that Mahdi Army members were perpetrators of the ethnic cleansing and displacement and that individual Sunni families were especially likely to be their victims. In both cases, when the results of the models are converted into more easily interpreted odds ratios, the results indicate that the odds are nearly double for a Sunni (compared to a Shia) to be victimized by Mahdi Army perpetrators (compared to other forces). The final fourth and fifth models indicate that the Mahdi Army used harassment and threats to accomplish the displacement (see also Appendix Table 4.4).

Of course, victims of ethnic cleansing and displacement in Baghdad were not only forced to move from their homes and neighborhoods, they also lost these homes and typically the jobs and businesses that were the foundation of their lives in Baghdad. Former international prosecutor Louise Arbour (2006) notes that international tribunals have recognized these costs and included

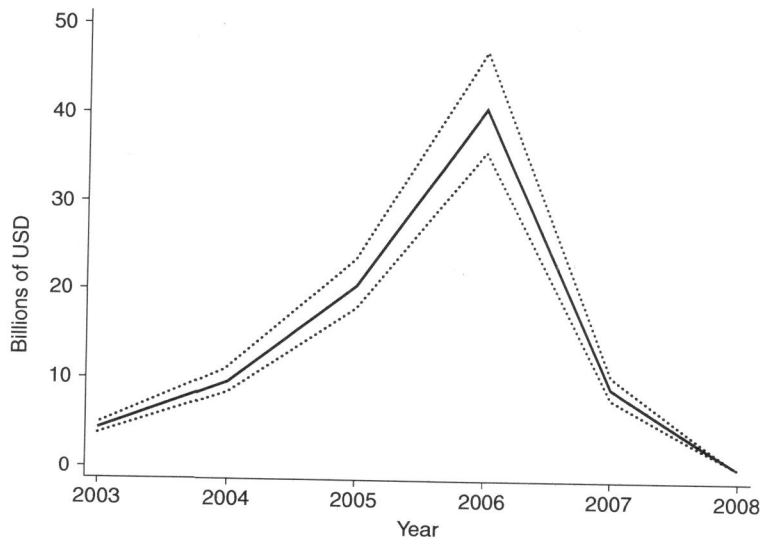

FIGURE 4.5. Annual Economic Losses in Baghdad, by Year of First Violation

them within cases of ethnic cleansing and crimes against humanity tried at the International Criminal Tribunal for the former Yugoslavia (ICTY). For example, she notes that the trial chamber of the ICTY in the *Kupresik* case recognized that widespread destruction of homes and property constituted crimes of persecution conducted as part of crimes against humanity.

Criminologists are especially well positioned by disciplinary emphasis to document and explain the collateral economic costs of ethnic cleansing and displacement within the context of their field's research on victimization (Hagan, Schoenfeld, and Palloni 2006). American researchers have assessed the economic costs of the war to the U.S. government, which Stiglitz and Bilmes (2008) estimate at over $3 trillion. The Costs of War project at Brown University reaches parallel conclusions. However, the economic costs to Iraqis who experienced the invasion and occupation are omitted from that work.

Using CVI data, Figure 4.5 shows the distribution over time of economic losses, revealing the same clear and expected peak found earlier for displacement in 2006, the year of the Samara bombing. We were able to use CVI respondents' comprehensive reports of monetary losses in 2003–8 to estimate in greater detail the costs associated with the political violence occurring during the invasion and post-invasion period.

Respondents reported monetary losses resulting from blackmail, payments for kidnapping/ransom, medical expenses related to violence, expenses related to changing houses because of security concerns, losses of businesses, homes, furniture, or cars, and any other large, unexpected expenses since the invasion. Losses were converted into 2008 U.S. dollars. The estimates we present in Figure 4.5 and Table 4.1 exclude outlying losses beyond the ninety-ninth percentile, removing the highest and perhaps least reliably reported losses. However, we also conducted an analysis that includes all outliers (see Hagan et al. 2012). In order to account for the possibility of unrepresentativeness in estimating monetary losses, we weighted CVI results according to each neighborhood's population and proportion of victimization reported in GP.

Estimated losses for Baghdad's full population, divided by security districts, appear in columns 3–5 of Table 4.1. The Rasheed district has by far the highest losses, which is consistent with it being one of the largest and most violent districts following the Samara bombing. Kadhimiyah also has relatively high median losses, consistent with its relative affluence; however, these losses are highly concentrated, limiting its total losses. With its dense population, Thawra (Sadr City) has large total losses, despite its relatively low victimization rate.

The lower part of Table 4.1 shows that, across Baghdad, the Sunnis are estimated to have lost notably more than the Shia. Weighted according to victimized population, economic losses suffered by Sunnis are over $40 billion, compared to about $27 billion for Shia and $21 billion for all others. Total estimated economic losses for the city of Baghdad approach $100 billion ($90,538,863,154), with a 95 percent confidence interval of $80–105 billion.

Because the CVI data are reported for all of Iraq, we also calculated an estimate for the entire country: about $309 billion. However, we are less certain about the sampling for this nationwide estimate, and the confidence interval is larger (nearly $100 billion). When we further calculated losses including outlying cases beyond the ninety-ninth percentile, the best estimate for Baghdad was over $254 billion and over $815 billion for the entire country. Although this inclusion of the top 1 percent of the CVI sample increases the estimates substantially, they are still quite plausible, given the concentration of wealth in the top 1 percent of the population. The upper bound estimate for Iraq is over $950 billion: *nearly $1 trillion USD.*

The largest and most statistically significant losses are associated with crimes – beheadings and kidnappings – that can involve large ransoms. On average, beheadings were associated with losses of $104,897, while kidnappings involved losses of $50,115. Losses associated with businesses are also large and significant, averaging $34,411. Our estimates consist entirely of monetary costs to households that were victims of human rights and humanitarian violations and do not include the principal costs to Iraq in terms of lost lives, injuries,

TABLE 4.1. *Estimate of total economic losses to victims in post-invasion Iraq circa 2003–2008, in USD*

	Median losses[a]	Sample losses[a]	Estimated total losses to victims[b]		
			95% Lower bound	Best estimate	95% Upper bound
District of Baghdad					
Rusafa	14,337.00	6,483,646.00	12,475,853,367.00	14,160,814,118.00	16,368,217,671.00
Adhamiyah	21,411.00	5,932,236.75	9,775,304,024.00	11,096,782,250.00	12,827,562,973.75
Thawra	19,010.00	1,456,849.00	8,479,854,681.00	9,624,641,360.00	11,124,775,631.00
Nissan	38,342.50	5,073,346.40	7,873,548,715.49	8,938,569,797.78	10,331,974,197.88
Karadah	14,286.00	3,955,867.12	6,694,468,233.74	7,599,607,469.98	8,783,927,901.59
Karkh	21,677.50	699,237.00	1,157,936,472.00	1,314,565,560.00	1,519,442,001.00
Kadhimiyah	44,854.00	2,948,474.00	4,059,591,264.00	4,608,714,720.00	5,327,484,842.00
Mansour	11,750.00	5,315,763.00	6,906,830,602.00	7,840,776,410.00	9,063,403,021.00
Rasheed	20,010.00	12,537,426.00	20,761,977,456.00	23,570,360,880.00	27,243,826,698.00
Sectarian Identity					
Arab Shia	11,822.50	13,949,855.65	24,149,028,189.66	27,413,206,077.34	31,686,719,554.03
Arab Sunni	25,040.00	20,452,998.00	36,325,109,360.00	41,235,850,466.00	47,663,687,636.00
Other	24,844.50	11,521,597.57	19,282,490,873.86	21,889,806,610.89	25,301,877,495.33
Total					
Baghdad	$20,010.00	$45,924,451.22	$79756628423.52	$90,538,863,154.23	$104,652,284,685.36
Iraq	$10,672.00	$75,671,686.36	$272221239745.36	$308,972,810,748.70	$357,117,069,273.99
***n* of households**					
Baghdad	675	675	1,299,164	1,474,407	1,704,293
Iraq	1,463	1,463	5,124,158	5,815,351	6,722,066

[a] Upper 1% excluded. For estimates including upper 1%, see appendix table 1 in Hagan et al. 2012.
[b] Population losses calculated using victimization estimates in tables 2 and 3 of Hagan et al. 2012.

infrastructure, civic institutions, and other kinds of public costs included, for example, in Stiglitz and Bilmes' (2008) estimates of the $3 trillion in costs to the U.S. government of the war in Iraq.

ANTICIPATION AND AMPLIFICATION OF ETHNIC CLEANSING

We were further interested in the extent to which the early post-invasion, neighborhood-based fears discussed earlier in this chapter were predictive of the *amplification* of displacement, beyond the intervening anticipation of the costs of ethnic cleansing and displacement that we have just described. We argued earlier that an independent effect of neighborhood fear in 2003 would likely produce what we have called the amplification of a self-fulfilling prophecy of fear leading to displacement – well beyond what might have been anticipated and resulting in ethnic cleansing. This self-fulfilling prophecy of fear is a larger self-reinforcing consequence of the war in Iraq. The *combined* effects of anticipation and amplification are key components of ethnic cleansing and the "accumulation of evil" associated with a criminal war of aggression in international criminal law.

Thus we argued that to the extent there would be a neighborhood-specific direct effect of early post-invasion neighborhood fear that exceeded the indirect processes of anticipation (Figure 4.2), that this influence of neighborhood fear could be understood as the result of a process of amplification – that is, as the predicted result of a prophecy of fear in the neighborhoods of Baghdad that compounded in a self-fulfilling way. The neighborhood measurement of this prophetic effect of fear in a data set separate from the neighborhood measurement of ethnic cleansing and displacement, with a further predicted peak three years later and following the Samara shrine attack, constitutes a demanding test of the self-fulfilling effect of neighborhood-specific sectarian fear in Baghdad.

Figure 4.6 gives a visual sense of the neighborhood-specific impact of fear in the peak 2006 year of violence in Baghdad. We used a model (Model (3) in Table 4.5 of the Appendix) to produce the graph in Figure 4.6 with the other significant variables in our analysis held constant. The graph is made more visually meaningful by randomly selecting a specified number – in this case fifteen – of the neighborhoods for presentation. Each line in the graph reflects movement up and down in a specific neighborhood of the odds of displacement associated with the year 2006 in which al-Qaeda struck the Samarra shrine. About half the neighborhoods presented are in the lower half of the distribution of fear soon after the invasion, while about half are in the upper half of this distribution.

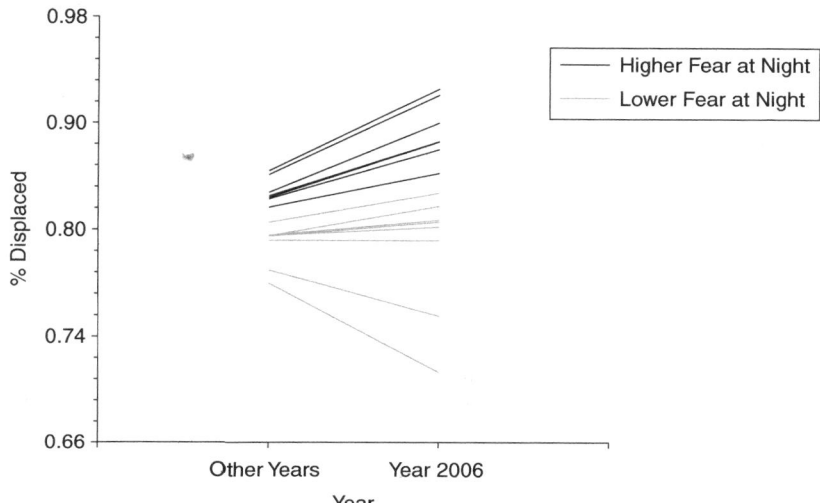

FIGURE 4.6. Amplified Impact of the Self-Fulfilling Prophecy of Fear on Displacement in Baghdad Neighborhoods with Varying Levels of Fear (2003) after the Samarra Shrine Attack (2006)

The lines in Figure 4.6 confirm that while most of the neighborhoods in the lower half of the fear distribution were little affected by the Samarra shrine attack, the neighborhoods in the upper half of the fear distribution were notably more likely to experience ethnic cleansing and displacement in the aftermath of the 2006 attack. This effect – with other variables held constant – is an indication of the amplified impact of the self-fulfilling prophecy of fear in the most fearful neighborhoods following the Samarra shrine attack. The results in this model implicate both al-Qaeda in Iraq and al-Sadr's Mahdi Army in the ethnic cleansing of Baghdad.

CONTEXTUALIZING FIGHT AND FLIGHT

We began this chapter with the thesis that the U.S. invasion, occupation, and presence in Iraq unleashed a self-reinforcing and self-fulfilling prophecy of fear, amplifying an increasingly brutal process of death and displacement that reconfigured through this ethnic cleansing a previously Sunni-dominated Baghdad into a Shia-controlled city. Fear about public security and safety is a major component of the theory of legal cynicism that is central to this book, and the theory predicts that a source of this fear is often skepticism about the legitimacy of state and non-state actors, and the action taken and not taken in responding to the circumstances that drive public fear, especially among targeted and vulnerable groups. We argued that there was much to cynically fear as the American presence brought resistance, militancy, insurgency, and terrorism to Iraq.

There is an inclination to see the battle for Baghdad as randomly chaotic – analogous to a mass fight-or-flight syndrome – without predictable order or discernible direction. Yet as widespread and chaotic as the conflict was, it was also systematic, for example, as displayed by the patterns of ethnic cleansing and forced displacement resulting from the harassment and threats identified in our analysis.

Our findings generally confirm the involvement anticipated in Figure 4.2 of Muqtada al-Sadr's Mahdi Army in harassing and threating Sunni individuals in Sunni and mixed neighborhoods, leading to the forced removal of Sunni residents from their neighborhoods. The attack of AQI on the shrine in Samarra is also shown to play a salient role in the resulting ethnic cleansing of Baghdad. Ordinary Iraqis' fears accurately anticipated the violence that followed the invasion, especially placing Sunni and other non-Shia groups at heightened risk of a process of sectarian ethnic cleansing involving harassment and threats by Shia militia. Even if ordinary Iraqis' inchoate fears could not have anticipated specific aspects of the Shia faction forming the Mahdi Army, it would have been unlikely for Iraqis based on their experiences in the 1990s and during and soon after the invasion not to have sensed collectively the looming prospect of Shia-on-Sunni sectarian conflict, and they therefore could foresee at the level of specific neighborhoods – especially in Sunni and mixed neighborhoods – the danger of the coming conflict that would seriously disrupt their lives.

Muqtada al-Sadr began as a non-state actor and became the leader of the largest political movement in Iraq. Al-Sadr was underestimated as the leader of the Sadrist movement previously developed by his father, who was assassinated by Saddam's Ba'athist regime. Following the invasion, Muqtada publicly voiced in his preaching his opposition to the U.S.-led coalition and occupation. He was excluded from the interim government that was composed disproportionately of Shia groups and leaders who had been exiled from Iraq for years, and he was intermittently pursued by U.S. authorities for alleged crimes. The pursuit of al-Sadr and his followers by the new authorities added to the Sadrists' legal cynicism and accumulated resentments.

The Sadrist movement had remained underground until the toppling of the Ba'athist regime. From this movement, al-Sadr built the Mahdi Army, which used the organized criminal tools of harassment, threats, and protection to expand its control from Baghdad's Sadr City. Al-Sadr in effect made this impoverished slum of several million people into a city-state within Baghdad. From there, he spread his territorial influence over much of eastern Baghdad and beyond, setting a foundation for his supporters to eventually enter Iraq's parliament and become a key part of the governing coalition.

We have argued that the opportunistic and coordinated "dual purpose" crimes involved in the ethnic cleansing by the Mahdi Army reflected a predictable outgrowth of the resentments and legal cynicism of the young and underemployed Shia followers of Muqtada al-Sadr who as a group had experienced the heavy-handed repression of Saddam Hussein's regime, and who received no American support when their predecessors and peers responded to the first President Bush's call to overthrow the Ba'athist regime. The Mahdi Army's harassment and threats leading to ethnic cleansing of the Sunnis in Baghdad reflected the kinds of organized collective criminal behavior depicted in Tilly's (2003; 1985) and Cloward and Ohlin's (1960) theories. Muqtada al-Sadr and the Mahdi Army successfully applied organized criminal methods that ethnically cleansed and changed the neighborhood demography of Baghdad.

The resulting population displacement from Baghdad peaked in 2006. However, when Muqtada al-Sadr staged a unilateral ceasefire in 2007, he and his Sadrist movement began a new phase of engagement with the Iraqi state that his mass movement and organized criminal methods had helped to shape. This new stage of engagement involved electing a bloc of Sadrists to parliament and forming a governing coalition with Prime Minister Maliki. Our findings are in this way consistent with the role that Tilly argues organized criminality can play in making and remaking states.

The fears expressed by Iraqi citizens in the 2003 post-invasion Gallup Poll correctly anticipated neighborhood-specific problems between Shia groups like the Mahdi Army and the Sunni, as well as other non-Shia residents. To the extent that there was an observable effect of these early post-invasion neighborhood fears exceeding the indirect processes of anticipation linking these fears to later ethnic cleansing and displacement, the added direct effect of neighborhood fear can be understood as the result of a cognitive process of amplification. The predicted result was a Mertonian prophecy of fear that compounded over time in a self-fulfilling way.

The final models we estimated included effects on displacement of the interaction of neighborhood fear soon after the 2003 invasion with the 2006 al-Qaeda attack on the Samarra shrine (see Appendix Table 4.6). This interaction effect helped to explain an earlier observed effect of neighborhood fear measured in 2003 on displacement. Thus, as predicted in our theoretical model in Figure 4.2, neighborhood fear measured soon after the invasion had its most significant impact three years later during the 2006 peak in the panicked displacement and resulting ethnic cleansing that followed the Samarra attack. This extends criminal responsibility for the ethnic cleansing of Baghdad's neighborhoods to the al-Qaeda attack on the Samarra shrine.

Expressed in sheer dollar terms, we found that the conservatively estimated total economic losses for the city of Baghdad were almost $100 billion. Annual losses peaked in 2006 at about $50 billion. We conservatively estimated that the total monetary losses suffered by members of Sunni groups in Baghdad were over $40 billion, which was almost $15 billion more than the also considerable losses to the Shia. We estimated that the losses across all of Iraq were more than triple the Baghdad total. These estimates were cautiously developed in a number of ways, including eliminating the highest outlier reports of losses, which indeed may actually be accurate.

These results from the battle for Baghdad are persuasive confirmation for Robert Sampson's thesis, developed in *Great American City*, that "the perceptual basis of action is contingent on neighborhood context, which in turn plays a role in shaping the long-term trajectories and identities of places" (2012:147). As Sampson more generally suggests, knowledge of place matters. *The American preemptive war in Iraq was waged with a willful ignorance and neglect of this kind of knowledge.*

It is of interest to speculate whether in some counterfactual way the U.S.-led coalition might have avoided the amplification of self-fulfilling fears of sectarian violence in Iraq. There is no certain way to know how different policies might have altered the post–Saddam Hussein era, but the dire consequences of the failure to engage or adequately acknowledge the concerns and uncertainties of underemployed youth, coupled with the devastating nature of the sectarian conflict, suggests less damaging outcomes might have been possible.

Certainly, the focus of U.S. policy on dismantling almost every aspect of centralized state control contributed to the uncertainty and chaos; disbanding the large military and security forces particularly produced mass employment problems and left management of social order to a foreign military with limited understanding of the Iraqi context. A broad policy of de-Ba'athification was crafted by the U.S.-led coalition to disempower authorities from the prior regime and exclude them from post-Saddam politics – and thus from reconstruction and stabilization efforts.

The sweeping scope of de-Ba'athification policy had the effect both of delegitimizing the U.S./coalition role in making a place for Arab Sunnis in the governance of Iraq, and of further undermining the faith of the Arab Sunni more generally that they would be provided the most basic security and safety by these forces. Illegitimacy and insecurity are core components of the theory of legal cynicism that we have argued can explain much of what went wrong in Iraq. In this chapter, we have seen how the problem of legal cynicism impacted both the Arab Sunni and Shia Sadrists in Baghdad. Neither group was well accommodated or integrated into a vision of the new Iraq.

A more conciliatory approach to the prior regime leadership who were not members of the Security Directorate or Hussein's repressive policies might have yielded a different outcome. Similarly, a more open embrace of the nation's inherent diversity coupled with specific policies (e.g., employment and economic stimulus programs) designed to link Iraqis, especially youth, with productive activities might have made violence less appealing.

There are perhaps two core elements of such counterfactual possibilities. First, there is the issue of timing, with what might have been possible before sectarian violence surged (2003 through mid-2004) not being possible after tens of thousands of residents had been killed and displaced (2005 through 2007). Second, there is the issue of political authority, with the U.S. and coalition forces clearly in control during early stages of the post-Saddam era, and a combination of foreign and Iraqi players later exercising increasing autonomy, authority, and power. With this in mind, the new Iraqi government could potentially have developed a less exclusionary process for vetting past leaders alongside more cooperative policies, including following through on promises to reintegrate the minority Sunni population into Iraq political life and providing security for its communities.

Much has been made in policy discussions about the unanticipated consequences of the American invasion and occupation of Iraq. The analysis presented in this chapter suggests that during the very period when the Bush administration that launched this war was celebrating its "accomplished" mission of the invasion and the toppling of the Saddam Hussein Ba'athist regime, Arab Sunnis in vulnerable Baghdad neighborhoods were already fearfully anticipating the dangerous consequences of the violence that this American invasion would unleash, and from which they would be left unprotected. This fearful anticipation was amplified by a compounding self-fulfilling prophecy of fear whose consequences were likely also anticipated by ordinary Iraqis – as night fell on Baghdad.

5

The Separate Peace of the Shia

After enduring years of increasing violence and domestic insurgency following the 2003 U.S. invasion and continuing into 2007, Iraq entered a period of relative peace and security. How this happened is not clear. Many military leaders, media pundits, and elected politicians have argued that a 2007 surge in U.S. forces and/or a Sunni Awakening movement led to a tentative period of peace in Iraq. Others have suggested that a partition of Iraq's sectarian groups alone could have delivered this result. Although there has been no official partition of the Sunni, Shia, and Kurdish groups in Iraq, we show and explain in this chapter how Iraq's sectarian groups moved into an unstable "separate peace" that more recently has been followed by renewed violence.

We take the surge and partition arguments into account in this chapter. However, unlike David Petraeus (2013), who before the advances of the Islamic State of Iraq and Syria (ISIS) claimed that the surge is "how we won in Iraq," we argue that unnecessary attacks on civilians reported by Arab Sunni civilians during the surge were actually a source of heightened perceptions of injustice and illegitimacy that are central to a theory of legal cynicism. Our further focus in this chapter is on using an endogenous conflict approach to supplement the theory of legal cynicism in explaining how an interim period of relative peace emerged and advantaged the Shia.

While journalists and soldiers continue to write a great deal about Iraq (e.g., Gordon and Trainor 2012), these accounts are highly anecdotal and view the Iraq conflict largely through an American lens that is framed by this nation's political debates about the Middle East. These debates reached a peak in 2006 over the decision to surge additional American troops or to partition Iraq's conflicting sectarian groups. There is relatively little social scientific work that locates these debates in relation to broader theoretical frameworks or that is based on nationally representative data collection that can illuminate how Iraqis have viewed the conflict around them, much less competing claims about this conflict.

Building on the work of Kalyvas (2008, 2006; Kalyvas and Kocher 2007), we postulate in this chapter that the opposing American arguments in favor of both the troop surge and partition positions had roots in an ethnic war theory – a theory that gives single-minded attention to unchanging sectarian divisions. We argue that the resulting surge/partition debate neither revealed nor stimulated understanding of an ongoing process of sectarian separation in Iraq that alternatively is best explained by a combined conflict and legal cynicism perspective. Rather than narrowly and exclusively focusing on the history of sectarian hatreds postulated in ethnic war theory, our perspective places its emphasis on newly evolving sources of collective violence. These evolving factors include the consequences of the U.S. war of aggression and a continued elite bargaining process with the Iraqi government of Nouri al-Maliki.

Thus our conflict-based approach addresses contradictory aspects of a counterinsurgency doctrine that underwrote the surge policy and deficiencies in an ethnic war theory that drove key aspects of the surge and partition perspectives. *Both proposals to surge troops and to partition the country ignored widespread legal cynicism in Iraq about a U.S.-led invasion and occupation that had replaced Saddam's legal authoritarianism with the presence of American troops whose recurrent acts of violent and unnecessary criminal militarism undermined peace and security.* In contrast, our approach reveals the backdrop to a divisively sectarian "separate peace" that advantaged the Shia and disadvantaged the Sunni in Iraq, creating a false, unequal, and unstable source of interim security. However, before we further develop this perspective and analysis, we first review the proposals that were made for the surge and the partitioning of Iraq.

THE SURGE AND THE COUNTERINSURGENCY (COIN) DOCTRINE

Wars often evoke taken-for-granted assumptions and related lay theories (Brubaker and Laitin 1998). In Iraq, the counterinsurgency doctrine was an example. Advanced by David Petraeus as a product of military social science at elite academic institutions as disparate as West Point and Princeton, the counterinsurgency doctrine – often called COIN – had a period of previous influence in the U.S. military during the Vietnam War.

Petraeus earned his doctorate at Princeton University, where he wrote a thesis about counterinsurgency efforts in Vietnam. After resigning as head of the CIA, he taught as a visiting professor at City University of New York. He also taught courses on COIN in the social sciences department at West Point, drawing on the work of French military analyst David Galula (1964) and others (e.g., Nagl 2005). Notwithstanding its earlier application in Vietnam, a popular journalistic account of COIN by Fred Kaplan (2013; see also Kagan 2009) argues that General David Petraeus redeveloped this "doctrine" as the foundation for an intellectually grounded "plot to change the American way of war."

Petraeus recruited followers for a redevelopment of the COIN doctrine as an alternative to what has been called conventional warfare theory, with an emphasis of COIN on "winning hearts and minds" and increasing cultural sensitivity to local populations. A major goal was to mitigate what we have called legal cynicism about the new American-led Iraqi state and the military failure to deliver peace and security. However, we argue that the COIN policy featured offensive operations and a criminal militarism that continued unnecessary violent attacks by U.S./coalition forces on civilians – especially Arab Sunnis – and as well underestimated the importance of ongoing community-level processes of sectarian separation.

When he was appointed commander of the coalition forces in an effort to turn around the failing Iraq war, Petraeus became the commander of a disliked and expanded occupying military force with little international credibility or effective knowledge of the community-level sectarian separation that was already well under way across Iraq. He promised to bring increased civilian protection and security to Iraq – core concerns of the theory of legal cynicism.

Petraeus (e.g., 1986) and his collaborators had written extensively about COIN in military and international relations journals, and they had produced a new counterinsurgency manual for the military (see Review Symposium 2008) that coincided with Petraeus's replacement of General George Casey. In 2006, Casey had adopted a "leave-to-win strategy" that removed American soldiers from population centers, restricting their exposure beyond heavily fortified bases to reduce casualties and initiate a path to a phased withdrawal. In early 2007, President Bush replaced embattled Defense Secretary Donald Rumsfeld with Texas A&M University President Robert Gates and announced General Petraeus as the new U.S. commander to replace General Casey in Iraq. Gates and Petraeus promised a new Iraq War strategy.

In Baghdad, a high-level advisor explained that "population protection became the driving mantra of the command environment" (Sky 2008:31). However, the new strategy also called for a surge of an additional 30,000 troops, and the repositioning of forces in neighborhoods and villages, that is, as French military theorist Galula recommended – "among the people." The point was to identify and displace the insurgents from the neighborhoods and villages, removing them from the civilian population, securing and protecting local communities, attempting to gain the trust of the people, and ideally committing community members to the then relatively recently reconfigured Iraqi government with its new, American-approved prime minister, Nouri al-Maliki. Yet we argue that the surge tactics were a problematic plan for improving feelings of insecurity – that are at the core of legal cynicism theory – because these tactics featured new offensive operations that continued unnecessary and violent attacks on civilians.

Attached to the surge was a program known originally as the Anbar or Sunni Awakening and later as the Sons of Iraq. This program involved hiring Sunni militiamen and former soldiers from the disbanded Iraqi military who were paid to patrol neighborhoods and villages and join in the fight against al-Qaeda in Iraq (AQI). One of the few published empirical assessments of COIN (Biddle, Friedman, and Shapiro 2012) argues that the Awakening interacted with the surge and amplified and entrenched its effectiveness in reducing violence in Iraq, although we cast doubt on this claim in the following chapter (see also Hagan, Kaiser, and Hanson 2013).

U.S. funds were used to pay the Awakening forces with the expectation that the Iraqi government would later assume the costs and integrate these forces into its army – an expectation that was never fulfilled. When the money stopped, the effectiveness of the Awakening withered. In a real sense, Awakening forces were "rented" as a means of dissuading them from leading or facilitating violence against the American forces. A further problem was that the Awakening forces would not be accepted in Shia communities, notably including Baghdad neighborhoods recently taken over by Shia militia, and thus could really only help to "stabilize" Sunni areas in what would turn out to be temporary ways.

Petraeus and other architects of the surge incorporated contradictions within their new counterinsurgency strategy, most notably increasing the use of force and coercion, which resulted in elevated military and civilian casualties while promising protection and security. The coercive aspect of the surge was expressed in a 2006 memo that was drafted by Vietnam veteran and former senator Charles Robb and presented to the Iraq Study Group.[1] Robb wrote, "My sense is that we need, right away, a significant short-term Surge in U.S. forces on the ground.... It's time to let our military to do what they're trained to do on offense – without being overly constrained by a zero casualties or controlled collateral damage approach" (quoted in Gordon and Trainor 2012:276). This attitude toward collateral damage, reminiscent of the American war in Vietnam, and cutting to the core of concerns of legal cynicism theory, raised the prospect of unnecessary attacks on civilians – which constitute war crimes[2] – and contradicted the trust-building, protection, and security mantra of COIN. This legally cynical contradiction perpetuated policies and practices of criminal militarism.

The demand for "offense" was further expressed in the final drafting of the new counterinsurgency field manual. The revision reflected conventional war theory thinking that "some of these insurgents – maybe a lot of them – were irreconcilable" (Kaplan 2013:219). This "assumption of irreconcilability" is a key premise of ethnic war theory – that sectarian conflicts have deep historical, if not primordial and essentialist, roots (Kalyvas 2006). The assumption that the insurgency was driven by Arab Sunni recruits, combined with the disregard for collateral damage indicated in the Robb memo, predicted new problems of legal cynicism among the Arab Sunnis, who already saw themselves as a population targeted by U.S./coalition forces.

Ethnic war theory is so widely taken for granted in popular policy circles that it is usually invoked without reference to its academic origins (e.g., see Kaufman 1996) – and more often advanced through the power of anecdotal argument. An influential surge advocate graphically illustrated the strength of commitment to this theory's premise of irreconcilable difference and a culture of criminal militarism when he recalled that during the Anbar Awakening his unit had "killed a particularly nasty insurgent, tied the corpse to the front of a tank, drove it around town for everyone to see, then phoned the dead man's mother to come pick up the body" (Kaplan 2013:221). Treating enemy dead in this manner is, of course, a war crime (see Dormann 2003).

COIN strategy also assumed a legitimate, established government for which counterinsurgency forces would fight. The Shia-dominated Iraqi government of Prime Minister Nouri al-Maliki was known for allowing if not supporting secret prisons for suspected Sunni insurgents who were subjected to torture and squalid living conditions – a poorly contained parallel to the earlier American torture policy – and for knowingly allowing and protecting Shia militia described in the previous chapter that harassed, threatened, and displaced Sunni residents from their homes and neighborhoods (see also Tripp 2010: chapter 7). These realities undermined the prospects for reducing legal cynicism among Iraqi citizens and creating an enduring trust between the Shia-dominated government and Sunni communities – especially during and beyond the relatively short period of the U.S.-led surge. However, we will show that Prime Minister Maliki briefly made some perhaps surprising progress toward this goal as the 2010 federal election approached in Iraq.

Finally, the surge commanded by General Petraeus also included the construction in selected neighborhoods of new twelve-foot cement blast barriers that rapidly snaked across Baghdad. These were sometimes called "Bremer's Barriers" – for their early appearance in Baghdad during Paul Bremer's leadership of the American occupation. The scale and impermeability of the barriers had a controversial purpose that offended a balance between nationalism and sectarianism in the symbolic politics of Iraq – by signaling that sectarian divisions were now literally set in concrete.

This was a symbolic expression of the key assumption of ethnic war theory – namely, that ethno-sectarian differences were so deeply unchangeable that they must be sealed and walled off. The U.S./coalition forces constructed barriers that locked in place communities that had only recently experienced sectarian purges. This had the effect of visibly solidifying and freezing in place a sectarian separation that was a recently emergent reality and still politically and culturally contested.

The COIN doctrine incorporated unnecessarily violent U.S./coalition attacks on civilians, endorsed and defended a less than legitimate government, allowed the building of highly visible barriers between sectarian groups, and invited a legally cynical response – especially from Iraq's Sunni communities – predicted by the endogenous conflict perspective considered later in this chapter.

PARTITIONING IRAQ

In the fall of 2006, when former senator Robb began his advocacy for the surge, then-Senator Joe Biden joined with the president of the Council of Foreign Relations, Leslie Gelb, to advocate the formal partition of Iraq – including a division of Baghdad potentially more permanent than Bremer's Barriers. This alternative strategy called for separating the contesting sectarian groups through a decentralized federal system of Kurdish, Sunni, and Shia regions that presumably would have also officially divided Baghdad itself. Like the argument for a troop surge, this policy drew prominently from ethnic war theory, particularly the versions reflected in Robert Kaplan's (1993) influential depiction of *Balkan Ghosts* in the former Yugoslavia and in related scholarly writings about civil wars (Kaufman 1996; Biddle 2006).

Kaplan argued that the ghosts of ethno-sectarian animosities were deeply entrenched in the history of the Balkans and created an insatiable appetite for violence. The Biden-Gelb model assumed that a formal and officially sanctioned separation of these kinds of long-time enemies could stop fighting in Iraq. This was widely thought to have been confirmed by the then-recent experience with the ethnic federation framework negotiated in Richard Holbrooke's (1995) Dayton Peace Accord between Bosnian Serbs, Muslims, and Croats.

The Biden-Gelb plan implicitly called for a decentralized yet still collaborative federalism as an alternative to a centralized and coercive legal authoritarianism that as noted in previous chapters was deeply entrenched in Iraq (see also Galbraith 2006). Tripp (2010; also Dodge 2013, 2012) copiously documents just how entrenched authoritarian governance has been in Iraq. Biden and Gelb (2006) launched their plan for an alternative decentralized power-sharing policy with a *New York Times* op-ed that advocated "Unity through Autonomy in Iraq." They emphasized that in Baghdad and the rest of Iraq, "things are already heading toward partition."

Of course, they needed to look no further for an example than Kurdistan, a semiautonomous region established after the first Gulf War and before the demise of Saddam Hussein that is home to almost all of Iraq's Kurds (82.1 percent of the nationally representative sample we introduce later in this chapter). They argued that Iraqis were growing too fearful of one another to avert a further countrywide sectarian separation. However, the internal evolution and devolution of this kind of official separation can be prohibitively complicated in its cultural dimensions – as has been argued in Iraq – where conceptions of nationalism and sectarianism persistently overlap in their symbolic expressions. Sunni and Shia groups in Iraq both persistently insist that they are committed to the nation of Iraq as well as to their own separate ethno-religious identities, with each group arguing that its own relationship to nationhood is essential to holding the country together (Haddad 2011).

Although the Biden-Gelb plan shared some ethnic war premises with the surge policy, it was also different in notable ways. In contrast to the proposed surge of 30,000 troops beyond the approximately 130,000 already in Iraq, Biden and Gelb proposed a reduction to 20,000–30,000 troops by the end of 2007. Biden and Gelb were looking for an alternative to both a combative reliance on increased U.S. troop strength and a continuing compromised reliance on a Shia-dominated al-Maliki government. However, President Bush announced and implemented the surge in early 2007 and the prospect of partition then largely dropped from view – except in Iraq, where the separation of the Sunni and the Shia groups mattered most – and where the "unmixing" of groups was well under way.

The approximately year-and-a-half-long surge ended during the 2008 U.S. election campaign. Presidential candidate John McCain insisted that the surge had succeeded in reducing Iraqi violence, while candidate Obama gave primary credit to the Awakening movement for reducing violence before the surge began. Missing in both accounts was an acknowledgment of the possibility that legal cynicism in Iraq about the continuing American military presence and its efforts at elite-bargained state making were as much or more a part of the conflict as the sectarian forces that both candidates implicitly blamed for the war. There was also little or no consideration of how extensive the separation of groups had already become in Iraq.

AN ENDOGENOUS AND EXCLUSIVE ELITE BARGAIN

Kalyvas and Kocher (2007; Kalyvas 2006) do not question that in Iraq most violence is between ethnic groups. Yet they draw an important theoretical distinction between exogenous and endogenous sources of the sectarian cleavages that underwrite this ethnic conflict. The exogenous cleavage thesis of ethnic war theory sees civil wars flowing directly from historically entrenched ethnic hostilities. The endogenous cleavage thesis adds crucial contingencies, for example, as we saw in the preceding chapter when the escalation of violence in Baghdad became catastrophically self-fulfilling and self-reinforcing following the American invasion and occupation (see also Brubaker and Laitin 1998; Fearon and Laitin 2000). A central prediction of endogenous conflict theory is that the existence of violence between groups will not necessarily or even usually in itself explain what is being observed as "group violence" without taking into account the contingent agency of state and non-state actors and their changing relationships with local ethnic communities.

Kalyvas and Kocher indicated that in Iraq "a key reason why the sectarian conflict has emerged with such force and violence is to be found in the handling of this country's occupation by the United States" (2007:185). This handling included not only the de-Ba'athification policies and dismantling of the military considered in earlier chapters, but also the subsequent implementation of the surge and the Awakening policies and the U.S. military collaboration with the Iraqi government led by Nouri al-Maliki.

Dodge (2013) refers to the post-invasion relationship of the United States with Prime Minister al-Maliki as an "exclusive elite bargain." This bargain was contextualized by the contingencies of the just noted post-invasion destruction of Iraq's last national and somewhat ethnically inclusive institutions: the central government's ministries, the army, and the Ba'ath Party. As noted in Chapter 2, the U.S. intervention in shaping the replacement state began with the selection of the Iraq Governing Council (IGC).

The IGC was dominated by previously exiled Shia parties and their elite leaders, most of whom were well educated, often with British and U.S. degrees, having taken expatriate refuge decades earlier from Saddam Hussein's Ba'athist regime. The IGC excluded from the outset important indigenous opposition leaders, including major Sunni figures and their followers, and ignored the rise described in the previous chapter of Shia cleric

Muqtada al-Sadr and his young and less-educated underclass Sadrist movement (Herring and Rangwala 2006). The limited representation of indigenous group leaders impacted the Arab Sunnis and the Sadrist Shia communities more than it did Kurdish groups because the latter had already become increasingly autonomous within their own self-governing region of Iraq. The exclusion of Sunnis and Sadrists from the new central government triggered a new level of legal cynicism and resulting recruitment from among these groups into local sectarian militias, which in turn stoked the smoldering fires of civil war.

The U.S./coalition-driven elite bargain was a wedge that widened the gap between Iraq's dominant groups and became a key source of the kind of endogenous ethnic cleavage Kalyvas and Kocher (2007) described. It was another macro-level source of cynicism about the U.S. and Iraqi political, military, and legal elites who were directing the war (especially the newly empowered Shia governing elite) linked and leading to the micro-level cynical attitudes among groups (especially the Arab Sunnis) who felt ignored and excluded. Dodge argues that "the political settlement created by the United States after the invasion, institutionalized by the new constitution and legitimized by two national elections in 2005, was undoubtedly an elite bargain of the exclusive variety" (2013:41). Like Kalyvas and Kocher, Dodge concludes that this exclusive elite settlement inflamed Iraqi politics with what we have called legal cynicism, intensifying divisions between the religious and ethnic groups. These group identities increasingly were linked to legally cynical justifications of collective violence (Haddad 2011).

Thus the post-invasion American Coalition Provisional Authority initiated and swiftly consolidated a new network of privilege, exclusion, and power around the Shia majority who were repressed under Saddam. Nouri al-Maliki emerged as the beneficiary of this emergent network. Al-Maliki was a long-time member of the exiled opposition Dawa Party who, before fleeing Iraq and later becoming the party's political leader, had aspired to be an educator. His grandfather was recognized for his poetry, which expressed a mixture of nationalist and sectarian themes. In the early years following the U.S. invasion, al-Maliki served in the second tier of the Iraqi government bureaucracy, emerging most visibly as a member of Ahmad al-Chalabi's de-Ba'athification commission (Parker and Salman 2013).

As noted, al-Maliki became prime minister in an elaboration of the exclusive elite bargain that followed the 2006 peak in sectarian violence associated with the al-Qaeda attack on the Samarra shrine. Ibrahim al-Jaafari, who had been confirmed by members of parliament after the 2005 federal elections, was forced from office in the face of the rapidly escalating violence. Al-Jaafari's fate was sealed when the American ambassador in Baghdad, Zalmay Khalilzad, was pointedly asked by President Bush in a videoconference, "Can you get rid of him?" (Filkens 2014a). Khalilzad later insisted that he did not choose al-Maliki, but that he had "merely exerted American leverage to maximum effect" (Filkens 2014a:53).

Although al-Maliki, like many other educated Shia, fled Saddam Hussein's regime, he differed in that he had stayed in the region and never became fluent in English or other aspects of Western culture. He did not know and distrusted Americans, and he quickly emerged as a truculent and uncertain ally, often finding ways to insist on his autonomy. He criticized the United States when its soldiers in 2006 killed family members after an ambush in Haditha, and again in 2007 when Blackwater USA security guards shot into a crowd at a Baghdad square and killed civilians (Apuzzo 2014b).

In 2008, when the United States insisted on continued immunity of its soldiers from prosecution in Iraq's courts, al-Maliki set a timeline for their departure, boasting that "I am the owner of the idea of withdrawing the U.S. troops" (Filkens 2014b:19). This led to the departure of the last U.S. combat troops from Iraq at the end of 2011, although as we note in the Epilogue, it is increasingly apparent that this particular elite bargain was driven by the direct influence of Iran.

An endogenous conflict perspective acknowledges the likelihood that domestic political elites such as Nouri al-Maliki will often if not usually be better prepared and positioned to manage local conflicts than external state actors who know less about national and local community-based political relationships. Although al-Maliki and his Dawa Party were explicitly Shia, he also developed a briefly expressed capacity – perhaps foreshadowed by his grandfather's poetry of nationalism and sectarianism – to strategically signal a national secular sensibility that temporarily resonated beyond his Shia base.

Al-Maliki expanded his political base among Arab Sunni voters in 2008 by challenging his rival and fellow Shia, Muqtada al-Sadr. As noted in the previous chapter, Al-Sadr's Mahdi Army and his Sadrist followers alternated between being an asset and a threat to al-Maliki. As explained further later in this chapter, al-Maliki intermittently gained support from the Sunni community by joining the Iraqi Army with the U.S. forces in attacking the Mahdi Army. By 2009, al-Maliki was benefiting from this strategy and peaking in his personal popularity.

Nonetheless, al-Maliki's coalition did not succeed in gaining the largest number of parliamentary seats in Iraq's 2010 federal elections. His leading opponent, Ayad Allawi, a more secular Shia with Sunni support, secured more seats, yet Allawi could not get U.S. support to form a coalition government. It took nine months, combined with ambivalent U.S. assistance and a dubious court decision, for al-Maliki to receive parliamentary approval for a second term as prime minister. Al-Maliki subsequently refused to grant the concessions demanded by the United States to maintain a residual military force in Iraq, and he would later instigate criminal charges and more violent measures in moves against leading Sunni members of his governing coalition.

Of course, al-Maliki's shifting tactics were hardly unprecedented: violent and legal authoritarian politics have been a core part of Iraq's history. Tripp (2010) warned that the continuing collective violence of local militias and insurgents represented determined efforts to counteract the al-Maliki regime's centralized assertion of a familiar type of authoritarian military control in Iraq. He lamented that "Western allies often failed to recognize how much they were part of this same history and thus ran the risk of once more succumbing to its baneful logic" (2010:317).

The overlapping accounts of endogenous cleavage by Kalyvas and Kocher, the elite bargain perspective of Dodge, and a new authoritarianism emphasized by Tripp share a concern that the invasion, occupation, and civil war in Iraq were the leading edges of a new regime that, notwithstanding effective campaign gestures of conciliation and inclusion, were committed to elite Shia domination and control. This endogenous conflict perspective suggests several hypotheses that are consistent with a theory of legal cynicism and that can be tested against the observed pattern of events and public opinion in post-invasion Iraq. Before we present these hypotheses, however, it is important to provide a sense of how U.S. military operations conducted with the cooperation of the al-Maliki government unfolded and impacted Iraqi civilians before and during the surge in Iraq.

U.S. OFFENSIVE MILITARY OPERATIONS AND CIVILIANS

Despite the focus on protection and security and "winning hearts and minds" in COIN doctrine, Dodge insists that "the major change in U.S. policy towards Iraq, launched in 2007, was dominated by military campaigns to the exclusion of all else" (2013:84). Operations Phantom Thunder and Phantom Strike marked the onset of the 2007 surge (Gordon and Trainor 2012), and U.S. military deaths, Iraqi civilian casualties, and insurgent attacks spiked during this period.[3]

Al-Maliki's Shia-dominated government facilitated attacks during the surge by coalition forces on Sunni insurgent groups throughout Iraq, while largely protecting Shia militia. Eventually Petraeus extracted an agreement from al-Maliki about "a zone in which special operations would be established for about a kilometer around the edge of [Shia-populated] Sadr City ... But the understanding was a far cry from the freedom the White House had presumed the American military would have in Iraq as it carried out the Surge" (Gordon and Trainor 2012:443). Finally, by 2008, U.S. surge operations took on al-Sadr's Shia militias in Basra and in Baghdad's Sadr City. But al-Maliki forbad further expansion of the surge-linked Awakening movement into the Shia south, and this movement never penetrated al-Sadr's Mahdi Army's domination of eastern Baghdad or Shia parts of western Baghdad (Hagan, Kaiser, and Hanson 2013). The surge focused more heavily on the Sunni-led insurgency than on the Shia militias, as we demonstrate in this and the following chapter.

Importantly, Operation Phantom Thunder expanded the previously largely classified role of the U.S. Joint Special Operations Command (JSOC) in violent attacks led by Major General Stan McChrystal. JSOC operated much like a CIA unit within the Department of Defense, gathering intelligence and conducting largely unreported raids and killings of targeted insurgent leaders. Gordon and Trainor suggest how these violent operations exposed the strategically motivated contradiction between use of military force and providing civilian protection during the surge:

> McChrystal's special operations forces were equally important given the offensive nature of the operation.... The commandos' mission was often described as "counterterrorism" – essentially, the killing or capture of important insurgent or militia leaders and operatives – and contrasted with the "counterinsurgency," protecting the population and isolating it from the enemy. In fact, the two had a synergistic relationship. (2012:418)

The raids and killings organized by JSOC, especially when they were based on faulty intelligence and resulted in civilian casualties, led to violent neighborhood and government clashes. JSOC played a role in pursuing Muqtada al-Sadr's Mahdi Army commanders, but it was much more extensively engaged in attacking the leadership of the Sunni insurgency and its presumed ties to al-Qaeda. For example, during one week alone in August 2007, JSOC strike forces launched eighty-seven missions in Sunni areas of northern Iraq that killed fifty-nine persons and detained 200 suspected enemy fighters (Gordon and Trainor 2012:419). These actions elevated legal cynicism about an American-led criminal militarism – especially in Sunni communities.

CVI reports later in this chapter and in earlier chapters of attacks against families were not exceptional, and they may have been part of "the new normal" during the peak period of 2005–7 violence. Hashim describes the methods of Operation Lightning:

> For much of June 2005 US and Iraqi troops stormed through largely Sunni neighborhoods, arresting thousands in a series of sweeps designed to put a halt to the suicide bombing campaign. Sunnis viewed Operation Lightning

as a form of collective punishment of the entire community. Those who were detained and then released because there was no evidence against them complained of being tortured by Interior Ministry security forces. A sweep of Abu Ghraib [neighborhood] was perceived as indiscriminate and the general in charge admitted as much. He reportedly told detainees who were about to be released, "The fire burns the wet leaves as well as the dry ones" (the innocent suffer with the guilty). (2006:333)

Such reports are part of a larger picture that, at least from the Arab Sunni perspective, seemed cynical about the casualties imposed on civilians.

In October 2010, WikiLeaks released nearly 400,000 U.S. Army field reports that further illuminated this picture. These reports revealed approximately 15,000 deaths not included in Iraq Body Count's (IBC) estimation of war-linked mortality based on media reporting, with about 80 percent of these deaths being civilians, and raising the IBC estimate to 150,000 deaths. Most of the "missed" deaths resulted from incidents involving one to three casualties, which is consistent with the assumption that IBC's use of a media report methodology and WikiLeaks' reliance on U.S. Army field reports can be viewed as most effectively enumerating larger incidents, and thus likely missing many or most individually occurring deaths (Bohannon 2010:575).

Unnecessary Attacks by U.S. Soldiers

There are numerous accounts of unnecessary attacks by U.S. soldiers in the Iraq History Project's Current Violations Initiative (CVI). A particularly disturbing example is the story of Hanisik from 2007 in Kirkuk:

Unfortunately, after a while, the Americans started killing people on the roads and public places like the terrorists ... myself, my husband and my daughter Hanisik were driving to my father-in-law's house which was nearby.... Suddenly, two American Humvees came in front of us. Hanisik loved American soldiers. So, she stood up in the back seat and with her little hands she started waving at the Americans. Sadly, the soldiers' response to her greeting was a ... bullet which hit her small head. I didn't feel a thing. All I saw was the window smash and Hanisik falling off the seat.

I got out of the car and reached for Hanisik. I saw blood pouring out of her forehead. After ten minutes her little heart stopped beating and she died in my arms. Then, one of the American soldiers arrived and said, "Sorry."

... Our relatives put her in a coffin. After a few days we were called by the American soldiers. Then, they didn't say anything other than the word, "sorry." Three more times they called and apologized. However, we were determined to see that American soldier taken to court. All our efforts and pleas were ignored. It was useless. They ignored our complaints.

A deadly incident was persuasively corroborated with documents from WikiLeaks Iraq War Logs. This incident involved civilian killings in Ishaqi, approximately eighty miles northwest of Baghdad and close to Saddam Hussein's town of Tikrit. The first reports of the killings appeared in the Western news media shortly after they occurred in March 2006 (Schofield 2006).

This was about a month after the bombing of the Samara shrine that set off the peak period of violence in Iraq. U.S.-trained Iraqi police in the Joint Coordination Center in Tikrit (set up with American military assistance) reported that American troops had killed in an execution-style manner as many as eleven people (listed by name in the police report), including a seventy-five-year-old woman and a six-month-old infant. The succinct but detailed police report indicated the map coordinates of the killings and that "American forces used helicopters to drop troops on the house of Faiz Harat Khalaf situated in the Abu Sifa village in the Ishaqi district. The American forces gathered the family members in one room and executed 11 people, including 5 children, 4 women and 2 men, then they bombed the house, burned three vehicles and killed animals."

An American military spokesman initially responded to the report by saying he had no information about the killings and that "we're concerned to hear accusations like that, but it's also highly unlikely that they're true" (Schofield 2006). Later, U.S. authorities acknowledged that the raid had occurred in response to a report that a member of AQI was at the home.

Neighbors confirmed that such a person had visited the home and reported that an exchange of gunfire had occurred. U.S. officials added that in the aftermath of the incident they had found one dead and another living al-Qaeda suspect in the rubble of the home. A brother who lived nearby the dead owner of the home said that as they left the area, U.S. troops fired six missiles from helicopters. A local police commander interviewed for the news report said that autopsies at a Tikrit hospital "revealed that all the victims had bullet shots in the head and all bodies were handcuffed," which is consistent with the execution-style description of the killings.

This case was not followed by any public report of a U.S. military investigation other than a public statement that U.S. military personnel "had implemented the correct military procedures" (Adriaensens 2013). Quite a different picture emerged five years later as a result of the WikiLeaks release of cables related to the Iraqi conflict (Schofield 2011b). The release included a communication from Phillip Alston – the United Nation's special rapporteur on extrajudicial, summary, or arbitrary executions – to U.S. authorities, just days after the Ishaqi killings. Alston posed a series of questions based on international humanitarian law and the original Iraqi Police report.

Alston summarized the report by saying that "It would appear that when the MNF [Multinational Force] approached the house, shots were fired from it and a confrontation ensued for some 25 minutes. The MNF troops entered the house, handcuffed all the residents and executed all of them. After the initial MNF intervention, a US air raid ensued that destroyed the house." Alston cited as a possible motivation for the attack a response to the earlier killing of two MNF soldiers in the area, and that an al-Qaida suspect was thought to have stayed in the house. He added that "Other reports indicate that over the past five months, there have been a significant number of lethal incidents in which the MNF is alleged to have used excessive force to respond to perceived threats either at checkpoints or by using air bombing in civilian areas."

Following the WikiLeaks release of the communications in 2011, Philip Alston reported (Schofield 2011b) that many such cables had been sent to U.S. authorities during the peak in Iraqi violence, and that the lack of response from the American military "was the case with most of the letters to the U.S. in the 2006–2007 period." The American military investigation of this incident was disconcerting because it focused so heavily on the success of the "raid" in taking into custody an al-Qaeda suspect. Yet there is evidence that this suspect was actually taken into custody a day before the incident and there is no explanation for why he should have survived the event in which the other family members – including the elderly woman and child – were all reportedly handcuffed and shot at close range – leaving no civilian witnesses to explain how this occurred. The attack on the house with six missiles seems also to have occurred after rather than before or during the killings, destroying physical evidence.

Where this kind of testimonial evidence ends, survey evidence can usefully follow. Survey evidence may not resolve questions of individual guilt, but it can do something perhaps even more useful by testing hypotheses and revealing patterns of events during and after the surge. These events included attacks on civilians and provoked a legal cynicism that is revealed in the analysis in this chapter of perceptions of security, and in the following chapter involving Sunni militancy.

ASSESSING ENDOGENOUS CONFLICT HYPOTHESES

The endogenous conflict theory introduced in this chapter and in the reports on military attacks predicts that Arab Sunni civilians and communities in Baghdad and elsewhere in Iraq will have experienced the greatest impact of the U.S. operations and associated violence during and after the surge. Thus our overarching premise is that attacks in and on Arab Sunni communities during the U.S. surge and afterward had notably distinguishable impacts on the lives of individuals within them. In particular, during the surge:

H_1: Individual Arab Sunnis and predominately Arab Sunni communities will most often have reported unnecessary attacks on civilians by U.S. forces.

Because of increased sensitivity to these tactics of criminal militarism during the surge of U.S./coalition troops:

H_2: Unnecessary attacks on civilians by U.S./coalition forces will have played a salient role compared to other sources of war violence in lowering perceptions of improved security resulting from the U.S. surge operations.

These hypotheses suggest how the surge increased legal cynicism among Arab Sunnis and how a foundation was set during the surge for "a separate peace" that marginalized and disadvantaged Arab Sunni groups in Iraq.

As noted earlier, although himself Shia, Prime Minister Nouri al-Maliki was aware of the political costs of the counterinsurgency's focus on the Sunnis. Al-Maliki created a newly named State of Law coalition in 2008 for his next electoral campaign, which included efforts to mitigate damaged relations with the Sunnis and to attract at least some Arab Sunni support. He temporarily and symbolically capitalized on the overlapping albeit distinct commitments among the Sunnis and Shia to nationalism as well as sectarianism. He attempted to minimize the costs of his involvement in the U.S. targeting of the Arab Sunni insurgency by stressing his government's efforts to quell violence involving *both* Shia and Sunni militias.

Thus in 2008, al-Maliki personally and very visibly entered into the conflict alongside his rebuilt Iraqi Army forces with an offensive aimed at regaining control of Basra from the violent domination of Muqtada al-Sadr's Shia-led Mahdi Army. Against the advice of U.S. military advisors urging caution, al-Maliki rallied a charge into an ensuing battle for Basra by personally joining a helicopter-led assault from Baghdad to Basra with his elite troops.

When the Iraqi Army and U.S./coalition troops regained control of Basra, al-Maliki claimed victory for the "rule of law" and followed with the formation of his "State of Law" campaign coalition. In Kalyvas and Kocher's (2007:184;

see also Haddad 2011) terms, al-Maliki was at least publically projecting the goals of a unified nation-state committed to reducing sectarian fragmentation. Al-Maliki ultimately failed to obtain the scale of electoral victory he sought in this campaign, but in 2008–9 he nonetheless benefited from a rising popularity based on his participation in military victories and intermittent displays of his autonomy from the U.S./coalition forces.

This leads to our second set of hypotheses that despite mainstream American media attention that dismissed the role of al-Maliki and framed the surge as a U.S.-initiated success story:

H_3: Prime Minister al-Maliki was credited especially by Arab Shia Iraqis for his leadership alongside U.S. forces during the surge and for helping to reduce war violence and for setting the foundation for improved security in Iraq.

And:

H_4: As a result of finally achieving reductions in violent victimization, especially in predominately Arab Shia neighborhoods and villages, these Arab Shia communities began to perceive themselves as more secure than other communities in Iraq.

These improvements in perceived security – at least for the Shia – did not immediately end with the peak of the surge in U.S. troops or with the withdrawal of these troops, especially because the latter withdrawal was associated with Muqtada al-Sadr's unilateral ceasefire. The hope of the U.S. surge policy was to create a momentum that would persist after the surge troops were withdrawn, although this interim momentum may have resulted in significant part from al-Sadr's turn away from organized violence.

It is important to recall that the surge came on the heels of the 2006 attack on the Samara shrine and the wave of violence and displacement of the Sunnis described in the previous chapter from many Baghdad neighborhoods by al-Sadr's Mahdi Army (Rosen 2010). During the violence in Baghdad that had led up to the surge, the Mahdi Army had purged thousands of Sunnis from mixed and predominately Sunni neighborhoods. *The surge did not reverse this.*

In important respects, the effect of the surge and its Bremer's Barriers was to consolidate and entrench the resulting Shia domination of Baghdad neighborhoods, helping to change Baghdad into a Shia-controlled city (Allawi 2007; Rosen 2010). However, excesses associated with the advances of Muqtada al-Sadr's Mahdi Army across the neighborhoods of Baghdad eventually took their toll. Al-Sadr lost effective control of his militias and decided to issue his ceasefire. Still, his Shia-led Sadrist movement and its Mahdi Army had changed the sectarian balance in Baghdad. Whether called "The Shia

Revival" (Nasr 2006) or the "Eclipse of the Sunnis" (Amos 2010), the demographic shift to Shia control of Baghdad's neighborhoods was profound.

An endogenous conflict theory suggests that these results were set in motion in Iraq with the U.S.-led elite bargaining that favored the Shia following the invasion and during the occupation. The endogenous form of this theory suggests that the momentum of these effects would continue to increase and intensify. And in the immediate post-surge and post-ceasefire period, the momentum continued in the direction of declining violence, while the sectarian separation of communities also continued, and perceptions of security improved even for some Arab Sunnis. This marked a new period of less violent cleavage and fragmentation (Kalyvas and Kocher 2007:188), which leads to the following hypotheses that:

H_5: Improving perceptions of security will have continued among both the Arab Shia and some Arab Sunnis following the departure of the U.S. surge forces and the Mahdi Army ceasefire.

H_6: The improvement in perceived security will have been linked both to the perceived effects of the surge and to the newly established predominance of the Arab Shia in the separate communities where they lived.

H_7: Individual Arab Sunnis as well as Arab Shia living in predominately Shia communities will have benefited most from gains in the resulting perceived security.

The implication of the last hypothesis is that the benefits in the Shia communities of the separate peace predicted by an endogenous conflict approach extended beyond the Shia themselves to those Sunnis who also lived among the Shia, even though this benefit was proportionally limited by the fact that the better protected communities were now so predominately Shia in composition.

This last prediction of benefits to some Arab Sunnis living in predominately Shia areas is perhaps the least expected hypothesis, and it is significant with regard to ethnic war theory. Kalyvas and Kocher (2007; see also Kalyvas 2006:12) make the point that despite ethnic war assumptions, it is actually not the case that "disloyal" members of ethnic groups will necessarily find themselves targets of reprisals by their former enemies. They argue, consistent with our final hypothesis, that "In fact many people find that they are safer when living under the complete control of their ethnic rivals" (2007:212). This should result in a reduced legal cynicism expressed in improved feelings of security even among Arab Sunnis living in predominately Shia communities. We test this final and perhaps counterintuitive hypothesis in the analysis presented later in this chapter. The implication of this hypothesis is that fragmentation and cooptation can occur simultaneously, a contingency not anticipated in ethnic war theory and policies.

SURVEYING IRAQ DURING AND AFTER THE SURGE

We use a unique data set gathered within neighborhood communities as well as among individuals from the different sectarian groups of Iraq to test these endogenous conflict hypotheses. A consortium of international news organizations contracted with a survey organization in Istanbul to conduct four cross-sectional population surveys in Iraq from 2007 through 2009 – a period lasting from the beginning of the surge to seven months after its completion. The survey used sampling points in communities distributed proportionate to population in all 102 districts of all eighteen Iraq provinces.[4] Interviewers administered surveys in 62 percent of the households they contacted, in person and in Arabic or Kurdish. The two surveys analyzed in greatest detail in this chapter respectively include 2,186 and 2,213 respondents from within 452 and 443 sampling points that are nationally representative of Iraq.

Figure 5.1 displays the timing of all four Iraq surveys (totaling nearly 9,000 interviews) from the beginning of the surge of U.S. forces in February 2007, through the drawdown of the surge forces beginning in August 2007, to the completion of the drawdown in July 2008, and with the final survey completed seven months later in February 2009. The horizontal lines on Figure 5.1 summarize reports in the four surveys of war violence, approval of U.S. forces and Prime Minister Nouri al-Maliki, community separation of Sunni and Shia groups, and perceptions of security. There is little variation in these five factors in the first two surveys, which is why after reviewing Figure 5.1, we focus in the remainder of this chapter on the last two surveys.[5]

We initially see in Figure 5.1 that in the first pair of surveys about half (55.3% to 58.7%) of the communities were described as either completely Shia or completely Sunni. Individual reports of war violence remained at about two and a half (2.49 to 2.57) on an eight-point scale that included reports of nearby bombing, sniping, sectarian attacks, kidnappings, and unnecessary attacks on civilians by U.S./coalition forces, Iraqi Army, Iraq Police, or local militia.

Perceived neighborhood and family security remained just over five (5.55 to 5.14) on a thirteen-point scale.[6] Finally, approval of U.S./coalition forces declined by about 5 percent (from 23.4% to 18.9%), while approval of Prime Minister al-Maliki was nearly two times higher but decreased by about 10 percent (42.9% to 32.7%).

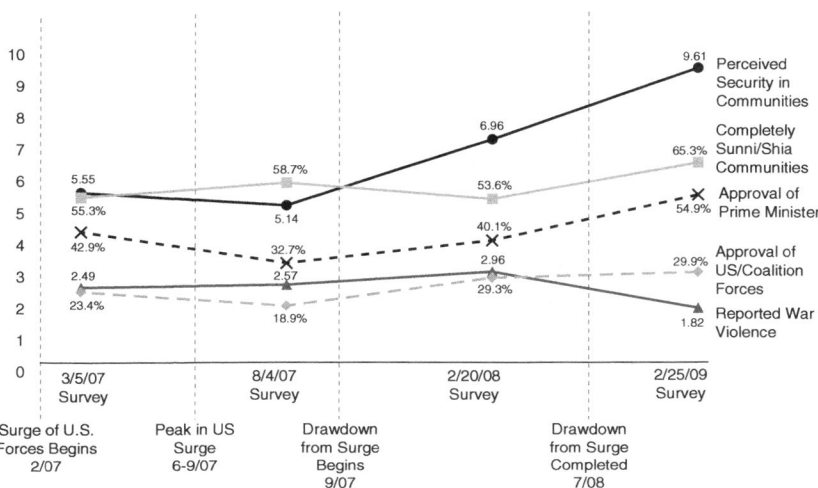

FIGURE 5.1. Reported War Violence, Sectarian Separation, and Perceived Security in Four Iraq Surveys, circa 2007–2009

So during the buildup and soon after the surge peak, according to Figure 5.1, these reports of community composition, war violence, perceived security, and approval of U.S. forces and al-Maliki stayed relatively constant or declined. Recall that the surge began several months after the escalation of war violence reported in the previous chapter and the community displacement that followed the February 2006 Samara shrine attack. As we have reported, in 2006 and the first half of 2007, Shia and Sunni militias across Iraq purged and separated communities, with Muqtada al-Sadr's Shia-based Mahdi Army seizing control of the majority of neighborhood communities in Baghdad. The initial pair of 2007 survey results in Figure 5.1 showing about half the communities in Iraq as being either predominately Sunni or Shia are consistent with the view that the buildup and peak of the surge coincided with a consolidation rather than a reduction or reversal of the sectarian separation of Sunni and Shia. Al-Sadr declared his unilateral ceasefire at the end of August 2007 and a drawdown in surge troops began the following month.

Reports of perceived security notably changed in the next two Iraqi surveys conducted *after* the drawdown from the surge began. About six months after al-Sadr declared his ceasefire, in the February 2008 Iraqi survey, the average score on the thirteen-point perceived security scale increased from about five to seven (5.14 to 6.96). On the other hand, reported war violence actually increased (from 2.57 to 2.96), and community separation remained about the same, with about half of the respondents still reporting their areas as being completely Shia or Sunni (from 58.7% to 53.6%).

In the fourth February 2009 Iraqi survey, the clearest signs of change emerged. Reported war violence dropped from about three to two (2.96 to 1.88), the proportion of completely Sunni and completely Shia communities jumped from about half to nearly two-thirds (53.6% to 65.3%), and perceived security continued its increase from about seven to over nine and a half (6.96 to 9.59) on the thirteen-point scale. The score on this security scale had now nearly doubled (from 5.14). While approval of the U.S./coalition forces remained constant (29.3% and 29.9%), approval of Maliki jumped into surprisingly positive territory (from 40.1% to 54.9%). So the third and especially the fourth surveys revealed change, and the remainder of this chapter therefore focuses on outcomes in these two later surveys during and after the surge.

PRELIMINARY FINDINGS ABOUT WAR VIOLENCE AND ATTACKS ON CIVILIANS

Our hypotheses included predictions about ethno-sectarian differences in reports of war violence and perceived security that we analyzed at individual and community levels,[7] with the sectarian identities of the communities measured for comparative purposes in terms of Shia predominance.[8]

We first examined respondents' specific reports of unnecessary violence against civilians in their communities by U.S./coalition forces. Almost half (46%) of respondents reported unnecessary U.S. violence against civilians during the latter part of the surge, while about a quarter (26%) reported this after withdrawal of the surge troops. This difference is evidence of the offensive aspect of the surge, and we have hypothesized that unnecessary violence against civilians by U.S./coalition forces is most likely to have been associated with U.S. targeting of Sunni insurgents and al-Qaeda. These reports of unnecessary attacks are likely sources of negative Iraqi perceptions of the surge.

Most Iraqi respondents did not view the effects of the increase in U.S./coalition forces during the surge as favorably affecting their security and were in this sense legally cynical.[9] When asked about areas where surge forces were sent, over half (53.1%) thought that security was worsened; when asked about other areas in Iraq, nearly half (48.7%) thought security was worsened; and in Iraq overall, more than 60 percent (61.2%) thought the U.S. troop surge made security worse. Respondents were only asked to indicate the effect of the Awakening councils in the areas where they were created. In these areas, about half the respondents thought their effect was to make security better (50.3%), versus about half concluding no effect (30.9%) or that security was worsened (16.1%). So the Awakening councils were perhaps better received than the surge forces, but neither was viewed particularly positively.

We focus here on the reports of unnecessary U.S./coalition attacks on civilians during the latter part of the surge, in March 2008, while we give more attention to these attacks at the peak of the surge in the following chapter. As we noted earlier, unnecessary attacks on civilians are war crimes and nearly half of Iraqi respondents reported in early 2008 that such attacks occurred in their neighborhoods. This indicates a prevalent perception that these unnecessary U.S. attacks on civilians occurred across a wide swath of Iraq. Similar proportions of respondents also reported nearby bombings (43%), kidnappings (49%), Iraqi militia attacks (39%), sectarian attacks (38%), and sniping and crossfire (37%), while somewhat fewer reported unnecessary attacks by Iraqi police (22%) and Army (22%).

We next briefly summarize prediction models (Table 5.2 in the Appendix) that we estimated for the purpose of seeing in relative terms how influential other forms of violence (and other variables) were in explaining the attacks on civilians by U.S. forces during the surge. Reports of nearby bombings significantly increased reports of unnecessary U.S./coalition attacks. This is consistent with some of these bombs being directed at the U.S./coalition troops. It is also consistent with the suggestion that the Ishaqi killings and other U.S. attacks on civilians were in response to suspected civilian complicity in nearby and recent deaths of U.S. soldiers associated with explosive devices.

Reports of unnecessary Iraqi Army and Police attacks on civilians also were associated with the reports of unnecessary U.S./coalition attacks – and may have occurred alongside them. Kurds were significantly less likely to report unnecessary U.S./coalition attacks. Perhaps most importantly, as predicted in Hypothesis 1, individual Sunni respondents were more likely to report unnecessary U.S./coalition attacks. By this logic, Arab Sunnis had reason to feel legally cynical about the surge. Individual Shia also disproportionately reported these unnecessary attacks; this probably was a result of al-Maliki allowing attacks on al-Sadr's Shia militia in Baghdad in 2008, as we further discuss later.

At the community level, as also predicted in Hypothesis 1, unnecessary U.S./ coalition attacks were significantly more likely to occur in predominately Sunni than predominately Shia areas. So even though individual Shia as well as Sunni respondents often reported these sources of violence, overall, these effects were reported more often in predominately Sunni than predominately Shia communities. As indicated, this supports our first hypothesis of greater impact of U.S./coalition attacks on the Sunnis than on the Shia during the surge. This differential impact on the Sunnis and its link to legal cynicism is a major focus of the following chapter.

The specific community locations of respondents in several areas of high conflict in Iraq also mattered. As suggested earlier, respondents in Sadr City also reported more unnecessary U.S. attacks on civilians. Sadr City is virtually completely Shia, and as we noted earlier, in the later stages of the surge Prime Minister al-Maliki finally allowed U.S. forces to target Shia militias in this part of Baghdad. Holding constant in our models this limited targeting of al-Sadr's Shia militia revealed how concentrated the reports were of unnecessary U.S. attacks on Sunni civilians.

We also examined the relative impact of the eight different sources of nearby war violence on perceptions of security specifically resulting from the U.S. surge (see Appendix Table 5.3). As predicted in Hypothesis 2, reports of nearby unnecessary attacks of U.S. forces on civilians– more than any other measured source of war violence – reduced feelings of measured security associated with the U.S. surge. With the added sources of war violence and other variables taken into account, the unnecessary U.S./coalition attacks decreased scores by about three-quarters of a point on the six-point surge security scale. Sectarian attacks were the next most influential source of violence in decreasing perceived security. Unnecessary attacks by the Iraqi Army, bombing, and sniping and crossfire also significantly decreased scores on the surge security scale. Our analysis further revealed that taking into account the apparent targeting of the Sunnis for unnecessary attacks – which was predicted in Hypothesis 1 – notably decreased the degree to which the surge was associated with perceived security.[10] The reported unnecessary attacks on Sunni civilians and their effect on support for the Sunni insurgency are more fully explored in Chapter 6.

THE SEPARATE PEACE AND APPROVAL OF MALIKI

We turned next to the approval predicted by Hypothesis 3 during and after the surge of the role of Prime Minister al-Maliki in the Iraqi War. The data make clear that approval of al-Maliki was predictably strong among his fellow Shia respondents, although not in Sadr City, where Muqtada al-Sadr's influence over Shia Sadrists prevailed. We further used these data to simultaneously examine the effects of the location of respondents in predominately Shia versus predominately Sunni communities along with their own sectarian identities as Shia and Sunni. This allowed us to observe where and by whom al-Maliki was experiencing heightened approval during and after the surge (see Appendix Table 5.4).[11]

Figures 5.2a and 5.2b summarize the results of this part of the analysis. In Figure 5.2a, we predictably see greater approval of al-Maliki during the surge

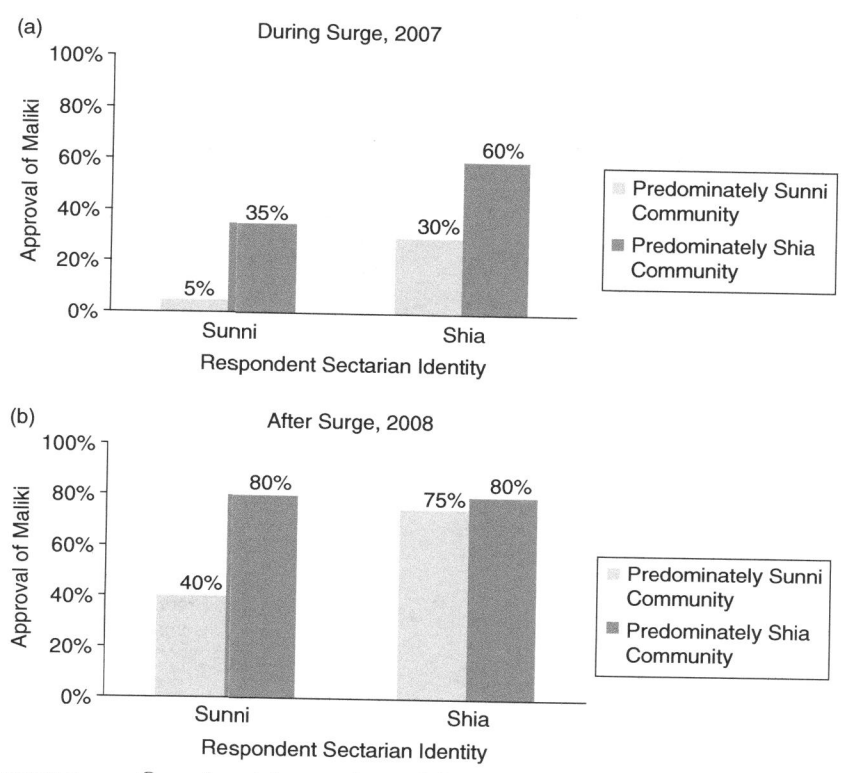

FIGURE 5.2. Cross-Level Interactions of Sectarian Community Predominance and Respondent Sectarian Identity on Approval of Prime Minister al-Maliki

among both Sunnis (35% compared to 5%) and Shia (60% compared to 30%) respondents who were living in Shia-dominated communities. More interestingly, Figure 5.2b displays – after the surge troops departed from Iraq – very high approval (75–80%) of al-Maliki among Shia who were living in *both* predominately Sunni *and* predominately Shia neighborhoods. Approval of al-Maliki even among Sunni respondents who lived in predominately Sunni neighborhoods reached 40 percent after the surge troops left, while this approval after the surge troops left reached 80 percent among Sunnis who were living in predominately Shia neighborhoods.

Of course, the overwhelming majority of Sunnis lived in predominately Sunni neighborhoods, and the majority (i.e., 60%) of these Sunni respondents still did not approve of al-Maliki. Even at this perhaps peak moment of al-Maliki's approval in Iraq, when legal cynicism about his government was at its low point, this disparity in approval – 40 percent approval in predominately

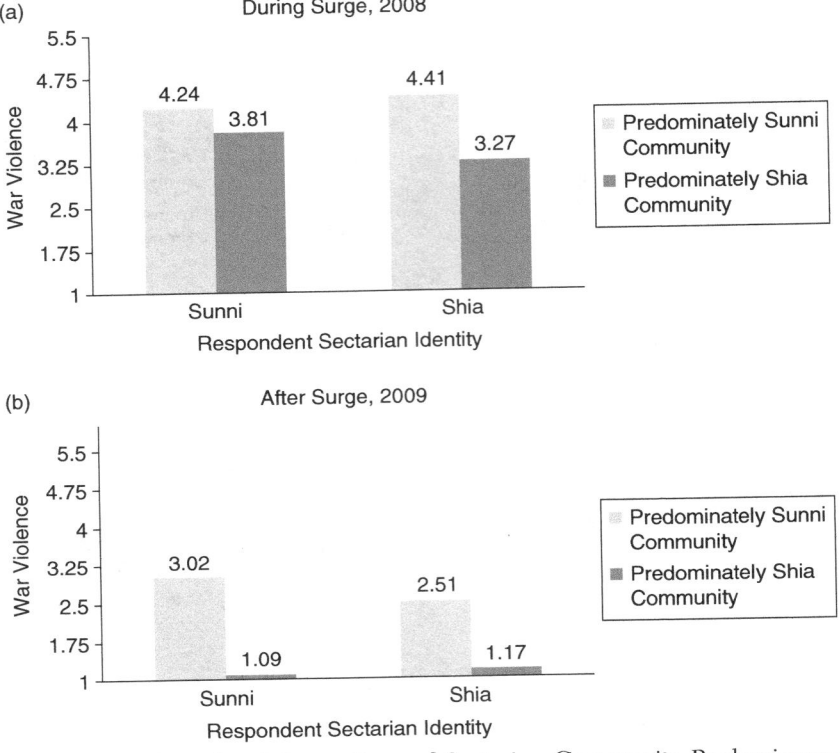

FIGURE 5.3. Cross-Level Interactions of Sectarian Community Predominance and Respondent Sectarian Identity on War Violence during and after the Surge

Sunni versus 80 percent in predominately Shia neighborhoods – is suggestive of the level of legal cynicism among the Sunnis and the separate kind of peace achieved among the Shia during and after the surge.

We turn next to an analysis of the war violence during and after the surge, which we measured as a sum of the eight separate sources of this violence considered earlier (see Appendix Table 5.5). As predicted in Hypothesis 3, we found that approval of the apparent role of Prime Minister al-Maliki in reducing war violence was significant and about equal in strength to approval of the role of the U.S./coalition forces.

Figures 5.3a and 5.3b display further information about the individuals and communities reporting reductions in war violence. During the surge, Shia respondents reported significantly less war violence (3.27 compared to 4.41) as a result of living in predominately Shia communities, while Sunni respondents reported slightly less war violence when they lived in predominately Shia communities (3.81 compared to 4.24). After the surge, both Sunni (1.09 compared to 3.02) and Shia (1.17 compared to 2.51) respondents reported lower war violence if they lived in predominately Shia communities. Overall, these results are consistent with Hypothesis 4 in that they show the greater reductions in exposure to war violence for those living in predominately Shia communities.

Finally, we consider the respondents' reported feelings of security during and after the surge (see Appendix Table 5.6). The results augment previous support for Hypothesis 3 by uniformly confirming that respondents' approval of al-Maliki was more strongly associated with perceptions of increased security than was approval of the U.S./coalition troops. This is consistent with feelings of legal cynicism about the latter forces. The results also strongly support Hypothesis 4 that after the surge – although not as clearly as during the surge – reductions in war violence were highly significant in predominately Shia communities in improving perceptions of security.[12]

As anticipated in Hypothesis 6, this part of our analysis also confirmed that the association between perceiving that the surge and the Awakening improved security significantly impacted overall perceptions of security. However, in these analyses, the Awakening coefficients were persistently negative. This implies that perceived security was still lowest where respondents perceived improvement resulting from Sunni Awakening involvement. Because promises by al-Maliki's Iraqi government about the continuation of compensation and integration of the Sunni Awakening forces into the Iraqi defense and security forces – about which there was always legal uncertainty and cynicism – were never fulfilled, the negative Awakening findings were both ominous and yet simultaneously unsurprising.

We can again compare the effects of living in predominately Shia and predominately Sunni communities. Comparison of the paired bars during and after the surge in Figures 5.4a and 5.4b confirm the prediction of Hypothesis 5 of overall improvement in security after the surge troops departed. In each case, the improvement in security between the period of the surge and after the surge troops left is from two to three points on the thirteen-point security scale. Thus, as predicted in Hypothesis 5, after the surge troops left, both Sunni and Shia respondents reported improved feelings of security.

Furthermore, as predicted in Hypothesis 6, both during the surge and after the surge troops left, living in a predominately Shia community yielded the highest security scores for Shia respondents. Shia respondents living in predominately Shia communities after the surge scored an average of 11.08 on the thirteen-point perceived security scale.

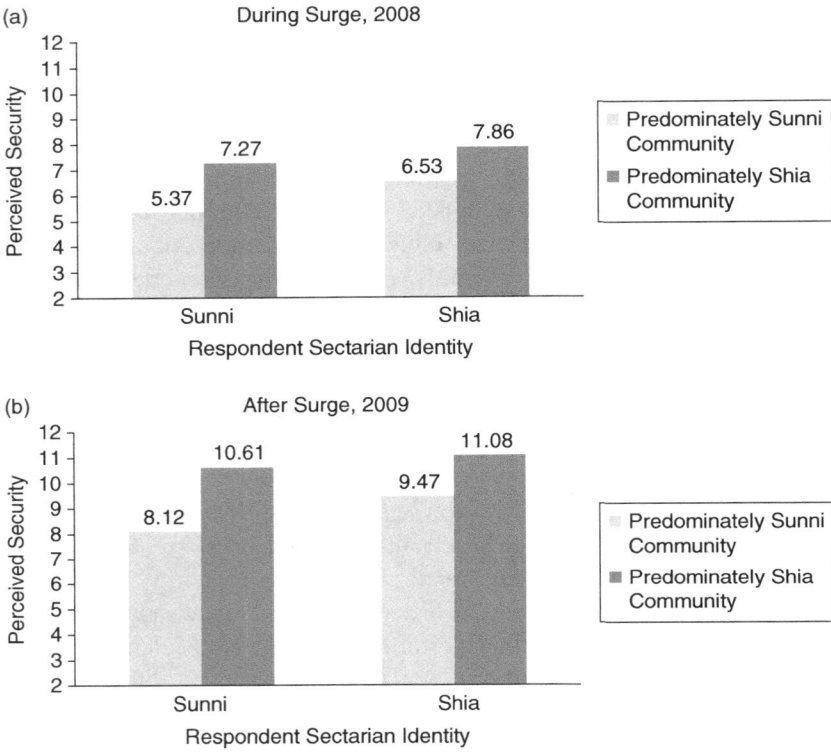

FIGURE 5.4. Cross-Level Interaction of Sectarian Community Predominance and Respondent Sectarian Identity on Perceived Security during and after the Surge

We highlighted Hypothesis 7 as making the most interesting predictions anticipated by Kalyvas and Kocher, namely, that both the Sunni and Shia respondents would report higher perceived security if they lived in predominately Shia communities. Figures 5.4a and 4.5b confirm this. During the surge, Sunni respondents' scores rose from 5.37 to 7.27 when they lived in predominately Shia communities, and after the surge troops had left their scores increased from 8.12 to 10.61. During the surge, Shia respondents' scores rose from 6.53 to 7.86, and after the surge troops had left their scores increased from 9.47 to 11.08. Of course, as noted before, Sunnis overwhelmingly live in predominately Sunni communities, while Shia overwhelmingly live in predominately Shia communities. As of 2009, the Shia clearly benefited the most from the post-invasion sectarian separation, or what we have called the separate peace.

SURGE AND SEPARATION

Iraq is a moving target for explanation that is buffeted by strong currents of external and internal change and that defies easy understanding, for example, with simplified ideas about deeply and inalterably opposed ethno-sectarian groups. From the Balkans, through Sudan and Darfur, to Iraq, a dominant view in U.S. policy circles has been that unchanging and irreconcilable differences between ethnic groups can sufficiently explain sectarian violence in conflict zones. The assumption of unchanging irreconcilable differences has motivated aspects of policy proposals as different as the military surge and the national partition of Iraq.

We have argued that the surge policy ultimately adopted in Iraq influenced the form and scale of sectarian conflict, as did the realignment of the elite political leadership of this country. At the very least, following Kalyvas, we have argued that the static and simplistic assumptions of an exogenously driven ethnic war theory must be modified and expanded to take into account the contingencies of endogenous change that have dynamically influenced sectarian conflict in Iraq, and by implication, elsewhere. Conflicts are not simply caused by historically enduring ethnic differences.

In place of an ethnic war theory, in this chapter we have proposed and tested hypotheses from an endogenous conflict perspective using survey data collected from 2007 to 2009 in Iraq – a period that included the surge and subsequent withdrawal of surge troops. We began with the overarching premise that disproportionate attacks in and on Sunni communities have had important impacts on the lives of individuals within them. We have found that unnecessary attacks by U.S./coalition troops on civilians were disproportionately reported by both Sunni and Shia individuals, but that they were most often reported in predominately Sunni communities. The notable exceptions seem to have involved the attacks of U.S./coalition forces on Shia militia in Sadr City. Thus the probability-based, representative survey data we have analyzed reveal widespread reports of violent and unnecessary U.S./coalition attacks on civilians, indicating ongoing patterns of criminal militarism. Moreover, the patterns we observed parallel reports from the Iraq History Current Violations Interviews, the military investigation of the Haditha killings, and the WikiLeaks Iraq War Log documents that include reports of killings by the Iraq police.

Unnecessary U.S. attacks of this kind directed at Arab Sunni individuals and communities were sources of legal cynicism among the Arab Sunnis. We further found that these reported attacks resulted in lowered perceptions of security attributed to U.S. surge operations, which were signals of Arab Sunni feelings of legal cynicism. These findings are consistent with the focus of an endogenous conflict perspective on the effects of interventions by outside states, and they further help to explain why the surge was relatively unpopular in Iraq, especially among the Arab Sunnis, despite beliefs of many American politicians about the success of this policy. These findings also begin to explain how the U.S. surge marginalized and disadvantaged Arab Sunni groups, likely increasing Sunnis' feelings of legal cynicism and setting the foundation for what we have called a separate peace – which proved not to be the hoped for lasting peace.

However, an endogenous conflict perspective does not simply focus on external state intervention. It also is concerned with domestic political leadership, and in the case of Iraq, with a leadership that was selectively installed by the U.S.-led coalition and that favored formerly exiled and elite Shia opposition figures. Nouri al-Maliki emerged out of this U.S.-led process as a multiple-term prime minister. In this role, he proved another source of endogenous influence on the unfolding sectarian conflict in Iraq.

Al-Maliki channeled and facilitated the U.S. concentration of offensive operations against Arab Sunni–based opponents, while he also for a time deflected legal cynicism among the Arab Sunnis for these operations by creating a newly named State of Law coalition with Arab Sunni and Kurdish representation in addition to the Shia. He strategically mounted electoral campaigns designed to mitigate the legal cynicism and political opposition emanating from the reversal of fortune suffered by the Sunnis following the defeat of Saddam Hussein's Sunni-dominated Ba'athist regime.

In Kalyvas and Kocher's (2007:184) terms, during this period al-Maliki was projecting the goals of a unified state and attempting to counteract the effects of state fragmentation in Iraq. At the time of the 2008–9 surveys we analyzed for this chapter, al-Maliki proved surprisingly adept in these efforts. For example, we found that Prime Minister al-Maliki for a time was credited by Iraqis for his leadership in reducing war violence alongside U.S. forces, as well as with improving perceptions of security involving war violence. Perceptions of security continued to improve among both the Arab Sunnis and Shia during 2008 and 2009, and favorable outcomes were especially evident for the Shia in the period immediately following the departure of surge troops.

While we found overall that the Shia benefited more than the Arab Sunnis from the reductions in violence and increased perceptions of security, we also found that both individual Arab Sunnis and Shia living in predominately Shia communities benefited from the new perceived security. This is a surprising outcome anticipated in the work of Kalyvas, and it notably complicates the sweeping premises of ethnic war theory. The implication is that the benefits in the Shia communities of the separate peace predicted by an endogenous con-flict perspective extended beyond the Shia to include some Arab Sunnis who lived among the Shia. Of course, we have also emphasized that the latter ben-efit was proportionally small and limited by the fact that the better protected communities in 2008–9 were now overwhelmingly Shia in composition – with most Arab Sunnis continuing to live in predominately Arab Sunni communi-ties where feelings of insecurity were significantly higher.

Thus, we have used an endogenous conflict perspective to predict a sepa-rate peace that in 2008–9 brought improvements for both the Arab Sunnis and Shia, but markedly greater benefits for the Shia. The nationally representative Iraq data we have analyzed from 2007 through 2009 are consistent with these predictions. Approval of the al-Maliki government noticeably grew between 2008 and 2009, and peaked in 2009. Yet even then there remained substantial differences, with the Arab Sunnis living in predominately Arab Sunni com-munities still least likely to approve of al-Maliki's governance. The disparities predicted by an endogenous conflict perspective and the findings we have reported therefore anticipated continued legal cynicism and instability in the separate peace observed for an interim period.

After the invasion and during the subsequent occupation, the U.S.-led Coalition Provisional Authority disbanded the military and security forces and purged the Ba'athists from government agencies. A replacement army and national police force were enlisted and trained under the supervision of the U.S. military. It was perhaps predictable going forward, then, that the new Iraqi Army and Police could be used to suppress Sunni citizens who contin-ued to protest and challenge disparities and imbalances between the Shia and Sunnis. When Sunni protesters mobilized peaceful demonstrations in 2012, they were met with a brutal military and police crackdown rather than nego-tiations or reforms. The result was a resurgence of legal cynicism in Sunni communities that reignited and further inflamed the sectarian conflict.

The Sunni-led uprising in Syria, just across the border from Iraq's Sunni-populated Anbar province, from the outset was perceived by the al-Maliki government as a threatening source of encouragement for a renewed Arab Sunni insurgency against the Shia-dominated central government. Already, in 2007, noted historian of Iraq Charles Tripp was writing that "there is a strong possibility that newly won privileges will be entrenched and Iraqis will have good reason to fear subjection once more to a regime that equates power with force and dissent with treason" (2010:322). The al-Maliki-led and Shia-dominated Iraqi government followed the American example of preemp-tion and concentrated the use of force by its security forces against Arab Sunni dissent (Dodge 2013).

The Shia and Arab Sunni communities have come to occupy separate and unequal places in Iraqi society that are the mirror image of the era of Saddam Hussein. The Shia are now markedly more advantaged and secure and the Arab Sunnis less advantaged and more insecure. The separate peace we have identified in Iraq as advantaging the Shia was imperiled from the outset by the prospect of mounting legal cynicism reflected in reports by the Arab Sunnis of their greater vulnerability to violence and insecurity, even during a period of relative peace.

Baghdad's Sunni Adhamiya community and the Shia Kadhimiya district provided a stark portrayal in 2014 of the aftermath of the 2003 U.S.-led invasion that exploded into violence in 2006 and 2007, temporarily gave way to a transitory separate peace from 2008 through 2011, and then entered a newly violent phase after the 2014 fall of Mosul. Adhamiya and Kadhimiya are joined by the al-Imans Bridge across the Tigris River and in better times residents walked peacefully through one another's neighborhoods to their separate places of work and worship. The bonds of trust that made this possible are now all but forgotten. Although Shia Kadhimiya eagerly expanded with its new government-nurtured advantages and protection, it is fearful of the renewed threat of potential violence resulting from the disadvantage that is the new reality in the now disenfranchised Sunni Adhamiya. What was lost by 2014 was perhaps most vividly on display during the breaking of the Ramadan holiday fasts that were once harmoniously celebrated with an intermingled casualness that hopefully but too briefly imagined the possibilities of a much more peaceful Iraq. "Now we have two Ramadans," a regretful resident of Sunni Adhamiya recently observed (Rubin 2014).

The challenge is to recognize the deeper roots of this despondency and the resulting militancy that were too optimistically concealed and ignored during the separate and transitory post-surge peace in Iraq. The persistent vulnerability and renewed Sunni militancy and insurgency are the subjects of our final chapter.

6

Legal Cynicism and Sunni Militancy

THE END OF AN INTERLUDE

A 2012 wave of protests and government crackdowns concentrated in Sunni areas of central and northern Iraq signaled the end of a peaceful period and the outbreak of new hostilities between the Shia-dominated government of Nouri al-Maliki and a Sunni insurgency that had challenged the U.S./coalition forces from 2003 through 2008. The December 2012 protests flared in Dignity Square of Fallujah after a raid on the home and the arrest of a popular Sunni federal finance minister, Rafi al-Issawi. The protests spread rapidly across the Sunni heartland.

In April 2013, the Iraqi Army stormed a protest camp in Hawija, killing 50 people and injuring 110. In December 2013, the Iraqi Army and Police in Ramadi killed more than a dozen among hundreds of protestors against government violence. The Ramadi protest had been ongoing for a year and leaders of major Sunni tribal groups – the Jumaila, Dulaim, and Mahamda – were centrally involved. Al-Maliki alleged al-Qaeda terrorists were responsible, but tribal leaders were in charge and challenged al-Maliki by calling for his resignation. The brutal assault by the army and the police included scores of Humvees, pickup trucks, and armored vehicles. Subsequent insurgent and counterinsurgent violence escalated to the highest levels since 2008.

The renewed conflict was evidence of a resilient Arab Sunni insurgency with its roots in the U.S. invasion and occupation. Although many insurgents previously had joined the Sunni Awakening movement, Cordesman and Khazai (2014:233) now reported, some factions had realigned with al-Qaeda in Iraq while others had reestablished themselves as independent Sunni militias with few ties or loyalty to the Shia-dominated central government.

By 2013, the war in Syria had raised the stakes and complexity of the situation (Alani 2014). Long-standing cross-border ties between groups of Syrian

and Iraqi Sunnis took on increased significance. Arab Sunnis in both countries were linked in their opposition to their respective Shia-dominated governments led by al-Assad and al-Maliki, with their overt and covert ties to
Iran. An important cross-border al-Qaeda alliance emerged in the form of the
newly named Islamic State of Iraq and Syria (ISIS), later calling itself simply
the Islamic State (IS). However, ties of this group to al-Qaeda "central" were
contentious and soon formally and very publicly severed.

This chapter addresses questions of how and why in this context a violent
Sunni insurgency reemerged. Following the recent outbreak of insurgent violence, experienced *New York Times* journalist Tim Arango (2013) speculated
that the worsening situation was a response to the antiterrorism tactics initiated by the U.S.-led occupation and counterinsurgency. The Shia-dominated
government of Nouri al-Maliki was even heavier handed in its use of these
tactics, and the U.S. government was either unwilling or unable to temper
their widespread and indiscriminant use against the Sunni insurgency. This
chapter assesses the capacity of a theory of legal cynicism that is focused on
such tactics to explain continued support for the militancy of an Arab Sunni
resistance and insurgency that tentatively allied itself with the Islamic State.

We ask in this chapter whether a theory previously used to understand
American street crime can explain widespread and systematic social support
for insurgent acts of collective violence in an international war zone. We
argue that the answer is yes, in part because these insurgent acts are characteristically treated by sovereign governments and occupying powers as terrorist
crimes. We argue that an elaborated theory of legal cynicism can play a key
role in accounting for the collective foundation of Sunni militancy and the
acceptance of insurgent acts of sectarian violence in Iraq.

The concept of legal cynicism has recently been applied to a wide range
of problems, from homicide (Kirk and Papachristos 2011) and bias in police
arrests (Carr, Napolitano, and Keating 2007; Kirk and Matsuda 2011) to teen
births (Sampson 2012:228–9). As noted in the Prologue, legal cynicism is a
concept Sampson and Bartusch (1998:782) introduced to refer to a state of
normlessness in which rules or laws are nonbinding. Similarly, we defined
criminal militarism as an anomic cultural framework or orientation in which
laws of war are often ignored.

Kirk and Papachristos extended the meaning of legal cynicism to include
a cultural frame or orientation in which law is viewed as illegitimate, unresponsive, and ineffectual in providing security – that is, "ill equipped to ensure
public safety" (2011:1191). Legal cynicism therefore involves illegitimate acts
of governments, elites, and their authorized agents that produce perceptions
of injustice and feelings of insecurity among nonelite and often specifically

targeted populations – such as the Arab Sunnis during the U.S.-led Iraq War (see also Hagan and Albonetti 1982; Hagan, Shedd, and Payne 2005; Ivkovic and Hagan 2006). These are what we have called the double and linked macro- and micro-level sources and manifestations of legal cynicism. The manifestations of legal cynicism thus subsume the feelings of insecurity that we considered with the measurement scale used in the preceding chapter, and these insecurities are linked to the governing policies of elites, in this case U.S. and Shia political and military elites.

Of course, the legal cynicism of the Sunnis did not rise fully formed and as an instant response to the U.S.-led occupation. It changed and evolved over time. Previous chapters have focused on a rough chronology tracking the consequences of the invasion and occupation. The challenge is to document and explain the process through which legal cynicism about U.S. criminal militarism in Iraq led to a corresponding legal cynicism – in the eyes especially of its Sunni targets – foretelling a trail of consequences and a *post bellum* "accumulation" that is a crucial outcome of the crimes of this aggressive war.

In this chapter, we focus on the way criminal militarism was individually and collectively experienced by Sunni civilians during the peak of the 2007 surge of U.S./coalition forces in Iraq. We specifically operationalize criminal militarism in terms of the reported unnecessary attacks of U.S./coalition forces on civilians we considered in the previous chapter. We further analyze legal cynicism individually and collectively in terms of several key measures of the perceived illegitimacy, unresponsiveness, and ineffectiveness of U.S./coalition forces and the Iraqi Army and police in protecting citizens from war violence. We then explore individual and collective links between civilian reports of U.S./coalition attacks and other forms of war violence, the indicators of legal cynicism, and social support for attacks against U.S./coalition forces. The latter attacks on U.S./coalition forces were core components of the insurgency in Iraq until these forces finally left the country in 2011.

A final part of our analysis considers whether the subsequently renewed insurgent attacks on Iraqi Army and Police forces may be the individual and collective product of the transference of legal cynicism from the U.S./coalition presence in Iraq to the Iraqi government and its national military and security police forces. We find evidence of this transference that is linked in particular to unnecessary attacks by the latter national security police. The origins of this problem date at least to the period leading up to the 2007 surge and Sunni Awakening when the data analyzed in this chapter were collected. We focused extensively on the surge in the previous chapter. In this chapter, we begin by considering the role of the Sunni Awakening.

QUESTIONS ABOUT THE SUNNI AWAKENING

In 2007, the U.S. military believed that the U.S. surge of forces successfully joined with the Sunni Awakening movement to bring the conflict in Iraq under control. However, we argue in this chapter that this view of the Awakening movement, as well as the surge that we questioned in the previous chapter, was overly optimistic. We begin by reanalyzing work of an influential research team led by Steven Biddle. Biddle is a widely known military analyst and is authoritatively cited as a key participant in a conclusive Oval Office meeting with President Bush leading up to the surge (Gordon and Trainor 2012:302; Kaplan 2013:237–8). He was a consistent advocate of the surge and the Awakening movement, arguing that they had a combined "synergistic" effect in bringing violence under control in Iraq (Biddle et al. 2012).

An interesting aspect of Biddle and colleagues' analysis is its observation that as early as 2004, Arab Sunni groups had repeatedly sought and failed to link up with the U.S./coalition forces in fighting al-Qaeda in Iraq. These Sunni groups included the Albu Nimr tribe in 2004, the Albu Mahal group early in 2005, and the Anbar People's Council and former members of the 1920 Revolution Brigades later in 2005. Biddle, Friedman, and Shapiro (2012) argue that these initiatives all failed because the U.S./coalition forces were not yet willing to provide necessary support and protection to these groups.

The Sahwa militia or Sunni Awakening – also variously known as the Anbar Awakening and the Sons of Iraq (SOI) – finally found a supportive U.S. ally in 2006, and fully mobilized alongside the surge in 2007. As many as 100,000 Sunni joined the Awakening effort during this period. Perhaps the best known of the Awakening leaders was Abdul Sattar Abu Risha, who is assumed to have been killed by an al-Qaeda assassin in the fall of 2007, just as the peak in violence in Iraq was beginning to subside.

The recruitment and tentative alliance of the Awakening forces was effectively motivated by the U.S. government's decision to pay individual Sunni fighters $300 a month, and more than a total of $30 million per month in the peak period of this program. One part of the plan was to take advantage of a rivalry between local tribal leaders and al-Qaeda in Iraq forces. The al-Qaeda-aligned portion of the insurgency had earned a reputation for excess in its use of extreme violence – both to provoke sectarian conflict and to enforce loyalty from local Sunni communities and fighters. ISIS, which later largely supplanted al-Qaeda in Iraq, similarly used extreme and retributive violence against other Arab Sunni groups, although it also sometimes strategically suppressed this tendency to broaden Sunni support and join forces against al-Maliki's Shia-dominated government.

In the lead-up to the Awakening and following the departure of U.S. combat forces from Iraq, it is important to note, the roles of AQI and ISIS were often difficult to separate from other Sunni-based groups. The earlier role of AQI, and subsequently ISIS, may sometimes have been exaggerated in the U.S. media. For example, in the early 2014 takeover of Fallujah, a Sunni military council was primarily formed by tribal leaders rather than ISIS, and various Sunni groups were allied to uncertain and differing degrees with ISIS in fighting the central government forces, including the Islamic Army, Hamas Iraq, the Mujahadeem Army, the Naqshibandi, Falluja Battalions, and the 1920 Revolution Brigades. The Sunni insurgency is a heterogeneous entity with extensive local tribal underpinnings. However, as 2014 unfolded, ISIS forces grew and took control of border crossings with Syria and one of Iraq's largest cities, Mosul, as well as other smaller communities and sites across central and northern Iraq.

Given the earlier failures of American-led alliances with the Sunni tribal groups to effectively materialize, it is reasonable to ask how strong the bond was between the Sunni Awakening and U.S. forces, and how impactful it might have been. Our hypothesis is that the bond was variable and that the impact was overestimated. We argue that the U.S. forces may primarily have been buying time, hoping that paying the Sunni militia would at least temporarily result in them stopping their attacks on U.S. forces, if not retaking control of areas from more extreme and less cooperative insurgent groups, possibly linked to AQI and ISIS. The goal of the U.S. forces seemed to be to reduce violence enough to comfortably leave Iraq.

This Awakening strategy assumed that the previously insurgent and now cooperating Sunni groups – who often had previously attacked U.S. forces – were the "good guys" and that their rivals were the "bad guys." One of the key claims of the U.S. forces was that the Awakening groups were crucial sources of human intelligence about the insurgency (Kaplan 2013). These alliances may often have involved taking sides in intra-insurgent conflicts and have resulted in U.S. forces acting on erroneous information that led to unnecessary attacks and casualties for civilians in Sunni communities.

Biddle and colleagues' evidence of the positive impact of the Awakening consists of before and after U.S. forces data from thirty-eight districts in Iraq where Sons of Iraq (SOI) units were "stood up." They report that in twenty-four of these thirty-eight districts, the "standing up" of the SOI units coincided with a decline in security incidents. However, when we closely examine these districts, we find that in nine of the twenty-four districts that they count in support of their argument, the evidence is actually doubtful. If our reading of the evidence is correct, there is good reason to doubt the degree of the impact of the Awakening movement.

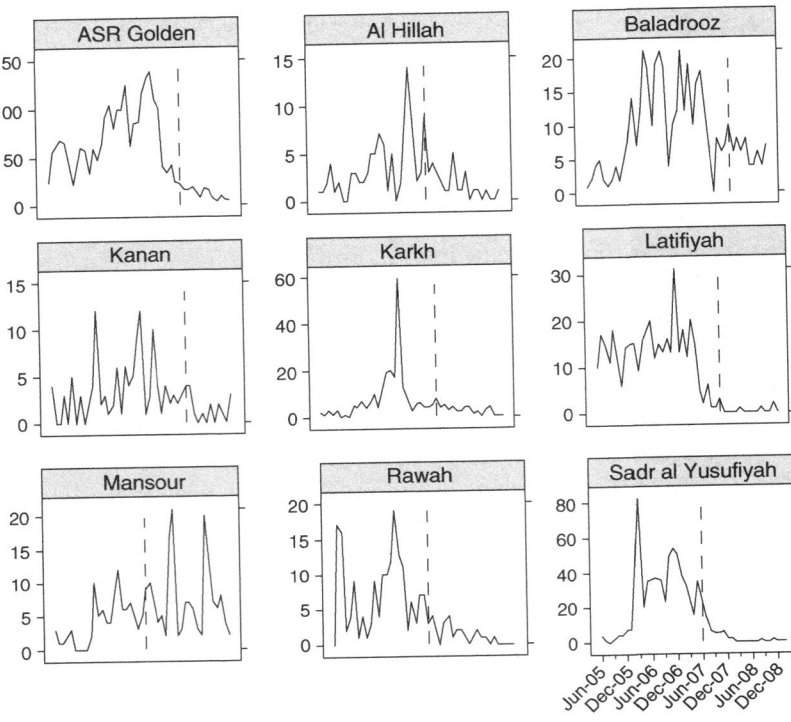

FIGURE 6.1. Reassessment of Nine "Confirming" AO Districts

We have abstracted and enlarged the line graphs Biddle and colleagues present for the nine doubtful districts in Figure 6.1. *In each of these districts – ASR Golden, al-Hillah, Baladrooz, Kanan, Karkh, Latifiyah, Mansour, Rawah, and Sadr al Yusufiyah – the trend line is already showing signs of decline before the SOI stand up and there is no sharp plunge downward reflecting a further change soon after the standup. The proportion of confirming districts by our reassessment is therefore actually below 40 percent.* That is, there is more evidence against than for Biddle and his colleagues' argument that the Awakening was a notable causal factor in reducing violence in Iraq (see also Hagan et al. 2012).

It is equally if not more plausible that the Awakening movement, like the surge, came during a period when AQI, ISIS, and other conflicting Sunni and Shia militias in Iraq had at least temporarily exhausted the strategic benefits and tactical capacities for sustaining high levels of violence. We saw evidence of this in Chapter 4 with Muqtada al-Sadr's August 2007 unilateral ceasefire, and we see further evidence of this decline in violence in Figure 6.1 before the "stand up" of the SOI.

Given Biddle and colleagues' account of failures from 2003 through 2006 of the United States to follow through on initiatives to form alliances with Sunni fighters, it seems unlikely that the Sunni forces who became involved in the Awakening movement would have trusted the promises that they would continue to be paid or be integrated into the Iraqi government military and national security police. It was clear by 2007 that the United States wanted to find a way of withdrawing most or all of its combat forces from Iraq. President Bush used a football analogy to describe the surge and the Awakening movement as a "slow motion lateral" to Iraqi control (Gordon and Trainor 2012:304). All parties could see this.

The acceptance of American money to reduce violent attacks, especially on U.S. forces, in anticipation of a U.S. departure made sense for all parties. It was a way of "buying time" to achieve this outcome. This did not mean that the Arab Sunnis now trusted the U.S.-led coalition or the Shia-dominated government. Indeed, we will show in this chapter that 2007 was a period in which the legal cynicism of the Arab Sunnis about the government and especially its national police forces remained a vital mediating source of the acceptance of insurgent violence.

It is not difficult to understand why large segments of the Arab Sunni public remained cynical about the U.S.-led coalition forces and the surge. The U.S. forces added during the surge adopted a divide-and-conquer strategy that intensified attacks targeting what were regarded as hostile and treacherous Arab Sunni communities. This left the Arab Sunni communities where the Awakening alliance had not taken hold vulnerable to what the residents of these areas regarded as unnecessary attacks on civilians. As noted in the previous chapter, it was not until 2008 that the U.S. surge finally pursued al-Sadr's Shia militias in Basra and in Baghdad's Sadr City; Prime Minister al-Maliki had forbidden further expansion of the surge and the Awakening movement into the Shia south, and the surge had never penetrated al-Sadr's Mahdi Army's domination of eastern Baghdad or Shia parts of western Baghdad. Instead, the surge concentrated its offensive operations on assumed al-Qaeda-linked elements of the Sunni-led insurgency thought to be located in or near sympathetic Arab Sunni communities. We describe the persistent pattern of U.S.-linked violence in Arab Sunni communities in the next section.

Attacks against U.S. forces trended markedly downward from the second half of 2007 through 2009. However, by 2010, especially following Sunni losses in the March elections, Arab Sunni fighters who had joined the Awakening movement began rejoining more militant Sunni militia, AQI, and subsequently ISIS. Concerns began to mount among U.S. forces and especially in the al-Maliki government that these former Awakening fighters were aiding the Sunni insurgency with information they had gained while allied with the U.S. and Iraqi government forces (William and Adnan 2010).

By July 2010, the U.S. Defense Department reported that less than half – 41,000 of 94,000 – of the Awakening's fighters had been offered jobs by the government. As well, many of these jobs were temporary and involved menial work. Fewer than one in ten Awakening members had been hired into the Iraq security forces, with officials blaming budget constraints. These Awakening members complained that they had been abandoned by the U.S. military (William and Adnan 2010). Furthermore, during this period, Iraqi security forces arrested hundreds of current and former Awakening members and accused them of acts of terrorism with AQI. A U.S. State Department report would later confirm that "many detainees were held for months or years after arrest and detention, sometimes incommunicado, without access to defense council or without being formally charged or brought before a judge within the legally mandated period" (cited in Cordesman and Khazi 2014:235).

From 2011 onward, after the United States' final withdrawal from Iraq, those Sunnis who at least temporarily shifted their alliances to the U.S. forces would have had growing reason to reconsider whether they would be better advantaged by rejoining AQI and ISIS factions to make common cause against the Shia government of Nouri al-Maliki. However, even at the probable peak of the Awakening movement in 2007, which coincided with the peak of the surge, as we will see, large portions of Sunni communities in Iraq continued to feel they were the targets of an illegitimate U.S. military presence and that attacks on these forces were justified.

COMMUNITY CONTEXTS OF SUNNI INSECURITY

The conviction of a single American soldier, Staff Sergeant Frank Wuterich, for "dereliction of duty" resulting in the deaths of twenty-four civilians in the town of Haditha in November 2005 is probably the best-known prosecution of criminal violence against Arab Sunni civilians by U.S. forces in Iraq. We presented evidence in the previous chapter that this kind of lethal violence was not isolated, and that a result was heightened individual and community perceptions of insecurity – which is a key factor in legal cynicism – especially in Arab Sunni communities. To understand this insecurity and why and how civilian deaths at the hands of U.S. soldiers occurred with some frequency in settings like Haditha, it is useful to first know something about this city and the details of the mass killing.

Haditha is an almost entirely Arab Sunni community of about 100,000 persons west of Baghdad and Fallujah on the Euphrates River, about halfway between Baghdad and the Syrian border. Saddam Hussein had protected this corridor as a lucrative smuggling route for goods and equipment from Syria. The threat posed by the new regime to this smuggling activity was one source of conflict that energized recruitment into the Sunni insurgency. When U.S. forces launched a massive assault to expel insurgents who controlled the city of Fallujah in 2004, many of the insurgents temporarily dispersed to towns along the Euphrates that were familiar to them. As a result, Haditha and nearby communities hosting insurgents remained highly threatening environments for U.S. soldiers.

This was a contrast to the relative safety of U.S. soldiers in Iraq during the first few months following the 2003 U.S.-led invasion and occupation. As shown in a graph from a U.S. Government Accountability Office (2007) report presented in Figure 6.2, attacks on U.S./coalition forces were rare at the outset of the occupation, but steadily increased in following years. Within two years, Arab Sunni areas of northern and central Iraq had become particularly dangerous for occupation forces.

For example, Hashim reports, "When marines reentered Haqlaniya during an operation in mid-2005, the front of practically every store in the main street had pro-jihad messages spray-painted on it, such as 'Allah is our God, Jihad is our way,' ... 'Long live jihad,' ... 'Death to those who collaborate with Americans'" (2006:336). The environment was even more perilous in Haditha. The Shia-dominated central government in Baghdad worsened the situation when it sent in unwanted and unappreciated Shia police. The result was predictable: attacks against the police intensified, followed by their withdrawal, and "into the vacuum thus created stepped the insurgents" (Hashim 2006:337).

Operation New Market and several other military sweeps during this period were similarly only briefly successful in clearing insurgents. By August 2005, Haditha was once more fully controlled by insurgents and serving as a waystation for foreign fighters headed from Syria to Baghdad. In early August, six U.S. Marines were killed in Haditha. A roadside bomb killed another fourteen Marines nearby.

In November 2005, a convoy of Marines entered Haditha and the last vehicle was blown apart by an improvised explosive device (IED), killing one soldier and wounding two others. The Marines reported they also confronted small arms fire from nearby houses. The squad leader named earlier, Staff Sergeant Frank Wuterich, set out to find the "trigger man" who exploded the IED. He spotted a car up the road carrying five young Iraqi males, four of whom were apparently being driven to school. Wuterich ordered them out of the car and onto the ground. When they refused, he shot all five men.

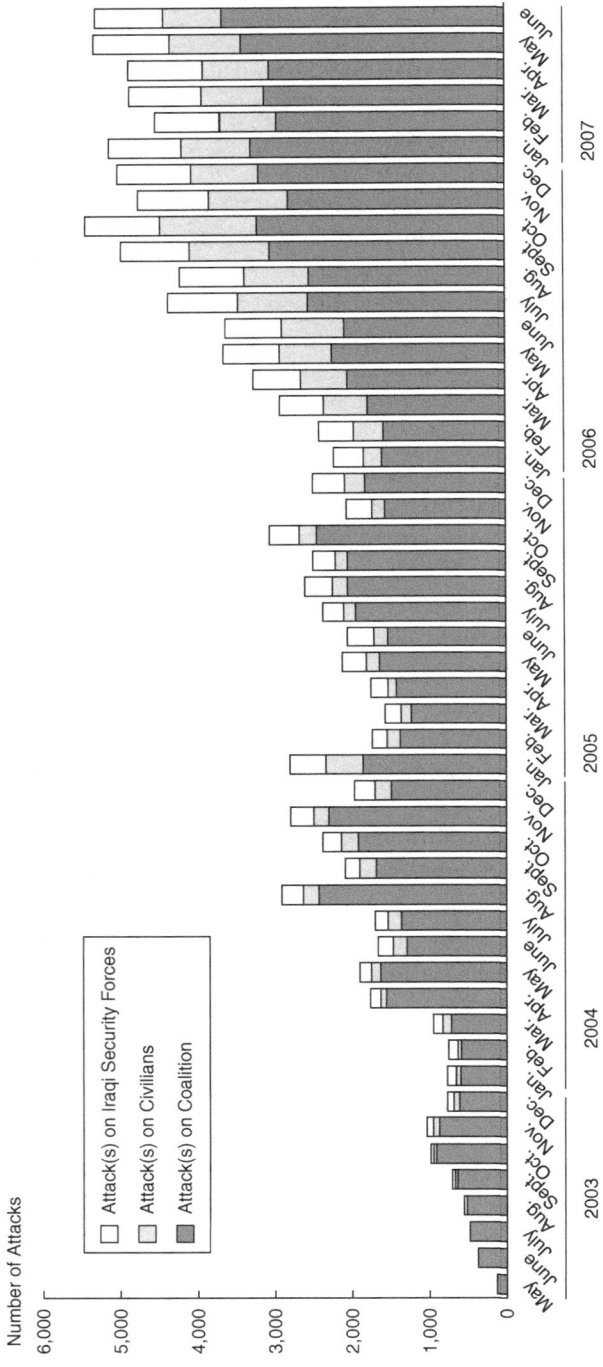

FIGURE 6.2. Enemy-Initiated Attacks against the Coalition and Its Iraqi Partners

Wuterich claimed they were trying to escape, although their bodies were all found just a few feet from the car.

Wuterich was ordered next by a superior officer who had arrived on the scene to lead an attack on nearby houses reported to have been the sources of gunfire. This attack killed another nineteen mostly women, children, and elderly Iraqi civilians in the houses. A report from a morgue where the bodies were taken indicated most were shot at close range in the head or chest.

The preliminary Marine report the next day indicated that the IED had killed one Marine and the nineteen Iraqi civilians, and that U.S. and Iraqi forces had killed eight insurgent combatants in a subsequent firefight. The following day, an Iraqi civilian videotaped the crime scene and the bodies at the morgue and the tape was passed to a *Time* magazine journalist. This video also became the subject of a *60 Minutes* television report. The killings would likely never have received public attention or military investigation without the media reporting (Savelsberg and King 2011: chapter 4).

The military investigation reprimanding officers for improperly reporting and investigating the killings resulted in charges against eight marines, including Frank Wuterich, who was charged with negligent homicide for the deaths of the women and children. However, charges against all of the Marines except Wuterich were subsequently dropped, while Wuterich was convicted through a plea bargain of a single count of dereliction of duty that resulted in no time served in prison. This was in spite of testimony from one of the other soldiers who had observed the first five shootings that "Sergeant Wuterich approached me and told me if anyone asks, the Iraqis were running away from the car and the Iraqi army shot them."

The larger implications of the Haditha killings became apparent when 400 pages of classified material from the military investigation unexpectedly were found in Baghdad and reported in the *New York Times* (Schmidt 2011). The material included testimony by General Johnson, who commanded American forces in Anbar province, and who forthrightly acknowledged the extensiveness of civilian killings by U.S.-led Multinational Forces (MNF) during the peak of violence in Iraq.

General Johnson testified that "It happened all the time, not necessarily in MNF-West all the time, but throughout the whole country." He went on to say that "So, you know, maybe – I guess maybe if I was sitting here at Quantico [Virginia] and heard that 15 civilians were killed I would have been surprised and shocked and gone – done more to look into it." "But, at that point in time," he recalled, "I felt that was – had been, for whatever reason, part of that engagement and felt that it was just a cost of doing business on that particular engagement."

Another retired army officer, U.S. Colonel Douglas McGregor, corroborated Johnson's testimony from his own experience in Iraq:

> Most of the generals and politicians did not think through the consequences of compelling American soldiers with no knowledge of Arabic or Arab culture to implement intrusive measures inside an Islamic society. We arrested people in front of their families, dragging them away in handcuffs with bags over their heads, and then provided no information to the families of those we incarcerated. In the end, our soldiers killed, maimed and incarcerated thousands of Arabs, 90 percent of whom were not the enemy. But they are now. (cited in Hashim 2006:326)

McGregor's point is that the U.S.-led war of aggression in Iraq did not include anticipation or preparation for the consequences of the brutal counterinsurgency tactics adopted in response to the violence they encountered during the military occupation.

The American and coalition soldiers were trained to conduct a conventional war and not prepared for the policing functions of military occupation. Hashim explains the significance of the unpreparedness for the unexpected dilemmas this occupation presented:

> Irregular warfare descends into barbarity, cruelty and planned dehumanization of the enemy much faster and more easily than does regular warfare. The rules of irregular warfare are not as well-codified as those for regular war because the irregular force does not follow them. Members of the latter often do not wear uniforms, and hide among the populace and hope government force sometimes goes out of its way to commit its own "barbarisms" to highlight the fact that the government forces are incapable of providing security. Of course the insurgency must balance this descent into barbarity against the possible loss of support among the people when it engages in such acts. It is incumbent upon the government/counter-insurgency side to prevent such a descent from taking place because it will rebound negatively against it. If the government/counter-insurgency side uses its security forces to engage in barbarities it loses the right to claim that it is on the side of law and order, or of morality and ethics. If it fails to prevent the insurgency from committing atrocities against the people or security forces, then it has failed to protect those it is supposed to. (2006:329–30)

The descent into barbarity that Hashim describes is a classic example of the consequences that Justice Robert Jackson warned unfold *post bellum* and accumulate in a war of aggression.

Our theory of legal cynicism maintains that the "loss of support among the people" described earlier is not simply the sum of the individuals who are directly affected, but also the further collective spillover effect on others who indirectly hear and become aware of the unnecessary violence imposed on civilians. This unnecessary violence against civilians is, of course, a war crime, and when this kind of violence is distributed widely, as it was during the surge, it is likely to be perceived as collective punishment. We elaborate next the more generalized role legal cynicism played in amplifying at the collective community level the experiences of individual civilians during the 2007 surge.

THE CULTURAL FRAMING OF SUNNI INSECURITY

It is not surprising in view of this context to suggest that the Arab Sunnis felt themselves to be a conspicuously undefended and militarily defeated group in Iraq. Sampson and Bartusch (1998) adopt the concepts of "defeated" and "defended" neighborhoods that we in turn respectively apply to Iraq's Arab Sunni and Shia communities. We will see that the legal cynicism of a defeated group can be especially consequential precisely because of counterinsurgent efforts to keep it militarily suppressed. We argue that legal cynicism provided an important cultural framing that linked experiences of counterinsurgent violence to its consequences. In this case, the framing did this by providing a cultural interpretation that justified collective and individual-level possibilities for present and future violence by otherwise victimized and defeated insurgents.

Originally introduced by Suttles (1968), the defended/defeated distinction was also used by Kapsis (1978) to account for differing levels of felt political powerlessness, anomie, and perceived normlessness among residents in legally unincorporated compared with incorporated parts of the city of Chicago. Kutnjak and Hagan (2011) similarly explained national differences in participation and perceptions of institutionally defended Bosnian witnesses as contrasted with defeated Serbian defendants at The Hague International Tribunal. The key idea is that cultural orientations and framings of defended and defeated groups can be drastically different.

This conceptualization of legal cynicism is grounded in Snow and Bedford's definition of a cultural frame as an orientation that "simplifies and condenses the 'world out there' by selectively punctuating and encoding objects, situations, events, experiences, and sequences of actions within one's present or past environment" (1992:137). Snow and Bedford were interested in understanding the cultural or symbolic logics that can make collective action possible. The Arab Sunnis in Iraq were motivated by a framing that justified the militancy of their insurgency as more than an impulsive resort to revenge.

The emergence of a legally cynical framing among the Arab Sunnis had its origins in response to the kind of problem Weber analyzed as involving the legitimation of state rule. Weber classically conceptualized the state as "a human community that claims the monopoly of the legitimate use of physical force within a given territory" (1919). Recall that the U.S.-led invasion and occupation of Iraq and the subsequent de-Ba'athification of its government ministries and demobilization of its military purged these institutions of a large class of mid-level Sunni technocrats and bureaucrats along with higher-level Saddam loyalists. This undermined the perceived legitimacy of the newly hollowed-out state's central institutions for a large and subsequently unemployed cadre of Sunni military and government workers. Once undone, the challenge of reestablishing legitimate state bureaucratic rule among the institutionally defeated Arab Sunni population proved overwhelming.

The 2004 decision to launch a massive assault on Fallujah was widely perceived as a turning point expression of the American determination to establish the defeated status of the Sunni insurgents. Hashim observes that "senior officials of the Bush Administration, for whom the idea of reducing the political power and importance of the Sunni Arabs was part of their unstated ideological vision for post-Saddam Iraq, were not averse to the liberal use of force to teach this intractable Sunni outpost a lesson" (2006:44). Most Sunni politicians withdrew from the Iraqi government in response to their perception of the disproportionality of the massive attack on Fallujah, which destroyed much of the city (Wong 2004).

Hashim uses the term *Sunniphobia* to describe an attitude of dismissal and disdain that filtered down from the Bush administration to the Coalition Provisional Authority (CPA) in Baghdad (2006:280). As noted in earlier chapters, de-Ba'athification of government ministries and demobilization of the military forces largely eliminated the previously ascendant Sunnis from centers of power in Iraq. Hashim describes these policy decisions and the attitudes that underlay them as "Sunniphobic."

Keith Mines, a former 7th Special Forces Group officer and the top CPA representative in Anbar province in 2003, drew from his unique experience with the CPA to reach a similar conclusion. He observed:

> Al Anbar was not only home to tens of thousands of disenfranchised soldiers and thousands of their officers, but several hundred intelligence officers and other thousands of ex-Ba'athist civil servants. I met with them frequently and they were looking for a way forward. They were angry.... No question that it fueled the insurgency, both indirectly by barring fathers from meaningful jobs and making them available for more nefarious lines of work, and indirectly by demonstrating to the ex-Ba'athists that they really did not have a

place in the new Iraq, thus motivating them to oppose the emerging new democracy. (2012)

Mines lamented that it took so long for the United States to enlist Sunni fighters in the Anbar Awakening and Sons of Iraq programs, and that the Iraqi government then failed to follow through on their promised integration into the Iraqi Army and security forces. He provocatively mixed the themes of legal cynicism and militarism with his speculation that "maybe Patton was right, Americans simply love to fight, and we would rather keep the glory for ourselves than sub-contract it out [i.e., to non-American groups]."

Hashim explains that the subsequent low turnout of the Sunnis for the 2005 elections was "symptomatic of their cynicism about and contempt for the entire process, which they saw as selling out Iraq to U.S. and Iranian interests" (2006:48). The failure to assure a meaningful place for the Sunnis in Iraq's governance was apparent from the initial selection of the Interim Governing Council through what Dodge (2012) has called the "exclusive elite bargain" that installed Shia Prime Minister Nouri al-Maliki as the multiple-term leader of Iraq, despite the failure of his party to win a plurality of seats in the 2010 parliamentary elections.

Recent conceptualization of legal cynicism by Kirk and Papachristos (2011) goes beyond the issue of legitimation to include concerns about unresponsiveness and ineffectiveness of governing institutions in providing public safety and security. Expanding on Kirk and Papachristos' conceptualization, our thesis is that together, the dimensions of illegitimacy, unresponsiveness, and ineffectiveness contributed to an Arab Sunni framing that justified individuals and groups in "taking law into their own hands." This kind of cultural orientation can be seen as producing responses ranging from individual and group withdrawal and refusal to communicate and cooperate with authorities, to resort to targeted crimes of individual and collective violence.

NEUTRALIZING AND ACCEPTING SUNNI REPRISALS AGAINST U.S./COALITION FORCES

Kirk and Papachristos indicate that "antagonism toward and mistrust of the agents of the law may propel some individuals toward violence simply because they feel they cannot rely upon the police to help them resolve grievances" (2011:1191). Here we broadly interpret the meaning of police and agents of the law to include military and security soldiers such as the surging U.S./coalition forces. Although in the nationally representative 2007 Iraq survey analyzed in this research only about 7 percent of the respondents ranked as acceptable attacks on the Iraqi Army, more than half (56%) indicated that they thought attacks on U.S./coalition forces were acceptable.

The extreme disparity in 2007 of the acceptability to Iraqi respondents of attacks on U.S./coalition forces versus Iraq Army personnel is consistent with the importance cultural sociology attaches to the specific conditions and circumstances under which social actors deem it appropriate to respond to events and experiences in non-normative ways (Lamont and Small 2008). We noted earlier that the onset of attacks on U.S. forces did not begin immediately after the 2003 invasion. It is unlikely that the majority of Arab Sunni respondents in Iraq immediately would have accepted the idea of attacking U.S./coalition soldiers. Broad acceptance of the attacks likely required some time for legal cynicism to fully develop about the U.S.-led occupation and its failure to provide a safe environment, especially for Arab Sunnis in Iraq.

During the Ba'athist regime, Arab Sunnis dominated the Iraqi Army and the Arab Sunni population was generally respectful of the military. This respect for the military as an important social institution could conceivably have extended to the U.S.-led forces, despite their removal of Saddam Hussein. Echoing Keith Mines's view, and based on his own CPA experience, Hashim remarks that "Indeed, many Sunnis were willing to play their part in the new regime, as I discovered in numerous discussions in fall 2003 and winter 2004" (2006:346). However, by the onset of the 2007 surge, Arab Sunnis now saw themselves as not only defeated but also as primary targets of the U.S. forces. These forces trained and worked with the new Iraqi Army under the direction of a Shia-dominated government during and after the surge, but during the surge it was the U.S. forces that Arab Sunni civilians initially held most responsible for their violent mistreatment.

Lamont and Small emphasize that cultural sociology sees individuals as malleable and adaptive as they creatively use and respond to cultural symbols (2008:79). The unnecessary violent attacks on civilians attributed to the U.S. forces constituted the conditions and circumstances that we argue heightened legal cynicism about the role of U.S.-led forces in Iraq. This legal cynicism in turn paved the way for the acceptance of attacks on these foreign occupiers and assailants. Yet we argue that such acts were not simply accepted as unthinking revenge for unnecessary and violent attacks by rogue U.S. military forces. Attacks on military forces would not have been acceptable to the majority of Arab Sunnis in the context of a legitimate, responsive, and protective military occupation. Rather, these attacks were accepted because they could be framed as symbolically representative of an illegitimate U.S.-led invasion followed by a belligerently nonresponsive and ineffectual occupation.

The redefinition of attacks by and on U.S. forces through this legal cynicism framing "neutralized" (Sykes 1957) conventional or mainstream Iraqi cultural prohibitions of violence against soldiers. An expanded cultural repertoire (Swidler 1986) now became available that endorsed attacks by Arab Sunnis on U.S. forces as forms of militant resistance, thus allowing the violation of a traditional cultural boundary norm (Lamont and Fournier 1992) that could previously have protected the military. From the Arab Sunni perspective, insurgent attackers were now destigmatized while the U.S. forces were newly stigmatized, with a reconfigured set of boundaries now distinguishing the Arab Sunni "us" from "them": the occupying U.S. foreign forces.

The implication is that the newly acceptable cultural repertoire included a resort to what Donald Black (1983) has called "self-help" strategies. This included the acceptance of attacks on U.S. forces as a self-help strategy of militant resistance. Of course, this did not mean that all Arab Sunnis engaged, aided, or abetted in these attacks. Kirk and Papachristos insist in the American context that "cynicism toward the law does not directly cause neighborhood violence yet it makes it more likely because mistrust of the agents of the law opens up the possibility that individuals will resort to illegal violence to redress a problem" (2011:1203).

In the Iraqi case, legal cynicism about the U.S.-led invasion, occupation, and ensuing insecurity made Arab Sunni insurgent attacks on U.S. forces both possible and likely. The legal cynicism frame was the justificatory bridge from the unnecessary violent attacks by U.S. forces on Sunni Arab civilians to Sunni Arab counterattacks on the U.S. forces. This framing extended collective consent to the latter attacks, and as we will see, multiplicatively increased the acceptance of these attacks in these communities.

MODELING THE CAUSES OF LEGAL CYNICISM AND SUNNI MILITANCY

The cultural framing thesis of Kirk and Papachristos about the effect of legal cynicism on Chicago homicides is an ecological argument that "individuals' own experiential-based perception of the law becomes solidified through a collective process whereby residents develop a shared meaning of the behavior of the law and the viability of the law to ensure their safety" (2011:1201). The logic of the argument is that the shared cultural meaning becomes so negative and collectively reinforced that it leads to an acceptance of violent strategies of action in response. In Iraq, our argument is that the violent insurgent strategies that became widely accepted notably included attacks on U.S./coalition forces.

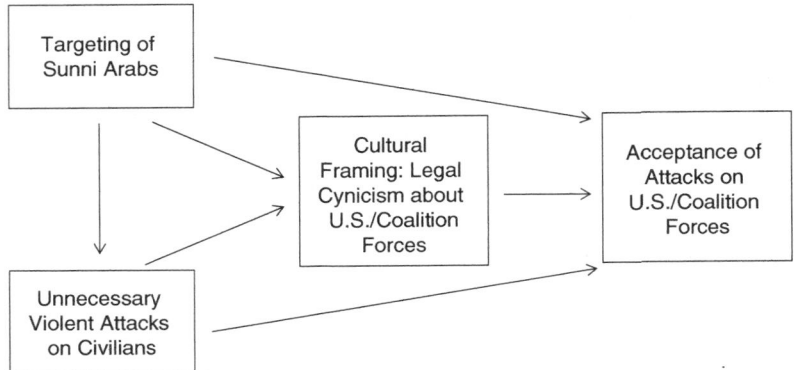

FIGURE 6.3. Conceptual Model of the Cultural Framing of Legal Cynicism that Made Attacks on the U.S./Coalition Forces Acceptable and Possible as a Strategy for Action in Iraq

Our conceptual model is summarized in Figure 6.3. We contend in this conception that the American targeting of Iraq's Sunni communities for unnecessary attacks that included civilians as victims played a major role in intensifying legally cynical attitudes about the invasion, occupation, and insecurity associated with the U.S./coalition forces, leading to the widespread acceptance of attacks on these forces. This conceptual model is not only consistent with the theoretical perspective of Kirk and Papachristos, it also subsumes Donald Black's (1983) theory of self-help as a response to the failings of official institutions to establish and maintain social order, safety, and security (see also Hannerz 1969).

The conceptual model presented in Figure 6.3 does not include all the possible causal forces that led to the acceptance of attacks on U.S. forces. Many other possible influences are included in our empirical models. However, the following variables and hypotheses are particularly important to our application of the theory of legal cynicism:

H_1: Unnecessary violent attacks on civilians by U.S./coalition forces were perceived and reported most often by Arab Sunni individuals, especially in Arab Sunni communities.

H_2: The cultural framing of legal cynicism about the U.S./coalition forces was most prominent among Arab Sunni individuals, especially in Arab Sunni communities.

H_3: Legal cynicism about U.S./coalition forces at the community level transmitted and intensified the acceptance by Arab Sunnis of attacks on these forces.

It is the last hypothesis that is ultimately most essential to our theoretical approach, because we have argued that attacks on U.S./coalition forces would not have been widely acceptable to the great majority of Arab Sunnis in the context of legitimate, responsive, and protective U.S./coalition forces. Rather, these attacks were more broadly accepted because they could be framed as symbolically responsive to an illegitimate U.S.-led invasion followed by a non-responsive and ineffectual occupation. The collective impact of legal cynicism about the larger U.S.-led invasion and presence in Iraq is essential in ultimately accounting for the breadth of the acceptance of attacks on the U.S.-led forces among Arab Sunnis in 2007.

We go one step further in the last part of our analysis to examine whether legal cynicism about U.S./coalition forces played a further role in developing a legal cynicism about the new Iraqi institutions it created and dominated:

H_4: Iraqis who were legally cynical about the legitimacy, responsiveness, and effectiveness of the U.S./coalition would extend this cynicism, albeit in reduced degree, to the Iraq government, military, and police.

The implication is that the effects and therefore theoretical significance of legal cynicism about the U.S. presence in Iraq were far-reaching and potentially long lasting. Indeed, this last hypothesis foreshadows the resurgence after the withdrawal of U.S. forces of AQI and ISIS attacks on Iraq government, military, and police that began to mount in 2012 and reached high levels in 2014.

SURVEYING LEGAL CYNICISM IN THE U.S. AND ARAB SUNNI CONFLICT

In the previous chapter, we focused on the two cross-sectional surveys conducted in early 2008 and 2009, which respectively included the later part of the surge and a period after the withdrawal of all surge forces from Iraq. In this chapter, we focus on the cross-sectional survey conducted in the fall of 2007, which included the peak of the surge – immediately preceding the beginning of the drawdown of these forces. As in the 2008 and 2009 surveys, the 2007 survey included sampling points in communities distributed proportionate to population in all 102 districts of all eighteen Iraq provinces. Interviewers administered surveys to more than 60 percent of the households they contacted, in person and in Arabic or Kurdish. The 2007 survey analyzed in this chapter includes 2,212 respondents within 456 sampling points that are nationally representative of Iraq.[1]

A distinctive feature of the 2007 survey was that it included an item asking whether respondents thought it was acceptable for attacks to be targeted at the U.S./coalition forces. The inclusion of this item at the peak of the surge allowed us to measure the amount, variation, and sources of support for the kinds of attacks targeted at U.S./coalition forces during the surge. As noted earlier, a clear majority – nearly 56 percent of Iraqis in this nationally representative sample – reported that they thought these attacks were acceptable. Our initial focus in this chapter is on explaining this acceptance of attacks on the U.S.-led forces, and we then consider whether there is evidence that this transferred to acceptance of attacks on Iraq government, military, and police targets.

We indicated in the previous chapter that more respondents during the latter part of the surge reported violence in their communities involving unnecessary attacks on civilians by U.S./coalition forces than from other specified sources. In the data analyzed in the previous chapter, 46 percent of the respondents reported these unnecessary violent attacks by U.S./coalition forces on civilians in their nearby areas. In the earlier 2007 survey we analyze in this chapter, 43 percent reported these attacks. The similarity of the results in the two surveys suggests the reliability of this reporting.

Thus during the surge, almost half of all Iraqis believed their communities were unnecessarily victimized by U.S./coalition attacks, and the similarity in the prevalence of these reports across surveys encourages the conclusion that the attacks actually occurred widely and frequently. However, even if this was not true, we hypothesize that the commonly shared belief in the widespread and frequent occurrence of these attacks would have had notable effects. This hypothesis is an extension of the self-fulfilling prophecy introduced in Chapter 4 and the classic theorem that a situation defined as real is real in its consequences (see Merton 1995).

Lower but still notable proportions of Iraqis also reported unnecessary attacks on civilians by the Iraqi Army (29%) and Police (20%). High proportions of Iraqis reported nearby bombings (41%), kidnappings (41%), violence between government and nongovernment forces (34%), sniping and crossfire (30%), and sectarian attacks (28%). These levels of reported violence are also relatively similar to the 2008 survey, indicating high reliability in reporting of war violence.

In this chapter, legal cynicism is measured directly and scaled separately in relation to U.S./coalition and Iraqi forces. We measured legal cynicism about U.S./coalition forces with four items that correspond to the dimensions of legal cynicism. The interviewers asked respondents to indicate the degree to which they (1) thought the U.S.-led invasion of Iraq was wrong, (2) opposed the presence of U.S. forces, (3) felt the way U.S. forces had conducted themselves was bad, and (4) thought the presence of U.S. forces had made the security situation worse.[2] The average score on this summed scale was eight out of twelve, which is skewed toward cynicism.

We measured legal cynicism about the new state institutions of Iraq with four related kinds of items. The interviewers asked respondents to indicate the degree to which they had (1) confidence in the national government of Iraq, (2) confidence in the Iraqi Army, and (3) confidence in the Iraqi Police; and (4) how well the national government had carried out its responsibilities. The average score on this summed scale was 6.13 out of twelve. While not fully comparable, this score suggests that in the fall of 2007, Iraqis were a bit less cynical and perhaps slightly more mixed in their feelings about their own new state institutions than about U.S. forces in Iraq.

We also included seven measures of background characteristics also used in the previous chapter. Our measure of individual-level sectarian identity was a self-designation as Arab Sunni (33%) or Shia (48%), with Kurdish and other groups (19%) as the omitted comparison group. The sample was otherwise about half male (51%), nearly thirty-five years old (34.77), with some secondary school education (3.31), a majority married (61%), and a large minority employed (41%).

We included seven indicators of community-level characteristics that were measured with mean scores for each community sampling point. We included three, separate community-level measures of reported unnecessary attacks on civilians. These measures again indicated the high level of unnecessary attacks reported on civilians by U.S./coalition forces, as well as by Iraqi Army and Police. Across the community clusters, an average of 44 percent of the respondents reported U.S./coalition attacks, 19 percent on average reported Iraqi Army attacks, and 20 percent reported Iraqi Police attacks. We also included a measure based on the average summed remaining sources of attacks (2.05 on a scale of six).

Finally, we included a measure that indicated the extent to which the area sampling points were predominately Sunni communities. This measure was calculated as the average score for individuals within the sampling points who reported their community was mostly or completely Sunni. This aggregate-level measure allows us to compare responses from predominately Arab Sunni communities in Iraq with an aggregation of other communities.[3]

SOURCES OF LEGAL CYNICISM AND ITS ROLE
IN THE U.S. AND ARAB SUNNI CONFLICT

As in the previous chapter, we next present results from prediction models[4] that summarize in relative terms the influence of variables in explaining reported attacks on civilians by U.S. forces during the peak of the surge in the fall of 2007 (see Appendix Table 6.2). Reports of nearby sniping and crossfire, sectarian attacks, and kidnappings were significantly associated with reports of violent and unnecessary U.S. attacks on civilians. The purpose of including these other sources of violence in this and the following prediction equations is as a means of holding their influence constant, especially in examining the role of the sectarian identity of respondents and their communities.

As predicted in Hypothesis 1, when compared to Kurdish and other respondents, individual Arab Sunnis were most likely to report unnecessary U.S. attacks. Individual Shia also more often reported these attacks, although less often than the Arab Sunnis. At the community level, as also predicted in Hypothesis 1, unnecessary U.S./coalition attacks were significantly more likely to be reported in predominately Arab Sunni areas. The fact that these attacks are reported as unnecessary implies that the Arab Sunnis perceived that their communities were singled out as targeted victims for collective punishment. This finding is net of controls for the levels of other war violence reported in these communities.

The bar graph presented in Figure 6.4 is estimated using the results from the prediction equation. Only about 25 percent of Shia and Kurdish respondents not living in predominately Arab Sunni communities reported nearby violent and unnecessary attacks on civilians by U.S./coalition forces, while about 70 percent of Arab Sunni individuals living in predominately Arab Sunni communities reported these violent and unnecessary attacks, with other sectarian combinations of individuals and communities in between. This high level of reported U.S. attacks in Arab Sunni communities is consistent with the expectation that civilians living in predominately Arab Sunni areas would be more influenced by legal cynicism about U.S./coalition forces in Iraq – which we examine next.

As predicted in Hypothesis 2, legal cynicism about U.S./coalition forces was higher among Arab Sunni individuals, and this cynicism was further elevated in predominately Arab Sunni communities (see Appendix Table 6.3). The cynicism about these forces was also intensified in communities with higher reported unnecessary and violent U.S. and Iraqi Army attacks on civilians. These community-level effects were highly significant even when

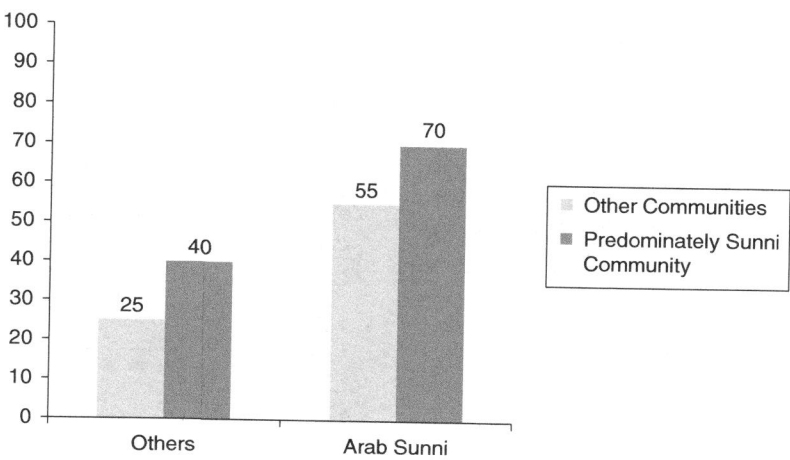

FIGURE 6.4. Unnecessary Attacks on Civilians by U.S./Coalition Forces in Iraqi Communities

individual-level measures of these variables and others were included in the prediction equations.

In Figure 6.5, we present the bar graph estimated using results from the prediction equation for the twelve-point U.S./coalition legal cynicism scale. Shia and Kurdish respondents not living in predominately Arab Sunni communities scored 6.75, while Arab Sunni individuals living in predominately Arab Sunni communities scored 10.50, with other sectarian combinations of individuals and communities in between.

We argued earlier and predicted in Hypothesis 3 that the latter heightened cynicism about U.S./coalition forces would mediate and intensify the acceptance of attacks on U.S./coalition forces in predominately Arab Sunni communities – by providing a broader justification than simple revenge for the unnecessary violent U.S. attacks on Arab Sunni civilians and communities.

Our next set of prediction equations supports Hypothesis 3 and our explanation of the effects of legal cynicism on Sunni militancy (see Appendix Table 6.4). The first of the results in this part of the analysis confirms the heightened acceptance in predominately Arab Sunni communities of attacks on U.S./coalition forces. The next result indicates that this Arab Sunni acceptance of these attacks is mediated by unnecessary U.S. attacks on civilians, both of which in turn are mediated by heightened legal cynicism about U.S./coalition forces.

The pronounced Arab Sunni community and legal cynicism effects on acceptance of attacks on U.S./coalition forces persisted even when a range

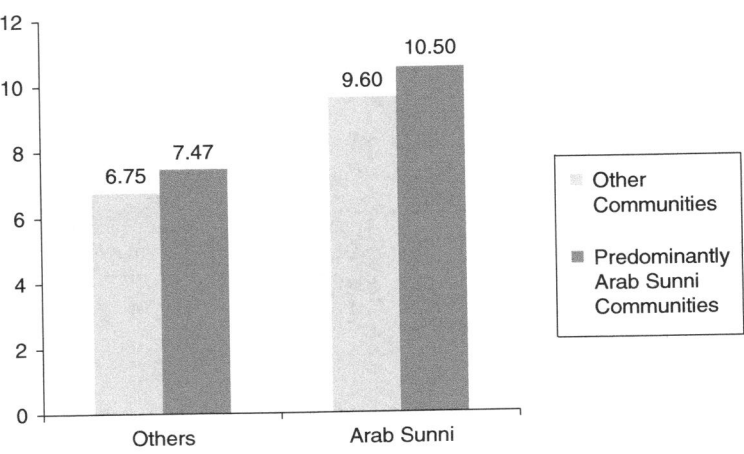

FIGURE 6.5. Legal Cynicism about U.S./Coalition Forces in Iraqi Communities

of individual-level measures is taken into account. Finally, we also found a highly significant interaction effect of being Arab Sunnis with legal cynicism about the U.S./coalition forces that explains the acceptance of the attacks among Arab Sunni individuals in predominately Arab Sunni communities (see Appendix Table 6.5).

Figure 6.6 presents a bar graph estimated using final results from the prediction equation for acceptance of attacks on U.S./coalition forces. This figure shows that about 20 percent of Shia and Kurdish respondents living in communities that were also only in the twenty-fifth percentile of legal cynicism accepted attacks on the U.S./coalition forces. In contrast, almost all (97%) Arab Sunnis living in communities that were in the seventy-fifth percentile of legal cynicism accepted these attacks, with other sectarian combinations of individuals and communities in between.

The overwhelming acceptance of the attacks on U.S./coalition forces in the latter communities with highly elevated cynicism about U.S./coalition forces reveals how pervasive acceptance of attacks on U.S./coalition forces became during the 2007 surge. Legal cynicism about the legitimacy, responsiveness, and effectiveness of the U.S./coalition forces among the Arab Sunnis was a key factor in creating a widespread acceptance of insurgent attacks against these forces. Our argument is that legal cynicism provided the broad justification that made these attacks possible and indeed frequent, as seen at the outset of this chapter in Figure 6.2.

Hypothesis 4 is a prediction that cynicism about the U.S./coalition forces in Iraq further served as a source of transference to cynicism about the Iraq

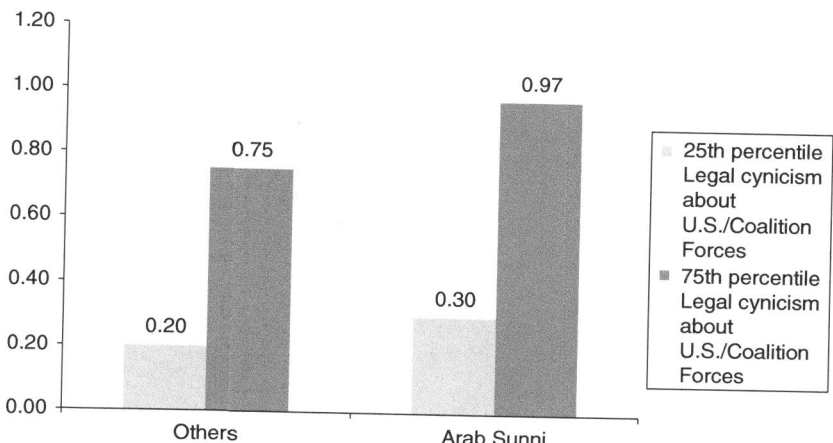

FIGURE 6.6. Acceptance of Attacks on U.S./Coalition Forces through Legal Cynicism

government, military, and police with long-lasting potential consequences in the nation. The new government of Iraq was, of course, influenced by the U.S.-led Coalition Provisional Authority. This was true from the establishment of the Interim Governing Council through the selection of Prime Minister al-Maliki, and this influence persistently favored the Shia in Iraq.

The prediction models we estimated strongly indicated that predominately Sunni communities and areas with more reports of unnecessary Iraqi Army and police attacks were likely to also express legal cynicism about the Iraqi government and its military and security police forces (see Appendix Table 6.3). We did not find a community-level influence of legal cynicism about the U.S./coalition forces, and there was also some indication of a negative impact of unnecessary U.S. attacks on civilians. Nonetheless, as predicted in Hypothesis 4, we found a highly significant influence at the individual level of legal cynicism about the U.S./coalition forces on legal cynicism about the Iraqi government/forces.

We next used the prediction model to estimate the impact of Arab Sunni individuals and communities in a bar graph using the twelve-point Iraq government/forces legal cynicism scale. These scores in Figure 6.7 were not as highly elevated as the scores seen in Figure 6.5 for legal cynicism about U.S./coalition forces. However, the scores were again much higher for Arab Sunni individuals living in predominately Arab Sunni communities (8.08) than for Shia and Kurdish individuals who did not live in predominately Arab Sunni communities (5.28).

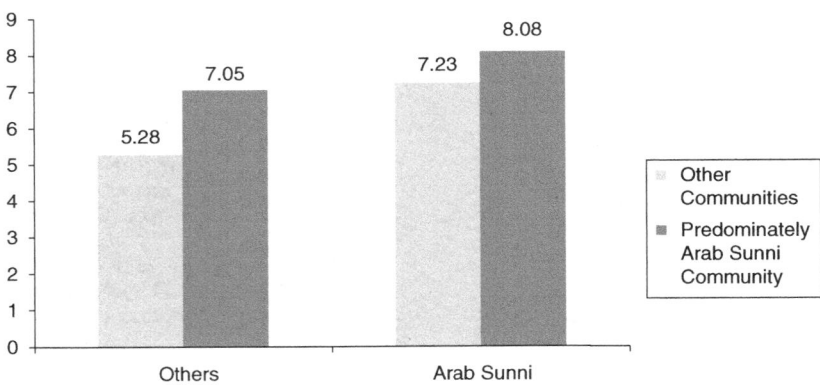

FIGURE 6.7. Legal Cynicism about Iraq Government/Forces in Iraqi Communities

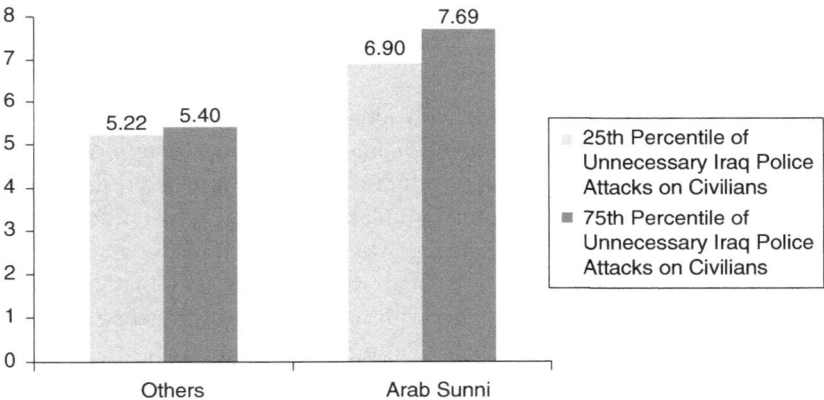

FIGURE 6.8. Legal Cynicism about Iraq Government/Forces through Unnecessary Attacks on Civilians

Finally, Figures 6.8 and 6.9 respectively present a bar graph and a line graph estimated with interaction effects added to the prediction equations involving legal cynicism about the Iraqi government and its military and police security forces (see Appendix Tables 6.6 and 6.7). These figures provide added information about the impact of unnecessary Iraqi Police attacks on civilians on legal cynicism about the Iraqi government/forces. Figure 6.8 shows that Shia and Kurdish respondents who lived in communities that were in the twenty-fifth percentile of unnecessary Iraqi Police attacks on civilians scored 5.22 on the Iraqi government/forces legal cynicism scale. However, Arab Sunni individuals living in communities that were in the seventy-fifth percentile of

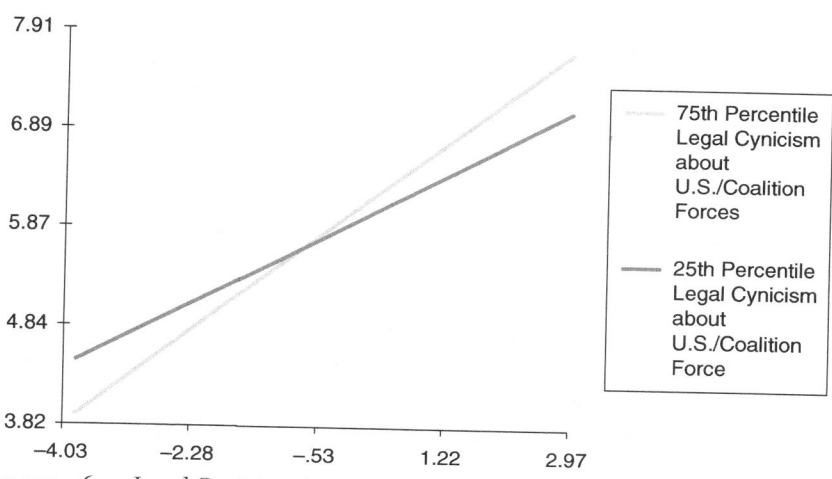

FIGURE 6.9. Legal Cynicism through Unnecessary Iraq Police Attacks on Civilians

unnecessary Iraqi Police attacks on civilians scored 7.69, with other sectarian combinations of individuals and communities in between.

Figure 6.9 shows that while there is a notable (i.e., relatively steep) relationship between unnecessary Iraqi Police attacks on civilians and legal cynicism about the Iraqi government, military, and security police forces even in communities at the twenty-fifth percentile of legal cynicism about U.S./coalition forces, the impact of these unnecessary police attacks on civilians is even stronger (i.e., steeper) in communities at the seventy-fifth percentile of legal cynicism about the U.S./coalition forces.

The implication is that going forward from the peak of the surge, not only the unnecessary attacks of the U.S. forces, but also the unnecessary attacks by the Iraqi security forces would play an important role in the conflict that continued once the American forces left Iraq. These findings foreshadow the rise in attacks by Sunni insurgents, including AQI and ISIS, on the Iraqi government/forces in 2012 through 2014.

"HEARTS AND MINDS" OR "BUYING TIME"?

The thesis of this chapter is that the roots of the Arab Sunni insurgency were the perceived and reported unnecessary attacks by U.S./coalition forces on civilians that increased cynicism about the role of these forces in Iraq, and that in turn mediated and intensified the widespread acceptance of attacks on these forces that were the hallmarks of the Arab Sunni insurgency. We argued that unnecessary attacks by U.S./coalition forces on civilians would have been understood as collective punishment of the Arab Sunnis as the defeated group in the Iraq War, and therefore that beyond effects on Arab Sunni individuals, we argued, there would also be broader spillover effects of resulting legal cynicism in predominately Arab Sunni communities that would mediate and intensify the widespread nature of support for attacks on the U.S./coalition forces in these communities. The data presented in this chapter are consistent with our argument about the causal processes that led to this expansive Arab Sunni community support and that made the Sunni insurgency's attacks on the U.S. forces possible.

The final argument presented in this chapter is that the role of the U.S./ coalition forces in Iraq was connected as well to rising legal cynicism about the Iraqi government and its military and security forces. Our premise was that the U.S.-led Coalition Provisional Authority intervened to form and shape the Iraqi government and its key institutions, and that legal cynicism about the former would foster legal cynicism about the latter. We found support for this final argument that again involved the Arab Sunnis, and a further parallel to the reported attacks of U.S./coalition forces on civilians in the form of unnecessary attacks by the Iraqi Police on civilians. Legal cynicism about the Iraqi government/forces was most intense among those who reported unnecessary Iraqi Police attacks on civilians and who lived in communities with high cynicism about the U.S./coalition forces, as well as among Arab Sunnis who lived in communities with high reported levels of unnecessary Iraqi Police attacks on civilians.

The implication of these final findings is that the U.S.-led coalition likely played an explicit or implicit role in facilitating the aggressive tactics of the Iraqi security forces – which would also be understood by the Arab Sunni as collective punishment. These final findings recall Justice Robert Jackson's observation at Nuremberg that a war of aggression is the most serious violation of international criminal law because it incorporates so many other kinds of war crimes within it. The longer-term, path-dependent possibilities extend to the renewal of the Sunni insurgency and to the rise of ISIS-led violence.

The sources of the fateful cynicism we observed especially among the Arab Sunnis about the Iraq national security police periodically found expression as well in international news reports about sweeps, arrests, prolonged imprisonments without charges, and torture. In 2006, the Iraq Interior Ministry suspended an entire brigade of about 800 special national police commandos for suspected participation in Shia militia kidnappings and killings in Baghdad's Sunni and mixed neighborhoods. Insurgent Sunni militia also conducted kidnappings and killings, but the coordination of the Shia-dominated national police with Shia militias was distinctive (Dodge

2012:124–6). Both the Shia Badr Brigade and the Mahdi Army gained deep footholds in the Iraqi Police.

When the *New York Times'* Tim Arango (2013) wrote about the beginning of the renewed Sunni insurgency, he drew an explicit connection between Sunni grievances and the laws and practices adopted by the U.S.-led coalition at the beginning of its occupation. He referred to the continued banishment of former Ba'athists from government employment and the reliance of Iraqi security police on undercover informants to identify suspected insurgents for lengthy detention without charges.

The resulting dragnet tactics overwhelmingly targeted Arab Sunni suspects and ensnared innocent civilians as well as active insurgents in an authoritarian and repressive regime of collective punishment. Arango warned that the consequence was that many ordinary Arab Sunni citizens were left "not only fed up with politics but … sympathetic with those who have recently taken up arms against the government." This is the kind of widespread and militant Arab Sunni support of insurgent violence that we have argued was a legacy of U.S.-led criminal militarism and legal cynicism in Iraq.

Arab Sunni detainees often insisted the U.S. forces allowed Shia-dominated national police units to conduct torture in Ministry of Interior prisons. WikiLeaks memos confirmed that U.S. forces were instructed not to report on Iraqi torture. In 2005, the Iraqi Ministry of Interior itself was found to be holding 625 malnourished and abused detainees in squalid conditions in a Baghdad building (BBC News 2005). In 2006, the United Nations reported systematic abuse and torture at an Iraqi government-run Baghdad prison. This facility reportedly held 1,400 prisoners in overcrowded and inhumane conditions. Also in 2006, the U.S. State Department reported that Iraq's national police force practiced widespread atrocities (U.S. Department of State 2006). These policies and practices were deeply rooted and persistent, and they provided fertile conditions and settings for AQI and ISIS recruitment of new fighters.

Sunni insurgents throughout the Iraqi conflict used suicide bombers and car bombs to attack police recruitment offices, presumably to deter volunteers from joining this national force. In theory, members of the Sunni Awakening movement were to be integrated by the government into the Iraqi Police, but as we noted early in this chapter, these plans were either blatantly ill-conceived or patently legally cynical. In either case, relatively few members of the Awakening forces were recruited into the Iraqi Police, and those who were recruited often later deserted and were suspected of being double agents for the Sunni insurgency and AQI and ISIS. The success of the Awakening was overestimated.

As Iraq entered a new phase of violence in 2011, it became increasingly apparent that the surge and the Awakening movement had not marked the end of the Sunni insurgency. In 2013, the International Crisis Group issued a report that concluded Iraqi security forces were "disproportionately deployed in Baghdad's Sunni neighborhoods as well as Sunni-populated governorates (Anbar, Salah al-Din, Ninewa, Kirkuk and Diyala)" (International Crisis Group 2013). The report concluded that the al-Maliki government has "resorted to both legal and extrajudicial means to consolidate power." In late 2013, the U.S. Department of State (2013) collated evidence of "credible cases of torture and abuse in Ministry of Interior (MOI), Ministry of Justice (MOJ), and Ministry of Defense detention facilities, including MOI and MOJ facilities where women were held." In 2014, Human Rights Watch (2014) issued a lengthy account of sexual abuse and assault in these facilities. The latter evidence of sexual torture returns us full circle to some of the worst practices of Saddam Hussein's Ba'athist regime described in detail in Chapter 1.

A recent analysis by Cordesman and Khazai places responsibility squarely with the U.S.-picked Prime Minister al-Maliki for the consolidation of power and repression of groups and individuals labeled as threatening and dangerous.

> Initially Sunni had been denounced or arrested as "Ba'athists" even when it was unclear they had any ties to current Ba'athist movements, had ever been supporters of the Ba'ath, or had only held more than low-level positions of the kind where party membership was necessary to have a job or career. From late 2011 onwards, however, criticism of the central government could be equated with the support of terrorism, protesting or active political opposition could be treated as support of Al Qaeda, arrests became increasingly arbitrary, detention became equally arbitrary, and the rule of law was at least partially suspended in suspect areas. (2014:142)

This made Iraq's Arab Sunnis inclined to fear and resist Iraq's central government as much or more than AQI or ISIS, who for their own part were involved in attacks on the Iraqi security forces, which the Arab Sunni community increasingly supported.

Events in the Anbar area of Iraq in 2013 and 2014 provide insight into the continuing nature of the conflict between Nouri al-Maliki's Shia-dominated central government, AQI, ISIS, and the Sunni insurgency more broadly. In December 2013, Prime Minister al-Maliki decided to respond to an ISIS-led ambush of government forces by shutting down a demonstration site in Ramadi and arresting one of the demonstration's Sunni leaders, Ahmed Alwani of the Iraqi Islamic Party. Maliki clearly hoped – much as in Basra and Sadr City in 2008 – that a show of government force could elicit widespread public support. But the attack on the Ramadi demonstration site conflated the violence of the provocations by ISIS with the nonviolence and popularity of the ongoing Sunni protests.

To this point, ISIS had been using the organized crime tactics described by Tilly that we associated with Muqtada al-Sadr and the Shia-based Mahdi Army and its incursions into Baghdad's Sunni and mixed neighborhoods in 2005–7. These tactics combined offers of protection from central government forces with threats against those who collaborated or cooperated with central government efforts to reestablish control. When al-Maliki ordered the shutdown of the Ramadi demonstration site, the effect was to provoke at least a temporarily strengthened alliance between ISIS, other Sunni militants, and tribal groups. The latter joined together in fighting Maliki's central government forces.

The period of greatly reduced violence, from 2007 through 2010, now seems most accurately characterized as a period of what Verta Taylor (1989) has called "abeyance." Taylor observes that when collective movements achieve concessions, in this case the recruitment of Sunni insurgent forces into the Awakening program, they sometimes enter into a period or pause that for all intents and purposes may convey the impression of relative calm and even passivity. Yet this does not mean that the grievances, demands, and cultural support for resistance have disappeared. Organized resistance may simply be in abeyance, awaiting new opportunities and incitements to action. Thus collective movements often are highly resilient in ways that anticipate renewal and reemergence. This is likely what happened with the Sunni insurgency during the surge and Awakening in Iraq.

Epilogue

President Barak Obama brought Prime Minister Nouri al-Maliki to the White House in December 2011 to mark the withdrawal of American combat troops from Iraq. The president optimistically observed that "the prime minister leads Iraq's most inclusive government yet," and that "violence remains at record lows." Less than two years later, with violence spiking to levels not seen since 2008, the prime minister returned to Washington to ask for Apache helicopter gunships with Hellfire missiles and F-16 fighter jets. When ISIS swept into Mosul in June 2014 – targeting prisons, freeing and recruiting thousands of detainees and inmates, robbing bank vaults, and targeting genocidal attacks on selected groups – al-Maliki urgently requested more help. However, the Obama administration opted for a change of leadership.

As strategically violent and tactically disciplined as ISIS had become by 2014, it was even more apparent when Mosul changed hands how hapless the U.S.-trained Iraqi Army was as a fighting force. Iraq's Shia-dominated army was ill prepared and badly supplied, with many units simply collapsing and abandoning the battlefield. Yet ISIS could not have so easily succeeded without the acquiescence and assistance of the Arab Sunni population and the support of local militias, many of whom previously were paid by the coalition to fight al-Qaeda in Iraq insurgents during the surge and Awakening period. Local support included remnants of Saddam's Republican Guard, now known as the Naqshbandia Order and reputedly led by Izzat Ibrahim al-Douri, a high-ranking general under Saddam (the "king of clubs" in the deck of cards American troops used to identify Saddam's henchmen). These former Ba'athists had strong roots in local Arab Sunni communities, which ISIS fighters often lacked.

By 2014, local Sunni groups were motivated to assist ISIS in wresting control from al-Maliki's Shia-dominated central government. The new, more disciplined tactics of ISIS included downplaying restrictions and punishments of

Sharia law among local Sunnis. This facilitated near-term alliances focused on regaining local control and expelling the Iraqi Army and Police. Leaders and fighters of local militias shared with ISIS a hatred for the Shia-dominated al-Maliki regime and its reliance on targeted violence, arrests, and detentions. Without the resulting legal cynicism of Arab Sunnis, ISIS could not have swept through northern Iraq, with the Iraqi Army melting away in the face of its well-planned, well-executed advances.

Of course, ISIS had not forsaken its violent interpretations of Islam, and members of non-Sunni ethnic and religious minorities felt the brunt of these beliefs and practices. The United Nations reported in July 2014 that Christian groups and a small but historic sect called the Yazidis were persecuted with kidnapping, killings, and destruction of their religious shrines near Mosul. Ethnic cleansing was first concentrated on the Yazidis, eliminating those who had not already fled with the arrival of ISIS; the Yazidis were now forcefully banished along with centuries of their cultural traditions from this part of Iraq. Meanwhile, also in July 2014, Human Rights Watch documented five mass revenge executions of Arab Sunni prisoners by the Iraqi Army, Iraqi Police, and Shia militias.

Given that levels of violence were already rising in 2011, it was an act of arrogance and hubris for David Petraeus to publish a 2013 article in *Foreign Policy* on "How We Won in Iraq." What would winning have meant in this context? Should there be pride in winning a war of aggression? Did it ever truly make sense to claim that the surge (or the Awakening movement) led to the inclusive government that President Obama's 2011 remarks suggested? Or, seen from the endogenous conflict perspective and the theory of legal cynicism adopted in this book, was the surge simply another part of an exclusive and aggressive elite bargain by the United States to support a Shia-dominated government in presiding over a separate and unsustainable peace that was especially disadvantaging to the Arab Sunnis in Iraq?

Of course, the surge was a Bush administration initiative that was not supported by the leading Democratic presidential candidates who sought their party's nomination in 2007. When General Petraeus traveled to Washington in September 2007 to present his PowerPoint slides to Congress on the progress of the surge, then-Senator Obama delivered a lengthy response. He summed up by characterizing the general's presentation of evidence as "selective." Then-Senator Hillary Clinton commented that "any fair reading of the advantages and disadvantages accruing post-surge ... end up on the downside."

We now have a "fuller reading" based on a longer time frame. The line graph presented in Figure E.1 charts Iraqi civilian deaths from the beginning of 2006 through the summer of 2010. This graph is likely a conservative

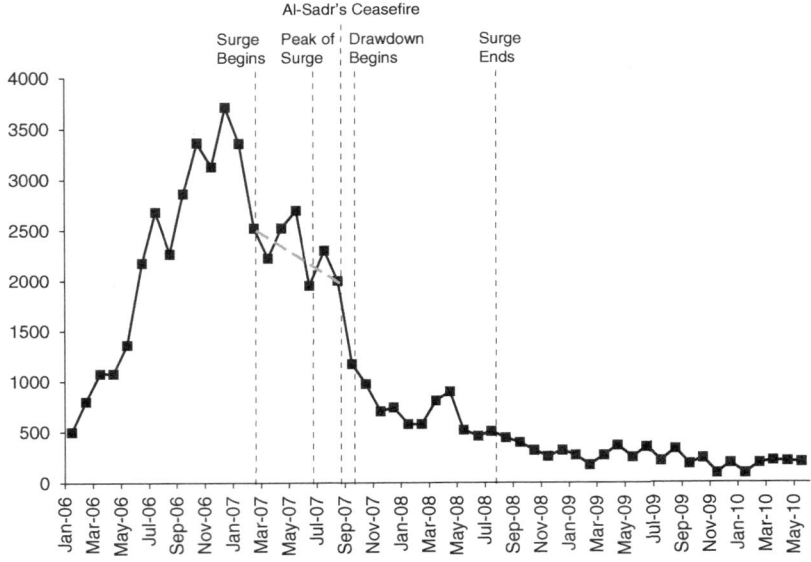

FIGURE E.1. Iraqi Civilian Deaths, circa 2006–2010

estimation given its reliance on the same U.S. military SIGACTS III Database General Petraeus used in his congressional testimony.

The line charting monthly deaths indicates a 2006 peak that parallels our analysis of the battle for Baghdad in Chapter 4. This graph shows that civilian deaths had already dropped by about a third – from about 3,700 to 2,500 deaths per month – before the surge even began in February 2007. This was followed by two near-term spikes in Iraqi civilian deaths associated with the peaking of surge force levels and offensive operations in the summer months of 2007 described in Chapter 5. The third-highest monthly number of U.S. soldier deaths occurred during this period.

A sharp decline in Iraqi civilian deaths followed between August and September 2007, as the drawdown in surge forces began. As emphasized in Chapter 4, this was also the month when Muqtada al-Sadr declared his unilateral ceasefire, which the U.S. leadership at first dismissed and then acknowledged was observed by most Mahdi Army units. We have included a broken line in Figure E.1 between the onset of the surge and the beginning of al-Sadr's ceasefire. This line traces a flattening out of the downward trajectory in the numbers of Iraqi civilian deaths during the 2007 peak of the surge.

The pace of the reduction in deaths resumed between August and September, with the onset of al-Sadr's ceasefire, and it continued as the drawdown of surge troops began. Yet none of the principals in the 2007 Senate surge hearings, including Petraeus himself, acknowledged the unexpected significance of al-Sadr in Iraq. Petraeus used an awkward metaphor to refer to al-Sadr and the Mahdi Army when he ironically commented, "In fact, a number of, we think, Shia militia elements took a knee for a while to sort of sort out."

The "take a knee" metaphor is a phrase that play-by-play sports commentators sometimes use to describe a winning football quarterback "running out the clock." The twisted syntax of Petraeus's sentence likely reflects a mid-thought discomfort in drawing a potentially victorious image of al-Sadr. Obama later tried to straighten out the metaphor when he said that "you've told us that, essentially, the Shias decided, even before we got there, to stand – to get on one knee and to wait it out." The reference to "waiting it out" was significant, given Obama's characterization noted later of the situation in Iraq as "good enough" and the subsequent return of Iraqi violence to heightened levels.

Neither Petraeus nor Obama foresaw that al-Sadr would effectively make a transition from an organized criminal to a political opportunist of the kind social theorist Charles Tilly noted has often occurred in modern state making. Tilly's perspective is highly relevant to the remaking of the Iraqi state. The widespread and systematic crimes against humanity perpetrated by al-Sadr's Mahdi Army in displacing Arab Sunni residents from many Baghdad neighborhoods – reconfiguring these neighborhoods under Shia control – was effectively locked in place by the U.S.-led surge in 2007. From this point, al-Sadr turned his attention to leading a bloc of parliamentary candidates and to increasing his control over selected government ministries. We return later to the significance of the recurring underestimation by the American leadership of al-Sadr's influence.

Obama's response to Petraeus's congressional appearance ended with an "everyman's" question about the surge that framed his approach to the U.S. combat role in Iraq in following years. "The question I think that everybody is asking," he remarked, "is how long will this take, and at what point do we say, 'enough'?" As he assumed the presidency and began maneuvering to withdraw all U.S. combat forces, Obama's position was that the situation was "good enough" to leave. His thinking was reminiscent of Vermont Republican Senator George Aiken's suggestion late in the American Vietnam War that we should essentially "declare victory and leave." It was a passive concession and expression of legal cynicism.

Less than a year later, in July 2008, with the Democratic presidential nomination now locked up, Obama visited Iraq and met with General Petraeus for an update on the surge and plans for troop withdrawals. Bush was still president, but he was now backing away from his earlier insistence that the United

States keep troops in Iraq until 2015. As we describe later in this chapter, Bush ultimately agreed to a 2011 departure that Obama eventually also accepted in a "good enough" elite bargain.

Violence was declining faster at the time of the Obama visit than when Petraeus had testified in Washington nearly a year earlier, and Obama cited the improvement in pressing for an earlier departure. He argued we should and could no longer sustain an expensive occupation, reasoning that "we can't pay $4.50 a gallon to Iraq because they are incompetent to spend it." Again echoing Senator Aiken's Vietnam formulation and his own remarks at the Senate hearing, candidate Obama challenged Petraeus's resistance to advancing the withdrawal date by suggesting, "at some point you have to ask, 'Do you just say this is good enough?' You are so invested. You are reaching for excellence, not just adequacy." Petraeus protested, "no, we are minimalists here," concluding, "we are very happy with adequate" (Gordon and Trainor 2012:539).

The polls were already forecasting Obama's presidential victory before his nomination. As noted, President Obama would ultimately add several months to his own departure schedule and accept Bush's negotiated date of December 2011 for the withdrawal of combat troops. However, Bush had also negotiated a status of forces agreement with the expectation that a residual commitment of noncombat troops would remain beyond that date to "advise and assist." Obama at first insisted that such a force must be small, and then late in the process decided against any residual forces at all. This was essentially an extension into 2011 of his "good enough" characterization of the situation in Iraq, but it was also the product of a series of convoluted elite bargains. To understand the logic of these bargains, it is necessary to go back to several watershed events in the Iraqi conflict.

The Blackwater case, which began with the 2007 mass shooting in Nisour Square and is discussed in further detail later, likely played a major role in convincing both Prime Minister al-Maliki and President Obama that the level of legal cynicism among Iraqis about U.S. military forces and contracted security guards was probably beyond repair. This encouraged the conclusion that a complete U.S. withdrawal was the likely path of least resistance. Even President Bush, who desperately wanted to believe in the benefits of a residual force in Iraq, came to realize in his final year in office that the terms of keeping military advisors in the country would require a carefully crafted and deceptive compromise.

Of course, elite compromise – in the form of what Dodge (2013, 2012) calls the "exclusive elite bargain" – had been the logic of American involvement in Iraq throughout. But a new phase of legal cynicism and what Hillary

Clinton had earlier called "the suspension of belief" now became necessary in the negotiations that Bush and then Obama used to find their way to the American withdrawal of combat troops. Assuring immunity from Iraq's courts was a publicly proclaimed American requirement for any of its military remaining in Iraq.

We noted in Chapter 3 how strong the contemporary as well as historical pressures were for Iraq's judiciary to comply and collaborate rather than resist the press of political influence in responding to the U.S.-directed conduct of the war, including the use of torture. In Chapter 3, we showed that more Iraqi judges were inclined to cynically collaborate than resist these influences, even when reaching hypothetical decisions about torture cases involving American forces. Still, notwithstanding such political protection from the will of the Iraqi judiciary, neither the American military leadership nor the Bush administration and its culture of criminal militarism had any inclination to contemplate U.S. soldiers – or themselves – being exposed to Iraq's courts.

Thus as the involvement of American forces in Iraq moved awkwardly to its conclusion, the Bush administration's negotiators had found themselves in a dilemma – namely, needing to consider compromises about accountability that they did not intend to make in order to keep U.S. forces in Iraq. *With many Arab Sunnis in Iraq reporting unnecessary violence by U.S.-led troops occurring near where they lived, there was an unyielding demand for Iraqi jurisdiction over U.S. soldiers' war crimes.* An apparent solution involved an improvisation in the rule of law based on a degree of legal cynicism that might seem remarkable even in this context of elite bargaining.

The Bush administration's solution was a negotiated formal legal framework – a status of forces agreement (SOFA) ostensibly promising an end to immunity for U.S. forces – but actually including carefully crafted provisions making it extremely unlikely that such prosecutions ever would take place. This was an agreement that provided a semblance of formal justice without the substantive content it implied; that is, it was a striking example of elite legal cynicism.

The Bush bargain was struck by an increasingly influential aide from the National Security Council (NSC), Brett McGurk, who had been one of the early advocates of the surge. McGurk was the source in 2008 of a proposal calculated to address the United States' unwillingness to relinquish immunity for its soldiers. McGurk's formulation met the al-Maliki government's need for the appearance of formal judicial authority over these soldiers – especially when they engaged in egregious forms of unnecessary violence in attacks on Iraqi civilians. He did this with a resort to legal indeterminacy of a kind that paralleled the U.S. interpretation of torture law described in Chapter 3.

McGurk explained his solution in a "Concentric Circles Paper" marked for NSC "Small Group Eyes Only" (Gordon and Trainor 2012:549). The crux of the dilemma was that the Iraqis wanted judicial authority over violent crimes committed by U.S. soldiers while away from their bases and off duty. "Off duty" is a highly indeterminate concept in the military context. One could argue that entire combat tours in Iraq were served "on duty." One of the "escape clauses" in the memo alternatively noted that, if necessary, soldiers could be further placed under orders not to leave their bases when "off duty." The SOFA also never actually defined the kind of "grave premeditated felonies" it would deliver to Iraqi jurisdiction, leaving this to be adjudicated by a joint U.S./Iraqi committee "to be named later" and that was never convened.

A further dimension of legal cynicism involved the participation of Sunni Vice President Tariq al-Hashimi in the SOFA process. Al-Maliki would later have al-Hashimi charged with plotting against the government and effectively have him run out of the country only a few days after President Obama had praised al-Maliki during his White House visit for the inclusiveness of his government. Al-Hashimi had demanded that the SOFA include enforcement of an amnesty law that would release thousands of Sunni detainees held by the Iraqis without charges. He also demanded a public referendum on the SOFA be held within six months as a source of leverage for the amnesty. The referendum was never conducted.

Nonetheless, the SOFA as modified by McGurk was adopted at the end of 2008 and was one of President George W. Bush's last initiatives in Iraq. Bush embraced the agreement to set the foundation for the U.S. presence of military advisors beyond the 2011 withdrawal of combat troops. To underline the importance of the agreement, Bush traveled to Iraq several weeks before Christmas. At the event meant to commemorate the SOFA, a reporter famously stood up in the audience and threw one and then the other of his shoes at the president, who bobbed and weaved to elude the flying projectiles.

The reporter's symbolic act was accompanied by his shouting of insults about the carnage of the war of aggression and his outrage about the transparently illegitimate elite bargain involved in the SOFA and its cynical celebration by the Iraqi prime minister and outgoing U.S. president. The public humiliation of George Bush in Iraq was captured by the international press for the entire world to see. Nonetheless, the legal cynicism and elite bargaining continued undiminished and unabated, albeit less conspicuously, during the Obama administration, when the new U.S. administration and Prime Minister al-Maliki confronted the still festering uncertainty about the continued presence of the U.S. military in Iraq and al-Maliki's disappointing 2010 election results.

After a period of indecision and vacillation, President Obama decided to end the prospect of even an advisory military force remaining in Iraq. This outcome was foretold when he insisted on terms that he knew al-Sadr and other governing bloc politicians would refuse. The terms were that any remaining U.S. soldiers must have immunity from prosecution for crimes committed in Iraq and that the continued presence of U.S. forces would also require the full approval of Iraq's parliament. These were terms Obama knew could not be met, and all U.S. combat troops finally left at the end of 2011.

Yet this is not the full story of the 2011 U.S. withdrawal (see Filkens 2014:57–8). After the disappointing showing by al-Maliki in the 2010 parliamentary elections (discussed further later), Qassem Sileimani, the head of Iran's powerful and clandestine Quds Force, invited Iraq's leading politicians to meet with him in Iran. Sileimani is a feared and distrusted figure. To cite only one source of concern, earlier in the war Sileimani's Quds Force is thought to have smuggled powerful explosives into Iraq that were used in insurgent attacks that killed many U.S. soldiers.

Dexter Felkins (2014b) reports that the United States obtained a transcript of the post-election 2011 meeting with Sileimani spelling out a brokered deal that was accepted in Iran by al-Maliki, and that was also agreed to several weeks later by the Obama administration's National Security Council. In exchange for supporting al-Maliki's second term as prime minister, and despite al-Maliki's party having won two fewer seats than the opposition that gained considerable Sunni support, Muqtada al-Sadr was promised control over several government ministries. Al-Maliki further agreed to make a pro-Iranian Kurdish politician the new president of Iraq. Finally, Sileimani's bargain required al-Maliki's agreement that all U.S. forces would leave Iraq by the end of 2011. As noted earlier, the reality was that neither the U.S. nor the Iraqi public wanted U.S. forces in Iraq, and this likely enhanced President Obama's willingness to accept the terms of the elite bargain, even though this bargain was brokered via a crucial Iranian intervention.

This book in various ways has documented the double and linked macro- and micro-level sources of legal cynicism about the criminal militarism of the American involvement in Iraq, and we now in a final way underscore the level of micro-level legal cynicism that this produced among the Iraqi public. Figure E.2 uses the nationally representative surveys analyzed in Chapters 5 and 6 to provide an overall picture of the persistent legal cynicism of Iraqis about American involvement from 2004 through 2009 – a cynicism that continued throughout the rise and fall in violence and that had among its roots sectarian-linked outrage about the evidence of criminal militarism involved in unnecessary violence against civilians by U.S. forces.

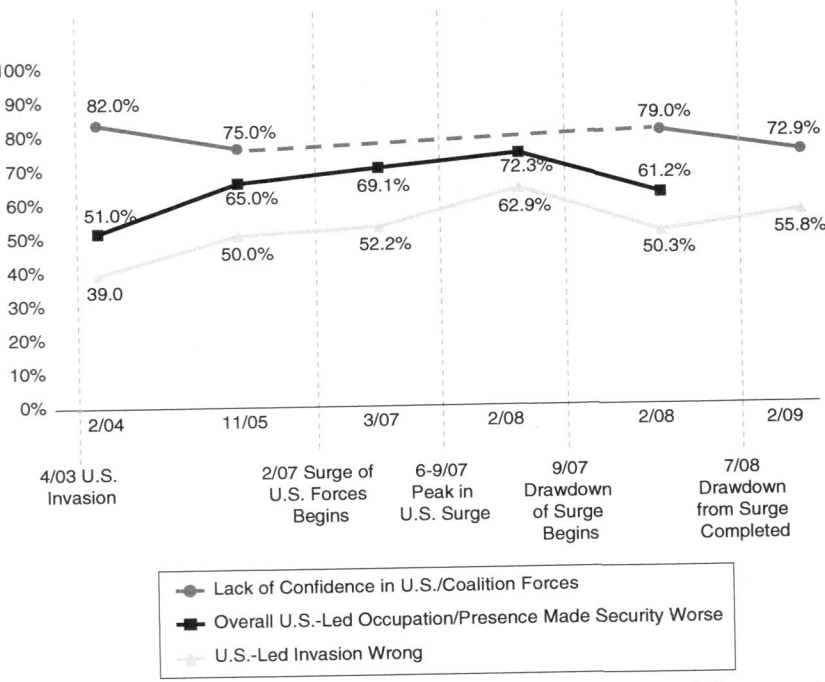

FIGURE E.2. Attitudes toward U.S.-led Invasion, Occupation and Presence in Iraq, circa 2003–2008

In Figure E.2, we see that from 2004 through 2009 about three-quarters of Iraqis lacked confidence in the capacity of U.S./coalition forces to improve security. When further asked from 2004 through 2008 (including the period of the surge) about the impact of the U.S.-led occupation and continued presence in the country, a stubborn majority reported these forces actually made security worse. And while a low of nearly 40 percent of Iraqis thought in 2004 that the U.S.-led invasion was clearly wrong, reflecting the initial and fleeting "shadow of hope" that we described in Chapter 2, a majority of Iraqis subsequently and consistently concluded that the invasion was wrong from 2005 through 2009.

Figures E.3 and E.4 focus on the concluding period of the presence of U.S. forces in 2008 and 2009. Although Figure E.3 reinforces the finding that Kurds compared to the other dominant groups were relatively happy with the U.S. decision to invade Iraq (with less than 20 percent saying this invasion was wrong), in other respects even the Kurds were not enthusiastic about the U.S.-led role in Iraq – while the Shia and especially the Arab Sunnis were

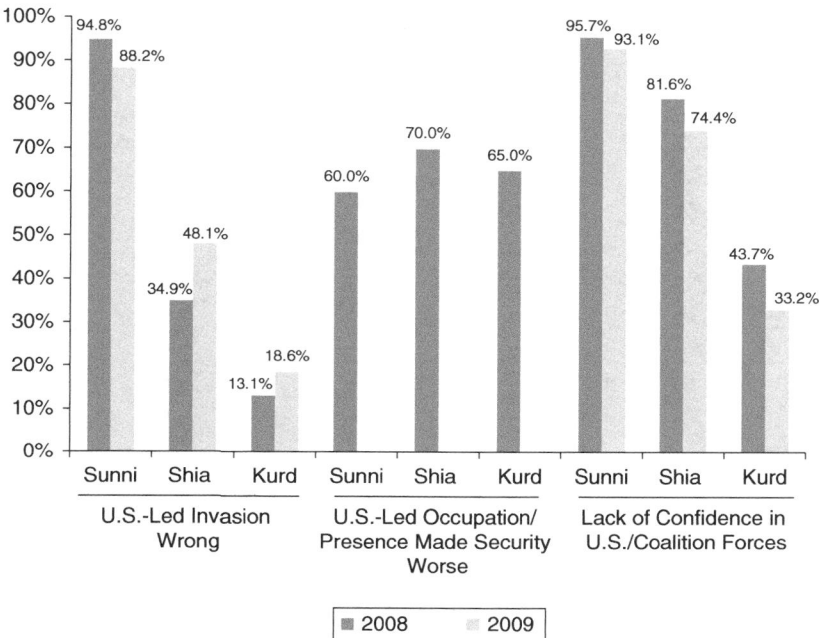

FIGURE E.3. Attitudes toward U.S.-led Invasion, Occupation, and Presence in Iraq by Community Composition, circa 2008–2009 (responses to presence available for 2008 only)

highly and especially cynical in their dissatisfaction. About 90 percent of the Sunnis thought the U.S.-led invasion was simply wrong, compared to a third to half of the Shia. More than 70 percent of all three groups thought the occupation/presence of the U.S.-led forces made security worse. And again, about 90 percent of the Sunnis lacked confidence in the U.S.-led forces, compared to about three-quarters of the Shia and about a third of the Kurds.

As we noted in Chapters 4 through 6, Arab Sunnis felt themselves to be targets of both Shia and U.S. policies. Figure E.4 brings us back to this issue of unnecessary crimes of violence by again focusing on attacks of U.S./coalition forces on civilians. The results presented in Figure E.4 consistently illustrate the ways this perception of unnecessary U.S. violence against civilians was correlated with the legal cynicism of Iraqis about the legitimacy of the U.S.-led role in Iraq in 2008 and 2009. Recall that this was the period in these data when war violence decreased and feelings of security improved.

The results in Figure E.4 indicate that this representative sample of Iraqis responded especially negatively to the U.S. role when unnecessary attacks

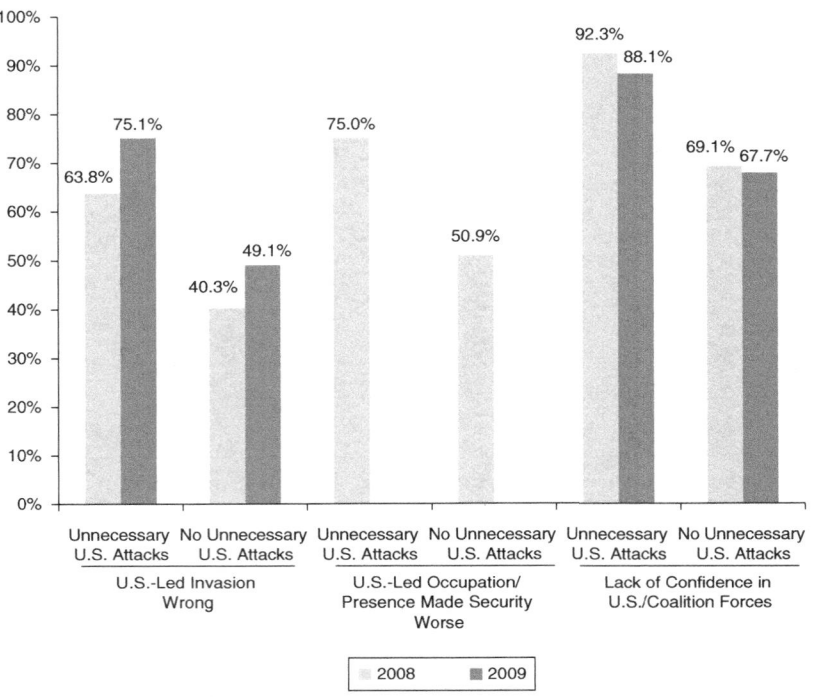

FIGURE E.4. Attitudes toward U.S.-led Invasion, Occupation, and Presence in Iraq by Unnecessary U.S./Coalition Attacks on Civilians, circa 2008–2009

on civilians occurred nearby. *These unnecessary attacks on civilians strongly provoked the Iraqi sense of legal cynicism about U.S. violence – a continuing manifestation of what we have more generally referred to as criminal militarism.* Recall that in Chapters 5 and 6 we reported that more than 40 percent – nearly half – of Iraqis reported the occurrence of these unnecessary U.S.-led attacks on civilians during the surge. Among these respondents, two-thirds to three-quarters thought the invasion of Iraq was wrong, three-quarters thought the occupation/presence made security worse, and more than 90 percent lacked confidence in the U.S./coalition forces. This is a high and persistent expression of legal cynicism about the U.S. role in Iraq.

Although the sources of this legal cynicism were many and varied, in the end three singularly impactful episodes stand out: the lack of accountability of U.S. leaders for torture at Abu Ghraib prison, the solitary conviction and single noncustodial sentence for the killings of twenty-four civilians at Haditha, and the long-delayed and problem-plagued prosecution of five Blackwater USA guards for killing seventeen civilians in Baghdad's Nisour Square. We have discussed Abu Ghraib and Haditha previously in this book, and we now finally consider the Nisour Square killings involving Blackwater.

Only a few weeks *before* the Nisour Square shooting, a U.S. State Department investigator, Jean Richter, reported problems in the billion-dollar contract for Blackwater security work in Iraq. More remarkable, however, was the Blackwater response. The top on-site Blackwater manager threatened, according to a memo Richter wrote several weeks *before* the Nisour Square shooting, "that he could kill" him and that "no one could or would do anything about it as we were in Iraq" (Risen 2014). The memo concluded that "Blackwater contractors saw themselves as above the law" and that as a result of "hands off" management "the contractors, instead of Department officials, are in command and control."

The massacre in Nisour Square took place several weeks later. Federal prosecutors concluded that Blackwater security guards shot their automatic weapons, machine guns, and grenade launchers indiscriminately into the crowded square. Blackwater's employees claimed they were receiving incoming fire, but there was no evidence of this. Witnesses reported the Blackwater guards fired wildly into the crowded traffic circle, leaving seventeen people dead, including women and children. The episode "helped cement the image of Blackwater, whose security guards were involved in scores of shootings, as a trigger-happy company that operated with impunity because of its lucrative contracts with the American government" (Apuzzo 2014).

One Blackwater guard, Jeremy Ridgeway, pleaded guilty to voluntary manslaughter, but charges against four other guards were dismissed based on prosecutorial errors – then these charges were reinstated on appeal. The four guards were finally convicted in 2014, seven years after the massacre. There was no acknowledgment of responsibility at the state department or at other high levels of the U.S. government for Blackwater's indiscriminant and extensively reported use of force in Iraq.

In the end, ideas about neither the rule of law nor principles of democracy fared well in Iraq. As we saw in Chapter 5, Maliki's popularity with the electorate peaked in 2008 and 2009, and his State of Law coalition was the winning party in the 2009 provincial elections. But by early 2010, the political winds were shifting in Iraq. The March 2010 national election brought out more than 60 percent of the electorate and produced a close and unexpected outcome, with the Iraqiya party led by Ayad Allawi winning a narrow two-seat parliamentary victory. Although Allawi was a secular Shia, his nationalist coalition was mostly Sunni. The Iraq Constitution provided that the party winning the "largest bloc" of seats should be provided the first opportunity to form a majority government.

Al-Maliki minced no words in responding to the 2010 election outcome, declaring, "No way we will accept the results." This response foretold al-Maliki's continued efforts to hold on to the prime ministership in 2014. Thus after his disappointing 2010 electoral results, al-Maliki demanded a recount and called on the de-Ba'athification commission to disqualify elected Sunni opposition candidates and prevent "a return to violence" (Parker and Ahmed 2010). However, al-Maliki's most damaging challenge to the legitimacy of a new democracy and a politically independent judiciary was a letter he sent to Iraq's highest court challenging the constitutional interpretation of the first right to form a government.

Just four days after sending his letter, al-Maliki received the decision he wanted: the court issued its determination that the "largest bloc" referred *either* to winning the most seats by election *or* assembling a majority bloc in parliament after the election. The intent of the constitutional drafters seemed clearly to have given electoral outcomes primacy over post hoc parliamentary maneuvering. It was hard to avoid the impression in 2010 that al-Maliki had his way with the highest court and thereby subverted democracy, the independence of the judiciary, and the rule of law. This impression only increased when the following month a judicial panel confirmed a decision to disqualify more than fifty elected Sunni Ba'athist candidates.

As the United States was preparing for its 2011 departure, Iraq confronted an electoral and constitutional challenge that went to the core of its already fragile commitment to democracy and the rule of law. The Obama administration resorted once again to exclusive elite bargaining. The new U.S. ambassador, Christopher Hill, was disinclined toward Ayad Allawi becoming prime minister, in significant part because of his base of Sunni support.

Reaching back to the Bush administration's SOFA negotiations, the Obama administration again turned to Brett McGurk to help resolve the legitimation problem posed by al-Maliki's refusal to concede the 2010 election. Al-Maliki was stubbornly staying put in the prime minister's office, just as he would try to do again in 2014. Like Ambassador Hill, McGurk opposed Allawi becoming prime minister, and President Obama eventually signaled his agreement that al-Maliki could continue despite the electoral outcome (Gordon and Trainor 2012). This outcome had already been sealed in Iran and in Washington, and the question was how to somehow make it appear democratically legitimate in Iraq.

The result was a new elite bargain with a government of national unity to be formed through what was called the Erbil Agreement (Dodge 2013:247). This agreement established a new entity, the National Council for Strategic Policy, not mentioned in the constitution. The agreement was that this council would recommend the direction of key foreign and economic policies and form the foundation for a "partnership government," exercising influence over important decisions – for example, in the oil sector – that were not already allocated by the constitution to the prime minister.

This new elite bargain provided that al-Maliki would continue for another four years as prime minister and that Allawi would become the first head of the envisioned council. However, the council was never established (Dodge 2013:248). When al-Maliki came to Washington in December 2011 to receive President Obama's praise of his inclusive government, he came without members of Allawi's Iraqiya party or other Sunni parliamentarians (Gordon and Trainor 2012). As noted earlier, only days after Maliki's return to Baghdad, the Sunni vice president, Tariq al-Hashimi, was charged with plotting against the government and effectively exiled from Iraq. Nonetheless, this concluding phase of the leadership transition was judged "good enough."

The former Iraqi ambassador to the United Nations, Feisel Istrabadi, later lamented that "there was a moment, when it was conceivable to imagine of Iraq getting out of this exclusive elite pact, and that was in 2010 when against all odds and all predictions the al-Iraqiya List won a bare plurality of two seats over the governing State of Law List" (2013:3). Istrabadi emphasized the greater national representativeness of Iraqiya's successful candidates compared to State of Law's failure to elect any candidates north of Baghdad. His prediction was that the Sunni would sooner or later give up on the centralizing influence of a government in Baghdad and, as our data similarly suggested, that a separation of Iraq's major sectarian groups would continue, with a new form of regionalism emerging in Iraq. Although Istrabadi did not specifically predict the dramatic new role of ISIS and its efforts to establish an Islamic state, his prediction was prophetic.

What should Americans make of this outcome? The hope we were asked to accept until the 2014 fall of Mosul and the advances of ISIS was that the results in Iraq were in President Obama's earlier words "good enough." Subsequent events and the results of the research presented in this book suggest otherwise. For Americans, this dubious belief in a "good enough" outcome expressed a stubbornly mistaken inclination to deny the lasting lessons to be learned about the criminal militarism of a war of aggression in Iraq.

Appendix

TABLE 2.2. *Descriptive statistics, Baghdad circa August/September 2003*

	μ $(n = 980)$	σ
Neighborhood Composition		
Shia Majority (0/1)	0.37	0.48
Sunni Majority (0/1)	0.08	0.28
Mixed Composition (0/1)	0.55	0.5
Demographic Background		
Male (0/1)	0.48	0.5
Age (10 groupings, 18–60+)	6.19	1.75
Education (7 groupings, none–university)	3.73	0.5
Married + Children (0/1)	0.61	0.49
Current Income (5 groupings, very low–high)	2.62	0.81
Rights Issues		
Religious Restrictions (1–3)	0.18	0.45
Political Expression (1–3)	0.86	0.61
Crime Victimization		
Assault (1–3)	0.04	0.27
Property (1–3)	0.07	0.39
Burglary (1–3)	0.04	0.24
Fear for Safety		
Fear at Night (1–3)	0.93	0.42
Fear during Day (1–3)	0.8	0.64
Baghdad Unsafe (1–3)	2.88	0.46

(*continued*)

TABLE 2.2 *(continued)*

	μ (n = 980)	σ
Non-access to Essential Services		
Medicine (1–3)	0.37	0.61
Food (1–3)	0.26	0.54
Gas (1–3)	0.5	0.69
Water (1–3)	0.92	0.75
Electricity (1–3)	1.13	0.41
Comparative Dis/Advantage		
Job Loss (1–3)	0.16	0.42
Income Gain/Loss (1–5)	2.92	1.04
Legitimacy of Coalition		
US/GB Leadership (1–3, α = 0.85)	7.28	4.34
CPA (1–5)	2.95	1.02
Legitimacy of Invasion		
Conditions Better/Worse since Invasion (6–21, α = 0.70)	14.62	3.52

TABLE 2.3. *Neighborhood- and individual-level predictors of perceived legitimacy of the Iraq invasion, Baghdad circa August/September 2003*

	Model 1 β	Model 2 β	Model 3 β	Model 4 β	Model 5 β	Model 6 β	Model 7 β	Model 8 β
Neighborhood Composition								
Shia Majority	1.42*	1.39*	1.41*	1.36*	1.50*	1.29*	0.87**	0.85**
Sunni Majority	−1.52*	−1.48*	−1.47*	−1.43*	−1.43*	−1.57**	1.19**	−1.21**
Demographic Background								
Gender	−0.1	−0.09	−0.07	−0.01	−0.05	−0.37	−0.53**	−0.53**
Age	−0.14	−0.15	−0.14	−0.14	−0.15*	−0.17	−0.08	−0.08
Education	−0.07	−0.07	−0.07	−0.06	−0.06	−0.01	0.01	0.01
Married + Children	−0.13	−0.11	−0.11	−0.16	−0.21	−0.12	−0.03	−0.02
Current Income	0.77***	0.78***	0.77***	0.72***	0.70***	0.23	0.21	0.21
Rights Issues								
Religious Restrictions		−0.18	−0.19	−0.1	−0.16	−0.19	0.07	0.05
Political Expression		0.48**	0.48**	0.48**	0.42**	0.38*	0.04	0.24
Crime Victimization								
Assault			−0.01	0.04	0.09	0.41	0.58	0.57
Property			−0.36	−0.32	−0.33	−0.26	−0.18	−0.16
Burglary			−0.62	−0.63	−0.53	−0.24	−0.06	−0.08
Fear for Safety								
Fear at Night				0.14	0.14	0.23	0.36	0.35
Fear during Day				−0.39*	−0.32	−0.22	−0.30*	−0.29*
Baghdad Unsafe				−1.14***	−1.09***	−1.02***	−0.68***	−0.18***

(continued)

TABLE 2.3 *(continued)*

	Model 1 β	Model 2 β	Model 3 β	Model 4 β	Model 5 β	Model 6 β	Model 7 β	Model 8 β
Essential Services								
Medicine					−0.32	−0.33[*]	−0.25	−0.24
Food					−0.29	−0.2	−0.1	−0.09
Gas					−0.26	−0.14	−0.22	−0.24
Water					−0.46	−0.43[**]	−0.06	−0.06
Electricity					0.89[***]	0.81[**]	0.43[*]	0.44[*]
Comparative Dis/Advantage								
Job Loss						−0.93[***]	−1.13[***]	−1.12[***]
Income Gain/Loss						0.81[***]	0.66[***]	0.67[***]
Legitimacy of Coalition								
US/GB Leadership							0.23[***]	0.23[***]
CPA							0.99[***]	0.89[***]
CPA × Shia								0.30[+]
Intercept							14.17	

CHAPTER 4 TABLES

TABLE 4.2. *Comparison between GP and CVI data sets of index-crime distribution across Baghdad neighborhoods*

		Pearson's χ^2			Fisher's exact test	
		Value	df	p	p	n
All Victims	2003–4	37.3864	32	0.275	0.225	105
	2003–5	63.6822	34	0.002	0	166
Excluding Displaced Persons	2003–4	32.7778	31	0.38	0.533	80
	2003–5	39.002	32	0.184	0.184	92

TABLE 4.3. *Descriptive statistics for individual and neighborhood characteristics, Baghdad GP (2003) & CVI (2004–2008)*

	μ $(n = 764)$	σ
Individuals (CVI)		
Male (o/1)	0.75	0.43
Sectarian Identity (o/1)		
Sunni	0.4	0.49
Non-Shia Others	0.24	0.43
(Shia Reference Group)		
Employed (o/1)	0.63	0.48
Perpetrator Identity (o/1)		
Al-Qaeda	0.13	0.34
Mahdi Army	0.33	0.47
U.S. Forces	0.1	0.31
(Other Perpetrators Reference Group)		
2006 Attacks (o/1)	0.35	0.48
Killings (o/1)	0.56	0.5
Harassment (o/1)	0.35	0.5
Threats (o/1)	0.59	0.49
Displaced (o/1)	0.81	0.39
Neighborhoods (CVI & GP)	$(n = 25)$	
Sectarian Identity (o–1)		
Sunni	0.2	0.41
Mixed	0.68	0.48
(Shia Reference Group)		

(continued)

TABLE 4.3 *(continued)*

	μ ($n = 764$)	σ
Fear at Night after Invasion (0–1) (GP)	0.96	0.09
Fear at Night before Invasion (0–1) (GP)	0.06	0.05
Killings (0–1) (CVI)	0.55	0.13
Harassment (0–1) (CVI)	0.35	0.08
Threats (0–1) (CVI)	0.5	0.65

TABLE 4.4. *Multilevel estimates predicting the log-odds of harassment and threats*

	Harassment β (se)	Threats β (se)	
Individual-Level Characteristics			
Male	−0.014	0.241	0.245
	(0.157)	(0.186)	(0.19)
Sunni	0.369*	0.411*	0.361
	(0.179)	(0.207)	(0.203)
Non-Shia Others	0.318	0.614**	0.592***
	(0.25)	(0.191)	(0.173)
Employed	−0.244*	0.281	0.336
	(0.114)	(0.183)	(0.187)
Al-Qaeda	0.448**	0.552*	0.502*
	(0.169)	(0.225)	(0.241)
Mahdi Army	0.785***	0.483***	0.324**
	(0.157)	(0.107)	(0.105)
U.S. Forces	0.661*	−0.533*	−0.705**
	(0.275)	(0.242)	(0.229)
2006	−0.031	−0.095	0.076
	(0.162)	(0.145)	(0.148)
Harassment	–	–	0.972***
			(0.196)
Neighborhood-Level Characteristics			
Sunni	0.420***	0.217	0.132
	(0.089)	(0.343)	(0.353)
Mixed	0.207*	0.186	0.152
	(0.102)	(0.189)	(0.183)
Intercept	−1.086	−0.141	−0.387

Robust standard errors in parentheses
* $p < 0.05$, ** $p < 0.01$, *** $p < 0.001$

TABLE 4.5. *Multilevel estimates predicting the log-odds of displacement*

	Model 1 β (se)	Model 2 β (se)	Model 3 β (se)	Model 4 β (se)	Model 5 β (se)
Individual-Level Characteristics					
Male			0.215 (0.199)	0.238 (0.206)	0.164 (0.227)
Sunni			0.667 (0.243)**	0.576 (0.243)**	0.464 (0.229)*
Non-Shia			−0.054 (0.173)	0.451 (0.271)	0.268 (0.297)
Employed			0.502 (0.252)*	−0.024 (0.176)	−0.121 (0.169)
Al-Qaeda			0.094 (0.344)	0.038 (0.359)	−0.185 (0.333)
Mahdi Army			0.638 (0.303)*	0.547 (0.307)	0.463 (0.331)
U.S. Forces			−0.925 (0.224)***	−1.014 (0.237)***	−0.814 (0.270)**
2006			0.237 (0.156)	0.248 (0.158)	0.281 (0.188)
Killings			−0.324 (0.179)	−0.286 (0.177)	−0.247 (0.183)
Harassment				0.651 (0.195)***	0.315 (0.225)
Threats					1.593 (0.229)***
Neighborhood-Level Characteristics					
Sunni	0.725 (0.331)*	−0.040 (0.431)	−0.051 (0.419)	−0.069 (0.424)	−0.100 (0.467)
Mixed	0.680 (0.283)*	0.332 (0.271)	0.273 (0.356)	0.304 (0.383)	0.246 (0.467)
Killings	0.874 (1.040)	0.512 (1.054)	0.898 (0.970)	1.436 (0.892)	1.023 (0.776)
Fear before Invasion	2.062 (3.033)		3.581 (2.689)	3.981 (2.241)	2.855 (2.463)
Fear after Invasion		4.153 (1.226)**	4.863 (1.340)**	3.974 (1.207)**	3.763 (1.375)**
Harassment				3.385 (1.310)**	1.970 (1.654)
Threats					0.492 (.760)
Intercept	0.843	1.245	0.83	0.694	0.187

Robust standard errors in parentheses
* $p < 0.05$, ** $p < 0.01$, *** $p < 0.001$

TABLE 4.6. *Trimmed models of displacement with cross-level interactions*

	Model 1 β (se)	Model 2 β (se)	Model 3 β (se)
Individual-Level Characteristics			
Sunni	0.539**	0.541***	0.558**
	−0.194	−0.198	−0.196
U.S. Forces	−0.820***	−0.787**	−0.825***
	−0.234	−0.246	−0.244
2006	0.279	0.318*	0.557**
	−0.185	−0.162	−0.196
Threats	1.793***	1.800*	1.809***
	−0.199	−0.993	−0.197
Neighborhood-Level Characteristics			
Fear after Invasion	4.288***	1.990*	2.632*
	−1.132	−0.993	−1.219
Cross-Level Interactions			
Fear after Invasion X U.S. Forces	−3.011+		−2.169
	−1.607		−1.717
Fear after Invasion X 2006		4.268*	3.931*
		−1.89	−1.929
Intercept	0.341	0.323	0.316

Robust standard errors in parentheses
+ $p < 0.1$, * $p < 0.05$, ** $p < 0.01$, *** $p < 0.001$

CHAPTER 5 TABLES

TABLE 5.1. *Individual and community descriptive statistics: surge-era Iraq surveys in 2008–2009*

	During surge, 2008		After surge, 2009	
	μ	σ	μ	σ
Individual-Level Characteristics	($n = 2186$)		($n = 2213$)	
War Violence and Security				
Reported War Violence (0–8) ($\alpha = .61$)	2.78	1.88	1.82	1.51
Iraqi Army (0/1)	0.22	0.41	0.2	0.4
Iraqi Police (0/1)	0.22	0.41	0.17	0.38
Local Militia (0/1)	0.36	0.48	0.2	0.4
Bombing (0/1)	0.4	0.49	0.26	0.44
Sniping and Crossfire (0/1)	0.35	0.48	0.22	0.41

Sectarian Attacks (0/1)	0.35	0.48	0.17	0.38
Kidnapping (0/1)	0.45	0.5	0.33	0.47
Unnecessary U.S. Attacks on Civilians (0/1)	0.44	0.5	0.27	0.45
Perceived Security from Surge (0–6) ($\alpha = 0.75$)	2.28	2.21	–	–
Perceived Security from Awakening (0–2)	1.36	0.74	–	–
Perceived Security (0–13) ($\alpha = 0.87$)	7.19	3.89	9.61	3.11
Support for U.S. Forces and Prime Minister				
Approval for U.S./Coalition Forces (0/1)	0.29	0.45	0.29	0.45
Approval for al-Maliki (0/1)	0.38	0.49	0.54	0.5
Background Characteristics				
Kurd (0/1)	0.15	0.36	0.16	0.37
Sunni (0/1)	0.3	0.46	0.29	0.46
Shia (0/1)	0.51	0.5	0.51	0.5
Other Sectarian Identity (0/1)	0.04	0.19	0.04	0.19
Male (0/1)	0.5	0.5	0.49	0.5
Age (18–83)	35.91	12.78	35.9	12.62
Education (1–5)	3.27	1.24	3.13	1.24
Married (0/1)	0.69	0.46	0.67	0.47
Employed (0/1)	0.37	0.48	0.38	0.49
Location				
Sadr City (0/1)	0.05	0.21	0.05	0.22
Rest of Baghdad (0/1)	0.16	0.37	0.16	0.37
Anbar (0/1)	0.05	0.22	0.05	0.2
Basara (0/1)	0.08	0.25	0.07	0.25
Kirkuk (0/1)	0.03	0.16	0.02	0.15
Mosul (0/1)	0.04	0.2	0.05	0.21
Other (0/1)	0.6	0.49	0.6	0.49
Community-Level Characteristics	($n = 452$)		($n = 443$)	
Predominately Shia Community (0–1)	0.45	0.38	0.47	0.43
Aggregate Reported War Violence (0–1)	0.34	0.19	0.23	0.15

TABLE 5.2. *HLM Bernoulli regression models of unnecessary U.S./coalition attacks on civilians reported during the surge, Iraq survey in 2008*

	During surge, 2008	
	β (se)	β (se)
Individual-Level Characteristics		
War Violence		
Iraqi Army	0.08 (0.12)	0.08 (0.13)
Iraqi Police	0.32 (0.12)**	0.38 (0.12)**
Local Militia	0.24 (0.11)*	0.29 (0.11)**
Bombing	0.47 (0.11)***	0.40 (0.12)***
Sniping and Crossfire	0.06 (0.11)	0.41 (0.11)
Sectarian Attacks	0.17 (0.11)	0.11 (0.11)
Kidnapping	0.22 (0.10)*	0.29 (0.11)**
Background Characteristics		
Kurd	−1.08 (0.36)**	−1.06 (0.36)**
Sunni	1.22 (0.27)***	1.08 (0.27)***
Shia	1.11 (0.26)***	1.07 (0.26)***
Male	0.02 (0.11)	0.05 (0.11)
Age	−0.01 (0.01)	−0.01 (0.01)
Education	−0.05 (0.05)	−0.07 (0.05)
Married	0.15 (0.10)	0.12 (0.11)
Employed	−0.14 (0.12)	−0.16 (0.12)
Location		
Sadr City	−	1.29 (0.18)***
Rest of Baghdad	−	0.63 (0.15)***
Anbar	−	0.19 (0.22)
Basara	−	−0.24 (0.25)
Kirkuk	−	0.51 (0.33)
Mosul	−	0.07 (0.33)
Security from Awakening Councils		
Improved Security	−0.25 (0.07)***	−0.21 (0.07)**
Community-Level Characteristics		
Predominately Shia Community	−0.58 (0.25)*	−0.75 (0.28)**
Intercept	−0.38	−0.38

Robust standard errors in parentheses
* $p < 0.05$, ** $p < 0.01$, *** $p < 0.001$

TABLE 5.3. *HLM regression models of perceived increase in security resulting from the surge, Iraq survey, 2008*

	During surge, 2008	
	β (se)	β (se)
Individual-Level Characteristics		
War Violence		
Iraqi Army	−0.32 (0.09)***	−0.18 (0.09)*
Iraqi Police	0.09 (0.11)	0.19 (0.11)
Local Militia	0.05 (0.09)	0.11 (0.08)
Bombing	−0.39 (0.09)***	−0.27 (0.09)**
Sniping and Crossfire	−0.36 (0.08)***	−0.24 (0.07)***
Sectarian Attacks	−0.41 (0.09)***	−0.28 (0.08)***
Kidnapping	−0.06 (0.08)	−0.03 (0.08)
Unnecessary U.S. Attacks on Civilians	−0.76 (0.09)	−0.49 (0.08)***
Background Characteristics		
Kurd	−	0.90 (0.33)**
Sunni	−	−1.17 (0.35)***
Shia	−	−0.39 (0.34)
Male	−	−0.05 (0.08)
Age	−	−0.00 (0.00)
Education	−	−0.07 (0.04)
Married	−	0.06 (0.08)
Employed	−	0.12 (0.09)
Location		
Sadr City	−	−2.31 (0.12)***
Rest of Baghdad	−	−1.63 (0.15)***
Anbar	−	−1.18 (0.19)***
Basara	−	0.94 (0.17)***
Kirkuk	−	0.24 (0.37)
Mosul	−	0.62 (0.31)*
Security from Awakening Councils		
Improved Security	−	0.43 (0.05)***
Community-Level Characteristics		
Predominately Shia Community	0.22 (0.19)	0.26 (0.25)
Intercept	2.28	2.28

Robust standard errors in parentheses

* $p < 0.05$, ** $p < 0.01$, *** $p < 0.001$

TABLE 5.4. *HLM Bernoulli regression models of approval for al-Maliki during and after the surge, Iraq survey, 2008–2009*

	During surge, 2008	After surge, 2009
	β (se)	β (se)
Individual-Level Characteristics		
Background Characteristics		
Kurd	0.57 (0.44)	−0.01 (0.28)
Sunni	−0.98 (0.42)*	−0.01 (0.32)
Shia	1.34 (0.41)***	1.20 (0.33)***
Male	−0.03 (0.12)	0.05 (0.11)
Age	−0.01 (0.01)	0.01 (0.01)
Education	−0.16 (0.06)**	−0.00 (0.04)
Married	−0.05 (0.11)	−0.11 (0.11)
Employed	0.29 (0.13)	0.01 (0.12)
Location		
Sadr City	−2.57 (0.23)***	−0.88 (0.21)***
Rest of Baghdad	−1.32 (0.15)***	−0.87 (0.13)***
Anbar	−	−0.38 (0.20)*
Basara	0.38 (0.21)	0.32 (0.17)
Kirkuk	0.10 (0.57)	0.33 (0.38)
Mosul	0.93 (0.47)*	−0.05 (0.32)
Community-Level Characteristics		
Predominately Shia Community	0.52 (0.32)	0.46 (0.24)
Cross-Level Interactions		
Predominately Shia Community X Shia	2.85 (0.88)**	−0.19 (0.72)
Predominately Shia Community X Sunni	5.50 (1.04)***	1.68 (0.74)*
Intercept	−0.77	0.39

TABLE 5.5. *HLM OLS regression models for war violence during and after the surge, Iraq surveys in 2008–2009*

	During surge, 2008 β (se)	After surge, 2009 β (se)
Individual-Level Characteristics		
Support for Prime Minister & U.S./Coalition Forces		
Approval for U.S./Coalition Forces	−0.48 (0.09)***	−0.14 (0.07)*
Approval for al-Maliki	−0.35 (0.08)***	−0.16 (0.06)
Background Characteristics		
Kurd	−0.62 (0.44)	−0.78 (0.38)
Sunni	1.23 (0.31)***	0.36 (0.33)
Shia	0.89 (0.32)***	−0.03 (0.34)
Male	0.01 (0.07)	0.08 (0.06)
Age	−0.01 (0.00)*	0.00 (0.00)
Education	−0.02 (0.03)	0.02 (0.03)
Married	0.03 (0.06)	−0.06 (0.05)
Employed	0.00 (0.07)	−0.09 (0.07)
Location		
Sadr City	0.39 (0.18)*	0.42 (0.13)***
Rest of Baghdad	0.68 (0.13)***	0.18 (0.10)
Anbar	−0.67 (0.20)***	−0.27 (0.19)
Basara	0.71 (0.20)***	−0.04 (0.10)
Kirkuk	0.02 (0.21)	0.81 (0.31)**
Mosul	0.60 (0.49)	0.51 (0.29)
Community-Level Characteristics		
Predominately Shia Community	−0.19 (0.25)	−0.42 (0.23)
Cross-Level Interactions		
Predominately Shia Community X Shia	−2.85 (0.85)***	−1.80 (0.73)**
Predominately Shia Community X Sunni	−0.93 (0.85)	−2.23 (0.82)**
Intercept	3.11	1.9

Robust standard errors in parentheses
* p <0.05, ** p <0.01, *** p <0.001

TABLE 5.6. *Individual- and community-level regression models of perceived security during and after the surge, Iraq surveys in 2008–2009*

	During surge, 2008			After surge, 2009		
	β (se)	β (se)	β (se)	β (se)	β (se)	β (se)
Individual-Level Characteristics						
Support for Prime Minister & U.S./Coalition Forces						
Approval for U.S./Coalition Forces	0.89 (0.77)***	0.92 (0.18)***	0.91 (0.18)***	0.25 (0.15)	−0.13 (0.14)	0.09 (0.14)
Approval for al-Maliki	1.50 (0.18)***	1.44 (0.17)***	1.40 (0.17)**	0.78 (0.13)***	−0.67 (0.12)***	0.67 (0.12)***
Reported War Violence	–	−0.13 (0.05)**	−0.13 (0.05)**	–	−0.28 (0.08)***	−0.28 (0.08)***
Background Characteristics						
Kurd	3.01 (0.57)***	1.80 (0.48)***	0.93 (0.55)	2.74 (0.63)***	−1.55 (0.57)**	0.72 (0.49)
Sunni	−1.45 (0.51)**	−0.75 (0.41)	−0.59 (0.41)	−0.77 (0.63)	−0.31 (0.57)	1.01 (0.62)
Shia	0.01 (0.50)	0.60 (0.41)	0.68 (0.42)	0.98 (0.69)	1.13 (0.61)	1.10 (0.62)
Male	0.07 (0.13)	0.09 (0.13)	0.08 (0.13)	−0.09 (0.13)	−0.02 (0.12)	−0.01 (0.12)
Age	0.00 (0.01)	0.00 (0.01)	0.00 (0.01)	0.00 (0.01)	−0.00 (0.01)	−0.00 (0.01)
Education	0.02 (0.06)	0.03 (0.06)	0.04 (0.05)	−0.01 (0.06)	−0.03 (0.06)	−0.03 (0.06)
Married	−0.10 (0.12)	−0.06 (0.12)	−0.06 (0.12)	0.01 (0.12)	0.04 (0.12)	0.04 (0.12)
Employed	−0.09 (0.14)	−0.09 (0.14)	−0.09 (0.14)	0.34 (0.14)*	0.24 (0.14)	0.24 (0.14)
Location						
Sadr City	−0.70 (0.30)*	−0.38 (0.26)	−0.41 (0.27)	0.38 (0.22)	0.70 (0.20)***	0.54 (0.31)
Rest of Baghdad	−1.20 (0.24)***	−0.44 (0.24)	−0.47 (0.24)*	0.60 (0.20)**	0.74 (0.18)***	0.75 (0.19)***

Anbar	2.75 (0.30)***	2.25 (0.28)***	2.53 (0.28)***	0.19 (0.28)	0.09 (0.25)	0.20 (0.26)
Basara	−1.19 (0.40)**	−0.61 (0.38)	−0.65 (0.39)	−0.30 (0.20)	−0.35 (0.20)	−0.31 (0.24)
Kirkuk	−0.61 (0.50)	−0.48 (0.49)	−0.37 (0.47)	−0.37 (0.38)	0.31 (0.42)	0.25 (0.31)
Mosul	−1.46 (0.46)**	−0.82 (0.47)	−0.72 (0.47)	−0.88 (0.45)*	−0.34 (0.43)	−0.29 (0.33)
Surge and Awakening						
Perceived Surge Increased Security	0.28 (0.04)***	0.25 (0.04)***	0.24 (0.04)***	–	–	–
Perceived Awakening Increased Security	−0.020 (0.08)*	−0.20 (0.08)*	−0.20 (0.08)*	–	–	–
Community-Level Characteristics						
Predominately Shia Community	1.57 (0.45)***	0.98 (0.40)**	0.77 (0.38)*	0.74 (0.44)	0.19 (0.37)	0.18 (0.29)
Aggregate Reported War Violence	–	−5.39 (0.72)***	−5.21 (0.69)***	–	−4.50 (0.99)***	−3.88 (0.72)***
Cross-Level Interactions						
Predominately Shia Community X Shia	–	–	2.66 (1.25)*	–	–	3.74 (0.84)***
Predominately Shia Community X Sunni	–	–	3.73 (1.22)**	–	–	3.29 (0.88)***
Intercept	7.21	7.22	7.19	–	–	–

Robust standard errors in parentheses

* $p < 0.05$, ** $p < 0.01$, *** $p < 0.001$

CHAPTER 6 TABLES

TABLE 6.1. *Individual and community descriptive statistics: Iraq survey in September 2007*

	μ	σ
Individual-Level Characteristics	($n = 2212$)	
War Violence and Security		
Bombing (0/1)	0.41	0.49
Sniping and Crossfire (0/1)	0.3	0.46
Sectarian Attacks (0/1)	0.28	0.45
Kidnapping (0/1)	0.41	0.49
Unnecessary U.S. Attacks on Civilians (0/1)	0.43	0.5
Unnecessary Iraqi Army Attacks on Civilians (0/1)	0.29	0.46
Unnecessary Iraqi Police Attacks on Civilians (0/1)	0.2	0.4
Government/Nongovernment Violence (0/1)	0.34	0.47
Support for U.S. and Iraq Government/Forces		
Legal Cynicism about U.S./Coalition Forces (0–12) ($\alpha = 0.73$)	8	2.59
Legal Cynicism about Iraqi Government/Forces (0–12) ($\alpha = 0.83$)	6.13	3.19
Accept Attacks on U.S. Forces (0/1)	0.56	0.5
Background Characteristics		
Arab Sunni (0/1)	0.33	0.47
Arab Shia (0/1)	0.48	0.5
Male (0/1)	0.51	0.5
Age (18–83)	34.77	12.86
Education (1–5)	3.31	1.24
Married (0/1)	0.61	0.49
Employed (0/1)	0.41	0.49
Community-Level Characteristics	($n = 456$)	
Unnecessary U.S. Attacks on Civilians (0/1)	0.44	0.34
Unnecessary Iraqi Army Attacks on Civilians (0/1)	0.19	0.24
Unnecessary Iraqi Police Attacks on Civilians (0/1)	0.2	0.25
Other War Violence (0–6)	2.05	1.28
Legal Cynicism about U.S./Coalition Forces (0–12)	8	2.1
Legal Cynicism about Iraqi Government/Forces (0–12)	6.17	2.48
Predominately Sunni (0/1)	0.29	0.43

Robust standard errors in parentheses
* $p < 0.05$, ** $p < 0.01$, *** $p < 0.001$

TABLE 6.2. *Individual and community-level HLM Bernoulli regression models of unnecessary U.S. atacks on civilians, Iraq survey in September 2007*

	β (se)	β (se)
Individual-Level Characteristics		
War Violence		
Bombing	–	0.16 (0.13)
Sniping and Crossfire	–	0.29 (0.14)*
Sectarian Attacks	–	0.31 (0.13)*
Kidnapping	–	0.39 (0.13)**
Government/Nongovernment Violence	–	−0.24 (0.15)
Unnecessary Iraqi Army Attacks on Civilians	–	−0.03 (0.15)
Unnecessary Iraqi Police Attacks on Civilians	–	−0.18 (0.15)
Background Characteristics		
Arab Sunni	–	1.20 (0.29)***
Arab Shia	–	0.91 (0.24)***
Male	–	0.12 (0.10)
Age	–	−0.01 (0.01)
Education	–	−0.000 (0.05)
Married	–	−0.03 (0.11)
Employed	–	0.08 (0.13)
Community-Level Characteristics		
Unnecessary Iraqi Army Attacks on Civilians	0.08 (0.30)	0.09 (0.34)
Unnecessary Iraqi Police Attacks on Civilians	−0.13 (0.32)	0.09 (0.36)
Predominately Arab Sunni	1.14 (0.14)***	0.65 (0.22)**
Other War Violence	0.60 (0.06)***	0.36 (0.84)***
Intercept	−0.31	−0.35

Robust standard errors in parentheses
* $p < 0.05$, ** $p < 0.01$, *** $p < 0.001$

TABLE 6.3. *Individual and community-level HLM regression models of legal cynicism about U.S./coalition forces, Iraq survey in September 2007*

	β (se)	β (se)
Individual-Level Characteristics		
War Violence		
Bombing	–	0.20 (0.11)
Sniping and Crossfire	–	0.44 (0.11)***
Sectarian Attacks	–	0.23 (0.11)*
Kidnapping	–	0.03 (0.10)
Government/Nongovernment Violence	–	0.51 (0.10)***
Unnecessary U.S. Army Attacks on Civilians	–	0.71 (0.10)***
Unnecessary Iraqi Army Attacks on Civilians	–	0.09 (0.10)
Unnecessary Iraqi Police Attacks on Civilians	–	0.47 (0.11)***
Background Characteristics		
Arab Sunni	–	2.82 (0.30)***
Arab Shia	–	1.53 (0.25)***
Male	–	0.23 (0.09)**
Age	–	0.00 (0.00)
Education	–	−0.01 (0.04)
Married	–	0.19 (0.10)*
Employed	–	−0.22 (0.11)*
Community-Level Characteristics		
Unnecessary U.S. Army Attacks on Civilians	1.82 (0.26)***	0.79 (0.27)***
Unnecessary Iraqi Army Attacks on Civilians	1.44 (0.35)***	1.00 (0.37)**
Unnecessary Iraqi Police Attacks on Civilians	0.56 (0.35)	−0.15 (0.36)
Predominately Arab Sunni	2.08 (0.14)***	0.67 (0.22)**
Other War Violence	0.02 (0.07)	−0.35 (0.10)***
Intercept	8.01	8.02

Robust standard errors in parentheses
* $p < 0.05$, ** $p < 0.01$, *** $p < 0.001$

TABLE 6.4. *HLM Bernoulli regression models of acceptance of attacks on U.S./coalition forces, Iraq survey in September 2007*

	β (se)	β (se)	β (se)	β (se)
Individual-Level Characteristics				
War Violence				
Bombing	–	–	–	−0.06 (0.17)
Sniping and Crossfire	–	–	–	−0.17 (0.16)
Sectarian Attacks	–	–	–	−0.26 (0.16)
Kidnapping	–	–	–	−0.28 (0.16)
Government/ Nongovernment Violence	–	–	–	0.26 (0.15)
Unnecessary U.S. Army Attacks on Civilians	–	–	–	0.41 (0.15)**
Unnecessary Iraqi Army Attacks on Civilians	–	–	–	0.02 (0.17)
Unnecessary Iraqi Police Attacks on Civilians	–	–	–	0.46 (0.18)**
Background Characteristics				
Arab Sunni	–	–	–	3.06 (0.42)***
Arab Shia	–	–	–	1.45 (0.36)***
Male	–	–	–	0.25 (0.13)*
Age	–	–	–	0.00 (0.01)
Education	–	–	–	−0.11 (0.06)
Married	–	–	–	−0.15 (0.14)
Employed	–	–	–	−0.12 (0.15)
Support for U.S. and Iraqi Government/Forces				
Legal Cynicism about U.S./ Coalition Forces	–	–	–	0.51 (0.04)***
Community-Level Characteristics				
Unnecessary U.S. Army Attacks on Civilians	–	1.13 (0.27)	0.03 (1.03)	−0.10 (0.40)
Unnecessary Iraqi Army Attacks on Civilians	–	–	–	−2.21 (0.48)***
Unnecessary Iraqi Police Attacks on Civilians	–	–	–	−0.83 (0.46)
Legal Cynicism about U.S./ Coalition Forces	–	–	0.56 (0.05)***	0.21 (0.07)**
Predominately Arab Sunni	3.55 (0.21)***	3.21 (0.21)***	2.02 (0.25)***	0.87 (0.39)*
Other War Violence	–	–	–	−0.10 (0.12)
Intercept	0.7	0.69	0.62	0.67

Robust standard errors in parentheses
* $p < 0.05$, ** $p < 0.01$, *** $p < 0.001$

TABLE 6.5. *Cross-level interaction effects from HLM Bernoulli models of acceptance of attacks on U.S./coalition forces, Iraq survey in September 2007*

	β (se)	β (se)	β (se)
Cross-Level Interaction[a]			
Sunni X Predominately Sunni	2.74 (1.26)*	–	0.15 (1.35)
Sunni X Legal Cynicism about U.S./Coalition	–	0.84 (0.17)***	0.83 (0.19)***

[a] Individual-level and community-level coefficients included in equations and suppressed to conserve space.
Robust standard errors in parentheses
* $p < 0.05$, ** $p < 0.01$, *** $p < 0.001$

TABLE 6.6. *Individual- and community-level HLM regression models of legal cynicism about Iraq government/forces, Iraq survey in September 2007*

	β (se)	β (se)
Individual-Level Characteristics		
War Violence		
Bombing	–	−0.09 (0.12)
Sniping and Crossfire	–	−0.11 (0.12)
Sectarian Attacks	–	0.15 (0.12)
Kidnapping	–	0.09 (0.12)
Government/Nongovernment Violence	–	0.36 (0.12)**
Unnecessary U.S. Army Attacks on Civilians	–	−0.41 (0.11)***
Unnecessary Iraqi Army Attacks on Civilians	–	0.75 (0.13)***
Unnecessary Iraqi Police Attacks on Civilians	–	0.20 (0.11)
Background Characteristics		
Arab Sunni	–	2.02 (0.32)***
Arab Shia	–	−0.98 (0.23)***
Male	–	0.22 (0.10)*
Age	–	−0.00 (0.00)
Education	–	0.03 (0.05)
Married	–	0.02 (0.11)
Employed	–	−0.03 (0.11)

Support for U.S. and Iraqi Government/Forces

Legal Cynicism about U.S./Coalition Forces	–	0.44 (0.04)***
Community-Level Characteristics		
Unnecessary U.S. Army Attacks on Civilians	−0.22 (0.28)	−0.63 (0.30)*
Unnecessary Iraqi Army Attacks on Civilians	1.27 (0.41)**	0.97 (0.41)*
Unnecessary Iraqi Police Attacks on Civilians	2.49 (0.35)***	1.35 (0.38)***
Predominately Arab Sunni	0.05 (0.05)	−0.31 (0.07)**
Other War Violence	3.53 (0.20)***	0.85 (0.32)**
Intercept	6.17	6.19

Robust standard errors in parentheses
* $p < 0.05$, ** $p < 0.01$, *** $p < 0.001$

TABLE 6.7. *Cross-level interaction effects from HLM Bernoulli models of acceptance of attacks on U.S./coalition forces, Iraq survey in September 2007*

	β (se)	β (se)	β (se)
Cross-Level Interaction[a]			
Sunni X Unnecessary Attacks by Iraq Police	2.46 (0.57)**	–	1.54 (0.53)**
Legal Cynicism about U.S./ Coalition X	–	0.67 (0.13)***	0.56 (0.11)***
Unnecessary Attacks by Iraqi Police			

[a] Individual-level and community-level coefficients included in equations and suppressed to conserve space.
Robust standard errors in parentheses
* $p < 0.05$, ** $p < 0.01$, *** $p < 0.001$

Notes

PROLOGUE

1 General Assembly Resolution 3314 (XXIX), annex, UN Doc. A/RES/29/3314 (December 14, 1974).

2 See http://www.icc-cpi.int/iccdocs/asp_docs/Resolutions/RC-Res.6-ENG.pdf. The Rome Statute for the International Criminal Court provided that "crime of aggression" means "the planning, preparation, initiation or execution, by a person in a position effectively to exercise control over or to direct the political or military action of a State, of an act of aggression which, by its character, gravity and scale, constitutes a manifest violation of the Charter of the United Nations" and that "'act of aggression' means the use of armed force by a State against the sovereignty, territorial integrity or political independence of another State, or in any other manner inconsistent with the Charter of the United Nations." In June 2010, a Review Conference on the Rome Statute held in Kampala, Uganda reached agreement on the prospective implementation of the Rome Statute's definition of the crime of aggression.

3 See Mark Mazzetti, "Ex-Chief of C.I.A. Defends Actions in Wake of 9/11," *New York Times*, July 26, 2014, P. 1.

4 For full resolution, see: http://www.gpo.gov/fdsys/pkg/PLAW-107publ243/pdf/PLAW-107publ243.pdf.

5 The Downing Street "Memo" consisted of the minutes of a July 23, 2002 meeting of advisors to British Prime Minister Blair that were published in *The Sunday Times* newspaper on May 1, 2005. These minutes were evidence of an early skepticism or cynicism about misleading ways evidence was being developed by the Bush administration to justify the invasion of Iraq.

6 Robert S. Mueller III indicated the inability of the FBI to find such evidence in a speech on "Partnership and Prevention: The F.B.I.'s Role in Homeland Security" presented to the Commonwealth Club of California, April 19, 2002, and President Bush acknowledged the absence of confirming evidence in response to news conference questions in February and September 2003. See Michael Hirsh and Michael Isikoff, "No More Hide and Seek," *Newsweek*, February 10, 2003, p. 46 and Helen Thomas, "Hussein Link Was Sales Job," *Miami Herald*, September 27, 2003.

7 The U.S. Central Intelligence Agency's Charles Duelfer concluded in his Comprehensive Report of the Special Advisor to the DCI on Iraq's WMD in September 2004 that "It now appears clear that Saddam, despite internal reluctance … resolved to eliminate the existing stocks of WMD weapons during the course of the summer of 1991 in support of the prime objective of getting rid of sanctions," which likely explains why a decade later UN inspections before the Iraq War and U.S. investigations afterward failed to find WMDs.

8 See transcript of IAEA Director General Mohamed ElBaradei's presentation to the UN Security Council, March 7, 2003, page 8 of UN Documents S/PV.4714.

9 James Mahoney defines path dependence as: "historical sequences in which contingent events set into motion institutional patterns or event chains that have deterministic properties" (2000:508).

10 President Barak Obama to the Minneapolis American Legion Veterans of the Vietnam War, August 30, 2011 and again in Remarks at the Commemoration Ceremony of the 50th Anniversary of the Vietnam War, at the Vietnam Veterans Memorial, Washington Mall, May 28, 2012.

11 Further details, translated testimonies, and an overview of the Iraq History Project and its data and methods are provided at www.law.depaul.edu/centers_institutes/ihrli/pdf/ihp1.pdf.

12 The sampling design and methodology of the Gallup Poll Survey conducted in Baghdad from August 28 through September 4, 2003, is presented in "The Gallup Poll Tuesday Briefing," Subscriber Report: 2003 Gallup Poll of Baghdad, The Gallup Organization, Princeton, New Jersey.

13 Further details of the sampling design and methodology used in developing these data are presented in an "Overview of National Opinion Surveys in Iraq" by D3 Systems, Inc., 8300 Greensboro Drive, Suite 450, McLean, Virginia, 22102.

3 JUDGING TORTURE IN IRAQ

1 Article 127 of the Iraqi Code of Criminal Procedure prohibits the use of "any illegal method to influence the accused and extract a confession from him … Mistreatment, threats, injury, enticement, promises, psychological influence, or use of drugs or intoxicants [are] considered illegal methods."

2 Article 333 of the Iraqi Penal Code states that "any employee or public servant who tortures, or orders the torture of an accused, witness, or expert in order to compel that person to confess to committing a crime, to give a statement or information, to hide certain matters, or to give a specific opinion will be punished by imprisonment or detention. The use of force or threats is considered torture."

3 Memo 6, U.S. Department of Justice, Office of the Legal Counsel, Office of the Assistant Attorney General, Washington DC, January 22, 2002, Memorandum for Alberto Gonzales, Counsel to the President, and William J. Haynes II, General Counsel of the Department of Defense, p. 81.

4 Katherine Seelye, "A Nation Challenged: The Prisoners; First 'Unlawful Combatants' seized in Afghanistan Arrive at US Base in Cuba," *New York Times*, January 12, 2002.

5 From Attorney General Alberto R. Gonzales' draft memorandum, January 25, 2002, to President George W. Bush on the subject of a Decision re Application of

the Geneva Conventions on Prisoners of War to Conflict with al-Qaeda and the Taliban.

6 See http://www.defenselink.mil/news/Aug2004/d20040824finalreport.pdf.

7 "Foreign Terrorist Organizations," Country Reports on Terrorism, U.S. State Department, April 28, 2006.

8 See, e.g., http://newyorkmetro.com/nymetro/news/people/features/11719/index3 .html.

9 As a result of the randomized design of the factorial survey method, the degree of injury is not notably associated with group membership. In contrast, if the fact situation in a sample of actual court cases involved an al-Qaeda prison guard torturing an Iraqi prisoner, one might assume that the degree of injury would be greater than when a coalition member tortures another coalition member. However, randomization minimizes the likelihood of any systematic associations among the case characteristics of this type.

4 NIGHT FALLS ON BAGHDAD

1 See "The Situation in Bosnia and Herzegovina, G.A. Res. 47/121, pmbl., U.S. Doc. A/RES/47/121 (Dec. 18, 1992). Drazen Petrovic provides this further definition: "ethnic cleansing is a well-defined policy of a particular group of persons to systematically eliminate another group from a given territory on the basis of religious, ethnic or national origin. Such a policy involves violence and is very often connected to military operations. It is to be achieved by all possible means, from discrimination and extermination, and entails violations of human rights and international humanitarian law" (1994:351).

2 While some traditional Baghdad ethnic-religious populations, such as Jews, fled the country en masse in the 1960s in response to repressive state policies directed against them (Batau), in 2003, Baghdad remained a very diverse city with large populations of Kurds and Christians as well as neighborhoods with Sabean Mandeans, Turcomans, and others.

3 http://www.nytimes.com/2004/05/26/international/middleeast/26FTE_NOTE .html.

4 Al-Maliki was selected as prime minister on April 22, 2006, after Ibrahim al-Jaa'fari was forced from office. Al-Jaa'fari had been selected as prime minister following the contentious elections of January 2005.

5 *Ethnic cleansing* is defined in footnote 1 of this chapter, while the term *crimes against humanity* was first evoked in the Nuremberg Trials and is now codified within the statute of the International Criminal Court, which defines such crimes as acts of murder, extermination, torture, rape, disappearance, forced displacement, and "persecution against any identifiable group or collectivity on political, racial, national, ethnic, cultural, religious, gender … or other grounds" where the acts are "committed as part of a widespread or systematic attack directed against any civilian population" (Article 7 Rome Statute).

6 http://portal.unesco.org/en/ev.php-URL_ID=13637&URL_DO=DO _TOPIC&URL_SECTION=201.html.

7 See http://gulf2000.columbia.edu/maps.shtml.

5 THE SEPARATE PEACE OF THE SHIA

1   See usip.org/isg/iraq_study_group_report.
2   Attacking civilians is a serious war crime and human rights violation. Targeting civilians violates the most fundamental requirement of international humanitarian law to distinguish combatants from noncombatant civilians and to treat the latter as immune from direct attacks (see Dormann 2003).
3   See csis.org/files/publication/100217_iraq_security_study.pdf.
4   The sampling was based on 2005 Iraq Ministry of Planning data. Supervisors selected sampling points using satellite images and maps or grids with starting places picked randomly within locations among Iraq's nearly 11,000 villages and neighborhoods.
5   Descriptive statistics for the latter surveys are presented in Appendix Table 5.1.
6   This scale included: a four-point ranking of neighborhood security "conditions" from very bad to very good, a three-point ranking of neighborhood "safety" from very safe to not safe, a four-point ranking of "your family's protection from crime" from very good to very bad, and a two-point ranking of the neighborhood security "situation" from good, to neither good nor bad, to bad.
7   We use hierarchical linear models (HLM) (Raudenbush and Bryk 2004) to estimate variation in outcomes within and between communities, with adjustments for non-independence resulting from the clustering within these sampling points. For example, our final within-community models of perceived security regress individual-level reports of perceived security on individual-level reports of sectarian group membership, war violence, and other independent variables:

$$y_{ij} = \beta_{oj} + \beta_{1j}(\text{male})_{ij} + \beta_{2j}(\text{ethnicity})_{ij} + \beta_{3j}(\text{age})_{ij} + \beta_{4j}(\text{education})_{ij}$$
$$+ \beta_{5j}(\text{married})_{ij} + \beta_{6j}(\text{employed})_{ij} + \beta_{7j}(\text{perpetrator})_{ij} + \beta_{8j}(\text{forms of victimization})_{ij} + \beta_{9j}(\text{unnecessary U.S. attacks on civilians})_{ij} + \beta_{10j}(\text{location})_{ij} + \beta_{11j}(\text{improved security from Awakening})_{ij} + r_{ij}.$$

Our between-community models regress perceived security in the more than 440 sampling points – after the individual-level variables are taken into account – on the predominance at the community level of Shia respondents and the aggregate level of reported war violence in these settings:

$$\beta_{oj} = \gamma_{oo} + \gamma_{o1}(\text{predominately Shia})_{ij} + u_{oj}.$$

From the resulting joined analyses of the individual and community-level models, we learn not only about individual-level sources of variation in perceived security in Iraq, but also with these variables controlled, about the influence of differences following from the separation of respondents into predominately ethno-sectarian communities, about the aggregate-level impact of war violence in these settings, and about the impact of respondents' evaluations of the U.S./coalition forces, the surge, and Prime Minister Maliki.

8   Shia predominance at the community level is based on modal respondent reports of communities being completely Shia (1), mostly Shia (0.6), mixed (0.5), mostly Sunni (0.4), or completely Sunni (0). Individuals also self-identified as Kurdish, Sunni, and Shia, as well as male, married, and employed, while individual educational levels were ranked from one to five and age was measured in years. We also developed a

community war violence measure based on the simple average on the individual eight-point scale of war violence described earlier within each community.

9 We used the survey reports to form a scale measure of the perceived security resulting from the surge of U.S. forces and the formation of Awakening councils. This six-point scale ranked the impact of the increase in U.S. forces as making perceived security worse (0), having no effect (1), or better (2) in the combined nearby area, elsewhere in Iraq, and overall. A similar ranking of the impact of the creation of the Awakening councils was scored from zero (i.e., worse) to two (i.e., better). The surge and Awakening measures were not available in the final survey because the surge by then had ended.

10 Several factors introduced in the second column of Appendix Table 5.3 largely mediate the negative effect of U.S. attacks on civilians on the effectiveness of the surge in increasing perceived security. These factors include the targeting predicted in Hypothesis 1 of the Sunnis in unnecessary U.S./coalition attacks on civilians and the impact of respondents' locations in Sadr City, elsewhere in Baghdad, and in Anbar province.

11 Individuals indicated their approval (1) or disapproval (0) of Prime Minister al-Maliki. As noted, this approval was still peaking at the time of the February 2008 survey, foreshadowing the response to his ultimately successful involvement in the March 2008 battle for Basra. By the 2008 survey, al-Maliki had gained control of Iraq's military and security services and was bringing lower-tier Sunni figures into his government while eliminating rivals (Parker and Salman 2013).

12 Thus the coefficient in Appendix Table 5.6 for predominately Shia communities is reduced after the surge in 2009 by more than one-third by controlling for war violence.

6 LEGAL CYNICISM AND SUNNI MILITANCY

1 The descriptive statistics discussed in this and following paragraphs are reported in greater detail in Appendix Table 6.1.

2 The alpha score coefficient was 0.73.

3 Although we considered other ways of coding this variable, such as the approach used in the preceding chapter, with similar substantive results, the coding adopted here was more parsimonious and clear for the purpose of providing attention to predominately Sunni communities that is the focus of this chapter.

4 We use the same essential analytical approach in this chapter based on HLM models that was described in the previous chapter.

Bibliography

Abdullah, A. J. Thabit. 2013. *A Short History of Iraq*. New York: Routledge.

Adriaensens, Dirk. 2013. "The 2006 Mass Murder of Iraqi Civilians by U.S. Forces." *Global Research*, January 28.

Alani, Feurat. 2014. "Violence and Power Struggles." *Le Monde Diplomatique*, January.

Allawi, Ali. 2007. *The Occupation of Iraq: Winning the War, Losing the Peace*. New Haven, CT: Yale University Press.

Al-Wardi, Ali. 2008. *Understanding Iraq: Society, Culture and Personality*. New York: Edein Mellen Press.

Amnesty International Annual Report on Iraq. 1985.

Amos, Deborah. 2010. *Eclipse of the Sunnis*. New York: Public Affairs.

Anderson, Phillip. 1999. "Complexity Theory and Organization Science." *Organization Science* 10: 216–32.

Apuzzo, Matt. 2014a. "Black Water Guards Found Guilty in 2007 Iraq Killings." *New York Times*, October 22.

———. 2014b. "In a U.S. Court, Iraqis Accuse Black Water of Killings in 2007." *New York Times*, June 25.

Arango, Tim. 2013. "Iraq's Worsening Sunni Protests Revolve around Antiterrorism Tactics." *New York Times*, May 7.

Arango, Tim, Kareem Fahim, and Ben Hubbard. 2014. "Rebels' Fast Strike in Iraq Was Years in the Making." *New York Times*, June 15.

Arango, Tim and Eric Schmitt. 2014. "Escaped Inmates from Iraq Fuel Syrian Insurgency." *New York Times*, February 27.

Arbour, Louise. 2006. "Economic and Social Justice for Societies in Transition." New York University School of Law, Annual Transitional Justice Lecture, October 25.

Baker, Peter. 2013. *Days of Fire: Bush and Cheney in the White House*. New York: Doubleday.

Batatu, Hanna. 1978. *The Old Social Classes and the Revolutionary Movements of Iraq: A Study of Iraq's Old Landed and Commercial Classes and of Its Communists, Ba'thists and Free Officers*. Princeton, NJ: Princeton University Press.

BBC. 2004. "Iraq War Illegal Says Annan." September 16.

———. 2005. "New 'Torture Jail' Found in Iraq." BBC News, December 12.

Becker, Howard. 1963. *The Outsiders: Studies in the Sociology of Deviance.* New York: Free Press.

1967. "Whose Side Are We On?" *Social Problems* 14: 239–47.

Bell-Fialkoff, Andrew. 1993. "A Brief History of Ethnic Cleansing." *Foreign Affairs* Summer: 110–20.

1996. Ethnic Cleansing. New York: St. Martin's Press.

Bengio, Ofra. 1998. *Saddam's Word: Political Discourse in Iraq.* London: Oxford University Press.

Biddle, Stephen. 2006. "Seeing Baghdad, Thinking Saigon." *Foreign Affairs* 85: 2–14.

Biddle, Stephen, Jeffrey Friedman, and Jacob Shapiro. 2012. "Testing the Surge: Why Did Violence Decline in Iraq in 2007?" *International Security* 37: 7–40.

Biden, Joseph and Leslie Gelb. 2006. "Unity through Autonomy in Iraq." *New York Times,* May 1.

Black, Donald. 1983. "Crime as Social Control." *American Sociological Review* 48: 34–45.

Bohannon, John. 2010. "Leaked Documents Provide Bonanza for Researchers." *Science* 330: 575.

Bonin, Richard. 2011. *Arrows of the Night: Ahmad Chalabi's Long Journey to Triumph in Iraq.* New York: Doubleday.

Bremer, L. Paul. 2006. *My Year in Iraq: The Struggle to Build a Future of Hope.* New York: Simon & Schuster.

Brown, Gordon. 2013. "Re: The 1991 Iraq War." May 12. Gulf2000 Blog. Edited by Gary Sick, Columbia University.

Brubaker, Rogers and David Laitin. 1998. "Ethnic and Nationalist Violence." *Annual Review of Sociology* 24: 426.

Burkle, Frederick and Richard Garfield. 2013. "Civilian Mortality after the 2003 Invasion of Iraq." *Lancet* 383: 877–9.

Burns, John F. 1992. "A Killer's Tale – A Special Report: A Serbian Fighter's Path of Brutality." *New York Times,* November 27.

Bursik, Robert and Harold Grasmick. 1993. *Neighborhoods and Crime.* New York: Lexington Books.

Bush, George W. 2002. "President Bush Delivers Graduation Speech at West Point." June 1.

2003. President Bush Discusses Freedom in Iraq and Middle East. Remarks by the President at the 20th Anniversary of the National Endowment for Democracy. November 6. Whitehouse: Office of the Press Secretary.

2005. OUR NATIONAL STRATEGY FOR VICTORY IN IRAQ: Helping the Iraqi People Defeat the Terrorists and Build an Inclusive Democratic State. National Security Council. November.

Bybee, Jay. 2002. Memorandum from Jay Bybee, Office of Legal Counsel, to Attorney General Alberto Gonzales, Counsel to the President, Standards of Conduct for Interrogation under 18 U.S.C. Sections 2340-2340A (August 1).

Carr, Patrick, Laura Napolitano, and Laura Keating. 2007. "We Never Call the Cops and Here Is Why: A Qualitative Examination of Legal Cynicism in Three Philadelphia Neighborhoods." *Criminology* 45: 445–80.

Chehab, Zaki. 2005. *Iraq Ablaze: Inside the Insurgency.* New York: I. B. Tauris & Co.

Cloward, Richard and Lloyd Ohlin. 1960. *Delinquency and Opportunity: A Theory of Delinquent Gangs*. New York: Free Press of Glencoe.

Cochrane, Marisa. 2008. "The Fragmentation of Sadrist Movement." *The Institute for the Study of War*, The Iraq Report 12.

Cockburn, Patrick. 2008. *Muqtada Al-Sadr and the Battle for the Future of Iraq*. New York: Scribner.

Cohen, Elliot. 2001. World War IV. *Wall Street Journal*. November 20.

Cole, Juan. 2003. "The United States and Shi'ite Religious Factions in Post-Ba'thist Iraq." *Middle East Journal* 57: 533–66.

Convention for the Protection of Cultural Property. 1954. http://portal.unesco.org/en/ev.php-URL_ID=13637&URL_DO=DO_TOPIC&URL_SECTION=201.html.

Cordesman, Anthony and Sam Khazai. 2014. *Iraq in Crisis*. Washington, DC: Center for Strategic and International Studies.

Coughlin, Con. 2002. *Saddam: His Rise and Fall*. New York: HarperCollins.

Costs of War Project. Brown University. http://costsofwar.org.

Cover, Robert M. 1986. "Violence and the Word." 95 *Yale Law Journal*, 1601 (1986). Vol. 28, No. 1I 13 #12.

Cressey, Donald. 1979. *Theft of a Nation*. New York: Harper & Bros.

Davis, Eric. 2005. *Memories of State: Politics, History and Collective Identity in Modern Iraq*. Berkeley: University of California Press.

Dershowitz, Alan. 2002. *Why Terrorism Works: Understanding the Threat, Responding to the Challenge*. New Haven, CT: Yale University Press.

De Waal, Alex. 2004. "Counter-Insurgency on the Cheap." *London Review of Books* 26: 25–7.

Dezalay, Yves and Bryant G. Garth. 2002. *The Internationalization of Palace Wars*. Chicago, IL: University of Chicago Press.

Dodge, Toby. 2005. *Iraq's Future: The Aftermath of Regime Change*. London: Routledge.
2012. *Iraq: From War to a New Authoritarianism*. New York: Routledge.
2013. "State and Society in Iraq Ten Years after Regime Change: The Rise of a New Authoritarianism." *International Affairs* 89: 241–57.

Dormann, Knut. 2003. *Elements of War Crimes under the Rome Statute of the International Criminal Court: Sources and Commentary*. New York: Cambridge University Press.

Farrell, Stephen. 2007. "Sadr Suspends His Militia's Military Operations." *New York Times*, August 30.

Fearon, James and David Laitin. 2000. "Violence and the Social Construction of Ethnic Identity." *International Organization* 54: 860. ,
2003. "Ethnicity, Insurgency, and Civil War." *American Political Science Review* 97: 75–86.

Filkins, Dexter. 2009. *The Forever War*. New York: Vintage Books.
2014a. What We Left Behind. *The New Yorker*, April 28.
2014b. Wider War. *The New Yorker*, June 23.

Fischer, Hannah. 2010. *Iraq Casualties: U.S. Military Forces and Iraq Civilians, Police and Security Forces*. U.S. Government: Congressional Research Service.

Gagnon, V. P. 2004. *The Myth of Ethnic War: Serbia and Croatia in the 1990s*. Ithaca, NY: Cornell University Press.

Galbraith, Peter. 2006. *The End of Iraq: How American Incompetence Created a War Without End*. New York: Simon & Schuster.

Galula, David. 1964. *Counterinsurgency Warfare: Theory and Practice*. Westport, CT: Praeger.

Garfinkel, Harold. 1956. "Conditions of Successful Degradation Ceremonies." *American Journal of Sociology* 61: 420–4.

Garland, David. 1990. *Punishment and Modern Society*. Chicago, IL: University of Chicago Press.

Gibson, Bryan. 2010. *Covert Relationship: U.S. Foreign Policy, Intelligence, and the Iran-Iraq War, 1980–88*. New York: Praeger.

Goldsmith, Jack. 2007. *The Terror Presidency*. New York: W. W. Norton.

Gordon, Michael and Bernard Trainor. 2012. *The Endgame*. New York: Pantheon.

Gordon, Michael R. and Judith Miller. 2002. Threats and Responses: The Iraqis; U.S. Says Hussein Intensifies Quest for A-Bomb Parts. *New York Times*, September 8.

Gottfredson, Michael and Travis Hirschi. 1990. *A General Theory of Crime*. Palo Alto, CA: Stanford University Press.

Green, Penny and Tony Ward. 2009. "The Transformation of Violence in Iraq." *British Journal of Criminology* 49(5): 609.

Greenberg, Karen J. and Joshua L. Dratel, P. C. 2005. *The Torture Papers: The Road to Abu Ghraib*. New York: Cambridge University Press.

Haass, Richard. 2009. *War of Necessity, War of Choice. A Memoir of Two Iraqi Wars*. New York: Simon & Schuster.

Haddad, Fanar. 2011. *Sectarianism in Iraq: Antagonistic Visions of Unity*. New York: Columbia University Press.

Hagan, John. 2010. *Who Are the Criminals? The Politics of Crime Policy from the Age of Roosevelt to the Age of Reagan*. Princeton, NJ: Princeton University Press.

Hagan, John and Celesta Albonetti. 1982. "Race, Class and the Perception of the Criminal Injustice in America." *American Journal of Sociology* 28(2): 329–55.

Hagan, John, Joshua Kaiser, and Anna Hanson. 2013. "Assessing the Synergy Thesis in Iraq." *International Security* 37: 173–98.

Hagan, John, Joshua Kaiser, Daniel Rothenberg, Anna Hanson, and Patricia Parker. 2012. "Atrocity Crimes and the Costs of Economic Conflict Crimes in the Battle for Baghdad and Iraq." *European Journal of Criminology* 9: 481–99.

Hagan, John, Joshua Kaiser, Anna Hanson, and Patricia Parker. 2015. "Neighborhood Sectarian Displacement and the Battle for Baghdad The Self-fulfilling Prophecy of Crimes against Humanity in Iraq." *Sociological Forum*. Forthcoming.

Hagan, John and Wenona Rymond-Richmond. 2009. *Darfur and the Crime of Genocide*. New York: Cambridge University Press.

Hagan, John, Heather Schoenfeld, and Alberto Palloni. 2006. "The Science of Human Rights, War Crimes, and Humanitarian Emergencies." *Annual Review of Sociology* 32: 329–49.

Hagan, John, Carla Shedd, and Monique Payne. 2005. "Race, Ethnicity and Youth Perceptions of Criminal Injustice." *American Sociological Review* 70: 381–407.

Hannerz, Ulf. 1969. *Soulside: Inquiries into Ghetto Culture and Communities*. New York: Columbia University Press.

Hare, David. 2004. *Stuff Happens*. New York: Faber and Faber.

Harris, Shane and Matthew Aid. 2013a. "The U.S. Knew Hussein was Launching Some of the Worst Chemical Attacks in History." *Foreign Policy*, August 26.

2013b. "CIA Files Prove America Helped Saddam as He Gassed Iran." *Foreign Policy*, August 26.

Hart, H. L. A. 1961. *The Concept of Law*. Oxford: Oxford University Press, p. 132.

Hashim, Ahmed. 2004. "Understanding the Roots of the Shi'a Insurgency in Iraq." *Terrorism Monitor* 2, 13 (2004): 1–5.

2006. *Insurgency and Counter-Insurgency in Iraq*. Ithaca, NY: Cornell University Press.

Hatfield, Michael. 2006. "Fear, Legal Determinacy and the American Lawyering Culture." *Lewis & Clark Law Review* 10: 511–29.

Herring, Eric and Glen Rangwala. 2006. *Iraq in Fragments: The Occupation and Its Legacy*. Ithaca, NY: Cornell University Press.

Hersh, Seymour M. 2004a. "Annals of National Security: Torture at Abu Ghraib." *New Yorker*, May 10, at 43.

2004b. *Chain of Command: The Road from 9/11 to Abu Ghraib*. New York: HarperCollins.

Hiltermann, Joost. 2004. "Outsiders as Enablers: Consequences and Lessons from International Silence on Iraq's Use of Chemical Weapons during the Iran-Iraq War." In Lawrence Potter and Gary Sick, *Iran, Iraq, and the Legacies of War*. New York: Palgrave, pp. 151–66.

Hirsh, Michael and Michael Isikoff. 2003. "No More Hide and Seek." *Newsweek*, February 10.

Hirschi, Travis. 1969. *Causes of Delinquency*. Berkeley: University of California Press.

Holbrooke, Richard. 1995. *To End a War*. New York: Random House.

Horowitz, David. 2000. *Ethnic Groups in Conflict*. Berkeley: University of California Press.

Human Rights Watch. 1990. *Human Rights in Iraq*. Human Rights Watch Books.

2014. *No One Is Safe: Abuses of Women in Iraq's Criminal Justice System*. New York: Human Rights Watch.

Humanitarian Information Centre for Iraq. 2003. HIC Baghdad-Districts and Neighborhoods map. (http://www.humanitarianinfo.org/iraq/maps/280a%20 A4%20Baghdad%20districts%20neighbourh%20300dpi.pdf).

Hurd, Ian. 2013. "Bomb Syria, Even If It Is Illegal." *New York Times*, August 27.

Ignatieff, Michael. 2004. *The Lesser Evil: Political Ethics in an Age of Terror*. Princeton, NJ: Princeton University Press.

International Criminal Court: http://www.icc-cpi.int/iccdocs/asp_docs/Resolutions/RC-Res.6-ENG.pdf.

International Crisis Group. 2006. "Iraq's Muqtada Al Sadr: Spoiler or Stabilizer?" July.

2007. "Shiite Politics in Iraq." November.

2008. "Iraq's Civil War, The Sadrists and the Surge: Executive Summary and Recommendations." February.

2013 "Make or Break Iraq's Sunnis and the State." Middle East Report Number 144, August.

International Military Tribunal (Nuremberg). Judgment of 1 October 1946.

Istrabadi, Feisel. 2013. "*Iraq 2014 and Beyond*." Woodrow Wilson International Center for Scholars, Washington, DC, September 25.

Ivkovic, Sanja and John Hagan. 2006. *Reclaiming Justice: The International Criminal Tribunal for the Former Yugoslavia and Local Courts*. New York: Oxford University Press.

Jabar, Faleh. 2003. *The Shi'te Movement in Iraq*. London: Saqi Books.

2004. "Post-Conflict Iraq: A Race for Stability, Reconstruction, and Legitimacy." *The United States Institute for Peace*, Special Report 120. May.

John, O. P. and Benet-Martinez. 2000. "Measurement: Reliability, Construct Validation, and Scale Construction." Pp. 339–69 in H. T. Reis and C. M. Judd, *Handbook of Research Methods in Social Psychology*. New York: Cambridge University Press.

Johnston, David and James Risen. 2004. The Reach of War; The Interrogations; Aides Say Memo Backed Coercion Already in Use. *New York Times*, June 27.

Kagan, F. W. 2007. *Choosing Victory: A Plan for Success in Iraq*. Washington, DC: American Enterprise Institute.

Kagan, Kimberly. 2009. *The Surge: A Military History*. New York: Encounter Books.

Kahneman, D., P. Slovic, and A.Tversky (eds.). 1982. *Judgment under Uncertainty: Heuristics and Biases*. New York: Cambridge University Press.

Kalyvas, Stathis. 2006. *The Logic of Violence in Civil War*. New York: Cambridge University Press.

2008. 'Review Symposium on "The New U.S. Army/Marine Corps Counterinsurgency Field Manual as Political Science and Political Praxis."' *Political Perspectives*, June: 351–3.

Kalyvas, Stathis and Matthew Kocher. 2007. "Ethnic Cleavages and Irregular War: Iraq and Vietnam." *Politics & Society* 35: 183–223.

Kamp, Nina et al. 2006. "The State of Iraq: An Update," *New York Times*, December 20, A29, available at http://www.nytimes.com/2006/12/20/opinion/20ohanlon.html.

Kaplan, Fred. 2013. *The Insurgents: David Petraeus and the Plot to Change the American Way of War*. New York: Simon & Schuster.

Kaplan, Robert. 1978. "Black Ghetto Diversity and Anomie: A Sociopolitical View." *American Journal of Sociology* 83: 1132–53.

1993. *Balkan Ghosts: A Journey through History*. New York: St. Martin's Press.

Kaufman, Chaim. 1996. "Possible and Impossible Solutions to Ethnic Civil Wars." *International Security* 20: 136–75.

Keller, Bill. 2003. "The I-Can't-Believe-I'm-a-Hawk-Club." *New York Times*, February.

Kirk, David and Mauri Matsuda. 2011. "Legal Cynicism, Collective Efficacy, and the Ecology of Arrest." *Criminology* 49: 443–70.

Kirk, David and Andrew Papachristos. 2011. "Cultural Mechanisms and the Persistence of Neighborhood Violence." *American Journal of Sociology* 116: 1190–1233.

Knowlton, Brian. 2006. "Iraq Police Accused in U.S. Rights Report." *New York Times*, March 9.

Kutnjak, Ivkovic and John Hagan. 2011. "The Politics of Punishment and the Siege of Sarajevo: Toward a Conflict Theory of Perceived International (In)Justice." *Law & Society Review* 40: 369–410.

Lamont, Michele and Marcel Fournier. 1992. *Cultivating Differences: Symbolic Boundaries and the Making of Inequality*. Chicago, IL: University of Chicago Press.

Lamont, Michele and Mario Small. 2008. "How Culture Matters for the Understanding of Poverty: Enriching our Understanding." Pp. 76–102 in Ann Lin and David Harris, *The Colors of Poverty: Why Racial and Ethnic Disparities Persist.* New York: Russell Sage.

Lemert, Edwin. 1967. *Human Deviance, Social Problems and Social Control.* Englewood Cliffs, NJ: Prentice-Hall.

Lewis, Neil. 2006. "Lawyers Seek to Free U.S. Citizen Held in Iraq," *New York Times,* October 15, at Al8.

Lins de, AlbuQuerque Adriana Michael, O'Hanlon, and Amy Unikewicz. 2005. "The State of Iraq; An Update," *New York Times,* February 2005.

Llewellyn, Karl and Edward Hoebel. 1941. *The Cheyenne Way: Conflict and Case Law in Primitive Jurisprudence.* New York: Hein.

Long, Jerry. 2004. *Saddam's War of Words: Politics, Religion, and the Iraqi Invasion of Kuwait.* Austin: University of Texas Press.

Mahoney, James. 2000. "Path Dependence in Historical Sociology." *Theory and Society* 29: 507–48.

Makiya, Kanan. 1998. *Republic of Fear: The Politics of Modern Iraq.* Berkeley: California University Press.

Marashi, Ibrahim. 2002. "Iraq's Security and Intelligence Network: A Guide and Analysis." *Middle-East Review of International Affairs Journal* 6: 1–13.

Matsuda, Mari J. 1987. "Looking to the Bottom: Critical Legal Studies and Reparations." 22 *Harv. C.R.-C.L.L. Rev* 323.

Mazzetti, Mark. 2014. "Ex-Chief of C.I.A. Defends Actions in Wake of 9/11." *New York Times,* July 25.

Mazzetti, Mark and David Johnston. 2007. "Justice Dept. and C.I.A. Watchdog Start Inquiry of Interrogation Videos' Destruction," *New York Times,* December 9.

Memo 6, U.S. Department of Justice, Office of the Legal Counsel, Office of the Assistant Attorney General, Washington DC, January 22, 2002, Memorandum for Alberto Gonzales, Counsel to the President, and William J. Haynes II, General Counsel of the Department of Defense.

Merry, Sally. 1998. "The Criminalization of Everyday Life." In Austin Sarat et al., *Everyday Practices and Trouble Cases,* 14, 15. Evanston, IL: Northwestern University Press.

Merton, Robert. 1936. "The Unanticipated Consequences of Purposive Social Action." *American Sociological Review* 1: 894–904.

———. 1995. "The Thomas Theorem and the Matthew Effect." *Social Forces* 74: 379–424.

Miller, Judith. 2001. "A Nation Challenged: Secret Sites. Iraqi Tells of Renovations at Sites for Chemical and Nuclear Arms." *New York Times,* December 20.

———. 2002. "Threats and Responses: The Iraqis; U.S. Says Hussein Intensifies Quest for A-Bomb Parts." *New York Times,* September 8.

Mills, Nicolaus. 2009. "9/11 and the Road to Iraq." In Michael Walzer and Nicolaus Mills, *Getting Out: Historical Perspectives on Leaving Iraq.* Philadelphia: University of Pennsylvania Press.

Mines, Keith. 2012. "How Anbar Province Showed Promise and Problems from 2003–2004, Interview with Keith Mines, Former Coalition Provisional Authority Governor." *Musings on Iraq,* November 19.

Moss, Michael. 2006. "American Recalls Torment as a U.S. Detainee in Iraq." *New York Times*, December 18.

Moss, Randolph. 2000. "Executive Branch Legal Interpretation: A Perspective from the Office of Legal Counsel." *Administrative Law Review* 52: 1303–30.

Nagl, John. 2005. *Learning to Eat Soup with a Knife*. Chicago, IL: University of Chicago Press.

Nasr, Vali. 2006. *The Shia Revival: How Conflicts within Islam Will Shape the Future*. New York: W. W. Norton.

Nettler, Gwynn. 1978. *Explaining Crime*. New York: McGraw-Hill.

New York Times. 2010. "Assessing the 'Surge': A Survey of Baghdad Neighborhoods." *New York Times*, December 15.

Norland, Rod. 2014. "For Iraq, Potential Leader with a Tarnished Past." *New York Times*, June 30.

Packer, George. 2006. *The Assassin's Gate: America in Iraq*. New York: Farrar, Straus, and Giroux.

Parenti, Christian. 2004. *The Freedom Shadows and Hallucinations in Occupied Iraq*. New York: New Press.

Parker, Ned and Caeser Ahmed. 2010. "Maliki Seeks Recount in Iraq Elections." *Los Angeles Times*, March 22.

Parker, Ned and Raheem Salman. 2013. "Notes from the Underground: The Rise of Nouri al-Maliki." *World Policy Journal*, Spring. 30.

Petraeus, David. 1986. "Learning Counterinsurgency: Observations from Soldiering in Iraq." *Military Review*, January–February.

2013. "How We Won in Iraq." *Foreign Policy*. October 29.

Petrovic, Drazen. 1994. "Ethnic Cleansing: An Attempt at Methodology." *European Journal of International Law* 5(1): 342–62.

Posner, Eric and Adrian Vermeule. 2004. "A 'Torture' Memo and Its Tortuous Critics." *The Wall Street Journal*, July 6.

Power, Samantha. 2008. *Chasing the Flame: Sergio Viera De Mello and the Fight to Save the World*. New York: Penguin Press.

Priest, Dana. 2005. "CIA Holds Terror Suspects in Secret Prisons." *Washington Post*, November 2.

Prunier, Gerard. 2005. *Darfur: The Ambiguous Genocide*. Ithaca, NY: Cornell University Press.

Quillian, Lincoln and Devah Pager. 2010. "Estimating Risk: Stereotype Amplification and the Perceived Risk of Criminal Victimization." *Social Psychology Quarterly* 73(1): 79–104.

Raudenbush, Stephen and Anthony Bryk. 2004. *HLM 6: Hierarchical Linear and Non-Linear Modeling*. Lincolnwood, IL: Scientific Software International, Inc.

Review Symposium. 2008. "The New U.S. Army/Marine Corps Counterinsurgency Field Manual as Political Science and Political Praxis." *Political Perspectives*, June: 351–3.

Ricks, Thomas. 2006. *Fiasco: The American Military Adventure in Iraq*. New York: Penguin Books.

2009. *The Gamble: General Petraeus and the American Military Adventure in Iraq*. New York: Penguin Books.

Risen, James. 2014. "Before Shooting in Iraq, a Warning on Blackwater." *New York Times*, June 29.

Rosen, Jeffrey. 2007a. "Conscience of a Conservative." *New York Times Magazine*, September 9.

——— 2007b. *The Supreme Court: The Personalities and Rivalries that Defined America.* New York: Times Books.

Rosen, Nir. 2010. *Aftermath: Following the Bloodshed of America's Wars in the Muslim World.* New York: Nations Books.

Rossi, Peter. 1974. "Measuring Household Social Standing." *Social Science Research* 3: 169.

Roundtree, Pamela Wilcox and Kenneth Land. 1996. "Perceived Risk Versus Fear of Crime: Empirical Evidence of a Conceptually Distinct Reactions in Survey Data." *Social Forces* 74: 1353–76.

Rubin, Alissa. 2014. "Bound by Bridge, 2 Baghdad Enclaves Drift Far Apart." *New York Times*, July 27.

Sampson, Robert. 2012. *Great American City: Chicago and the Enduring Neighborhood Effect.* Chicago, IL: University of Chicago Press.

Sampson, Robert and Dawn Bartusch. 1998. "Legal Cynicism and (Subcultural?) Tolerance of Deviance: The Neighborhood Context of Racial Differences." *Law & Society Review* 32: 777–804.

Sampson, Robert and Stephen W. Raudenbush. 2004. "Seeing Disorder: Neighborhood Stigma and the Social Construction of 'Broken Windows.'" *Social Psychology Quarterly* 67(4): 319–42.

Sanchez, Ricardo. 2008. *Wiser in Battle: A Soldier's Story.* New York: HarperCollins.

Savelsberg, Joachim and Ryan King. 2011. *American Memories: Atrocities and the Law.* New York: Russell Sage Foundation.

Scheffer, David. 2012. *All the Missing Souls: A Personal History of the War Crimes Tribunals.* Princeton, NJ: Princeton University Press.

Schmidt, Michael. 2011. "Junkyard Gives Up Secret Accounts of Massacre in Iraq." *New York Times*, December.

Schofield, Mathew. 2006. "Iraqi Police Report Details Civilians' Deaths at Hands of U.S. Troops." *Knight Ridder Newspapers*, March 19.

——— 2011a. "WikiLeaks: Iraqi Children in U.S. Raid Shot in Head, U.N. Says." *McClathy Newspapers*, August 31.

——— 2011b. "Five Years, and Visions of Dead Are Still Haunting." McClatchy Newspapers, April 22.

Seelye, Katherine. 2002. "A Nation Challenged: The Prisoners; First 'Unlawful Combatants' Seized in Afghanistan Arrive at US Base in Cuba." *New York Times*, January 12.

Seron, Carroll et al. 2006. "How Citizens Assess Just Punishment for Police Misconduct." *Criminology* 44: 925, 931.

Shadid, Anthony. 2005. *Night Draws Near: Iraq's People in the Shadow of America's War.* New York: Henry Holt.

Simons, Malise. 2013. "To Ousted Boss, Arms Watchdog Was Seen as an Obstacle in Iraq." *New York Times*, October 13.

Sky, Emma. 2008. "Iraq 2007 – Moving Beyond Counter-Insurgency Doctrine." *RUIS* 153: 30–4.

Snow, David A. and Robert D. Benford. 1992. "Master Frames and Cycles of Protest." Pp. 133–55 in Aldon D. Morris and Carol McClurg Muller, *Frontiers in Social Movement Theory*. New Haven: Yale University Press.

Solum, Lawrence B. 1987. "On the Indeterminacy Crisis: Critiquing Critical," *University of Chicago Law Review* 54: 462.

State Department: Country Reports on Human Rights Practices for 2013. http://www .state.gov/j/drl/rls/hrrpt/humanrightsreport/#wrapper.

Stickler, Angus. 2011. "Allegations of Prisoner Abuse by U.S. Troops after Abu Ghraib." May 23. Bureau of Investigative Journalism.

Stickler, Angus and Chris Woods. 2011. "U.S. Troops Ordered not to Investigate Iraqi Torture." May 23. Bureau of Investigative Journalism.

Stiglitz, Joseph and Linda Bilmes. 2008. *The Three Trillion Dollar War: The True Cost of the Iraq Conflict*. New York: W. W. Norton.

Sullivan, Margaret. 2014. "Covering New War, in Shadow of Old One." *New York Times*, June 28.

Sutherland, Edwin H. 1949. *White Collar Crime*. New York: Dryden

Suttles, Gerald. 1968. *The Social Order of the Slum: Ethnicity and Territory in the Inner City*. Chicago, IL: University of Chicago Press.

Swidler, Ann. 1986. "Culture in Action: Symbols and Strategies." *American Sociological Review* 51: 273–86.

Sykes, Gresham. 1957. "Techniques of Neutralization: A Theory of Delinquency." *American Sociological Review* 22: 664–70.

Taguba, Antonio M. 2004. Article 15–6 Investigation of the 800T1 ... Military Police Brigade. (http://news.findlaw.com/hdocs/docs/iraq/tagubarpt.html)

Taylor, Verta. 1989. "Social Movement Continuity: The Women's Movement in Abeyance." *American Sociological Review* 54: 761–75.

Thomas, Helen. 2003. "Hussein Link Was Sales Job." *Miami Herald*, September 27.

Tilly, Charles. 1985. "War Making and State Making as Organized Crime." Pp. 169–91 in Peter Evans, Dietrich Rueschemeyer, and Theda Skocpol, *Bringing the State Back In*. Cambridge: Cambridge University Press.

2003. *The Politics of Collective Violence*. Cambridge: Cambridge University Press.

Tripp, Charles. 2010. *A History of Iraq*. Cambridge: Cambridge University Press.

Turk, Austin. 1982. *Political Criminality: The Defiance and Defense of Authority*. Beverly Hills, CA: Sage.

Tushnet, Mark. 1983. "Following the Rules Laid Down: A Critique of Interpretivism and Neutral Principles." *Harvard Law Review* 96: 781–819.

2005. "Critical Legal Theory (without Modifiers) in the United States." *Journal of Political Philosophy* 13: 99, 105, 108.

UN General Assembly Resolution 3314 (XXIX), annex, UN Doc. A/RES/29/3314 (December 14, 1974).

U.S. Department of State. 2006. "Iraq: Country Reports on Human Rights Practices." U.S. Department of State, March 8.

2013. "Human Rights Reports: Iraq." Bureau of Democracy, Human Rights, and Labor, April 19.

U.S. Government Accountability Office. 2007. *Rebuilding Iraq: Integrated Strategic Plan Needed to Help Restore Iraq's Oil and Electricity Sectors.* Washington, DC: U.S. Government Printing Office.

Walzer, Michael. 1977. *Just and Unjust Wars: A Moral Argument with Historical Illustrations.* New York: Basic Books.

2004. *Arguing about War.* New Haven, CT: Yale University Press.

2007. "The Crime of Aggressive War." *Washington University Global Studies Law Review* 6: 635–43.

2009. *Getting Out: Historical Perspectives on Leaving Iraq.* Philadelphia: University of Pennsylvania Press.

2012. "The Aftermath of War: Reflections on Jus Post Bellum." In Eric Patterson, *Ethics: Beyond War's End.* Washington, DC: Georgetown University Press.

Warr, Mark and Mark Stafford. 1983. "Fear of Victimization: A Look at the Proximate Causes." *Social Forces* 61: 1033–43.

Weber, Max. 1919. "Politik als Beruf." *Gesammelte Politische Schriften* (Muenchen, 1921), pp. 396–450. Originally a speech at Munich University, 1918, published in 1919 by Duncker & Humblodt, Munich.

Whitaker, B. 2003. "Flags in the Dust." *Guardian Unlimited Iraq special report at guardian.co.uk*, March 24.

William, Timothy and Duraid Adnan. 2010. "Sunnis in Iraq Allied with U.S. Rejoin Rebels." *New York Times*, October 16.

Wing, Joel. 2012. "How Anbar Province Showed Promise and Problems from 2003–2004: Interview with Keith Mines, Former Coalition Provisional Authority Governor." *Musings on Iraq*, November 19.

Wong, Edward. 2004. "Falluja Assault Roils Iraqi Politics." *New York Times*, November 9.

Woods, Kevin, David Palkki, and Mark Stout (eds.). 2011. *The Saddam Tapes: The Inner Workings of a Tyrant's Regime, 1978–2001.* New York: Cambridge University Press.

Yoo, John. 2006. *War By Other Means: An Insider's Account of the War on Terror.* New York: Atlantic Monthly Press.

Zawati, Hilimi. 2007. "Impunity or Immunity: Wartime Male Rape and Sexual Torture as a Crime against Humanity." *Torture* 17: 27–47.

Index

Abu Ghraib prison, 64–65
  as source of legal cynicism, 202–3
  torture scandal, 65
ad bellum circumstances, 2, 36
aggressive war. *See* wars of aggression
Aiken, George, 195
Al-Qaeda, 96
Al-Qaeda in Iraq (AQI), 96
Al-Fao effect, 23
al-Hakim, Ayatollah Baqir, 42
al-Hashimi, Tariq, 198, 205
al-Jaafari, Ibrahim, 138–39
Allawi, Ayad, 53, 203, 204, 205
al-Majid, Ali Hassan (Chemical Ali), 19–20, 32
al-Maliki, Nouri, 4, 12, 108, 133, 138–40
  data on approval of, and Surge, 152–56
  refusal to concede 2010 election, 204
  Surge and, 140–41
  2010 elections and, 204
  U.S. relationship with, 137
Al-Sadr, Muqtada, 42, 43, 96–97, 100, 101–2, 103–5, 106, 126–27, 195
Al-Sistani, Grand Ayatollah Ali Al-Husayni, 104
Anbar Awakening, 133, 134
Annan, Kofi, 6
Arab Sunnis, Iraq's, 7
  accepting and neutralizing reprisals of, 175–77
  Ba'ath Party and, 18
  consideration of, in planning Iraq invasion, 37
  contexts of insecurity of, 168–73
  cultural framing of insecurity of, 173–75
  displacement of, 38, 96–97

  legal cynicism of, 163
  modeling causes of militancy of, 177–79
  role of legal cynicism, 179–81
Arango, Tim, 162, 189
attacks, civilian, preliminary findings on, 150–52

Ba'ath Party, 17, 97
  religious groups and, 18
Baghdad. *See also* Iraq
  about, 98
  anticipated consequences of displacement in, 118–24
  anticipation and amplification of ethnic cleansing in, 124–25
  battle for, 107–8
  battle for, and Mahdi Army, 111–12
  Current Violates Interview of family caught in violence of, 108–11
  Hussein regime and, 98–99
  modeling ethnic cleansing in, 116–18
Bell-Fialkoff, Andrew, 97
Biden, Joe, 135–36
Blackwater USA guards, prosecution of as source of legal cynicism, 202–3
Blix, Hans, 35
Bolton, John, 35
boundary activation, 101
Bremer, Paul, 8, 37–38, 43–44
  creation of Interim Governing Council (IRC), 48
  de-Ba'athification policies of, 47–48
Brennan, John, 3
Brown, Gordon, 25
Bush Doctrine, 33